Critical Praise for
Out of the Box

"This book knocked my socks off! As a coach, it challenged me, and will challenge you, to guide your clients past symptoms to transformation, and show you how to do this step by step. Authors Bast and Thomson write with extraordinary wisdom, clarity, compassion, and with deep understanding of human capacity for change. They vividly emphasize a way to BE with clients and remind us to remain committed to our own transformation."
— Debbie Call, MSW, Professional Certified Coach
www.movingspirit.com
Contributor to *The New Private Practice* (Lynn Grodzki, Ed.)

"I love Out of the Box: Coaching with the Enneagram. It is the book I use to get ideas and fresh perspectives, not just for coaching but also for interacting with people. People are multi-coloured, even within the same style, and the case histories demonstrate this diversity while showing the similarity. A very fine balance achieved! I particularly loved the material on coaching techniques and tips. Mary and Clarence have such creativity, compassion, wisdom and wit and it is all offered to you in this book. I can usually find something in their material to get my creative juices going again. Wonderful material, great to have on hand, would not want to coach without it. Thank you for writing it all down."
— Ella Kila, President, Insight Facilitations, Inc.

"Out of the Box Coaching has become a significant and most valuable resource in my work as an organizational consultant and executive coach in Israel. Bast and Thomson teach an advanced coaching process, in both spirit and essence. The authors combine rich experience with wisdom, art with science. Not only do they provide useful methods to coach with the Enneagram, and answers to coaching dilemmas, they also generously give the tools to continue creating your own skilled coaching interventions."
— Nira Adler, CEO, Knowing – Executive and Team Coaching
www.knowing.co.il

"This book is an innovative and invaluable resource for anyone who works with individuals or organizations. Bast and Thomson show how Enneagram-savvy coaches can help others solve personal and business problems in ways that are creative and transformative."
— Judith Searle, Author, *The Literary Enneagram*
www.members.aol.com/jsearle479

"Excellence in leadership is the root source of gaining the competitive advantage. It's the one 'edge' your competitors can't copy. The authors identify that edge as they draw from their rich experiences coaching business executives. You will see yourself, co-workers, and employees in the stories they tell. Most importantly you will learn to identify the blind spots of your own operating style and of the people you are responsible to lead and find an important key to diminish or eliminate those blind spots. This book has been invaluable for me and continues to provide the 'gift' so necessary for excellence in leadership."

— Doris Pooser, President, AIS Marketing Services, Inc. and
Always In Style
www.alwaysinstyle.com

"As an engineer trained in scientific certainty, I was not prepared to recognize the wide range of personalities and behaviors I had to work with in a large corporation. Understanding the Enneagram helped me know where other people were 'coming from' and communicate more effectively with subordinates, peers, and superiors. I also learned how to deal with my own personal weaknesses. Reading this book will introduce you to what Enneagram coaching can do for you and your whole organization."

— Thomas P. Schmidt, Vice President, CSX Transportation, Retired

"Bast and Thomson share decades of coaching experience leveraging a powerful diagnostic tool: the Enneagram. Their methods and insights have been beneficial to our company's leadership development program. This practical guide shows those familiar with the Enneagram system how to apply its knowledge to effect profound change. Those who are not familiar with the Enneagram will gain a new dimension that will take their work to a deeper level."

— John Howe, President and CEO, MicroMass Communications
www.micromass.com

"If you are interested in the Enneagram and coaching, only one book is essential and this is it. The authors are highly experienced coaches and Enneagram teachers whose insightful, practical approach is grounded in respect, wisdom, humor, and heart."

— Michael J. Goldberg, Author, *The 9 Ways of Working*
www.9WaysofWorking.com

Out of the Box
Coaching with the Enneagram
Second Edition

Mary Bast
Clarence Thomson

Ninestar Publishing
Louisburg, KS

Published by
Ninestar Publishing
35439 Mission Belleview
Louisburg, KS 66053

ISBN 0-9763159-0-4

Cover art
 "The Portal" by Lawrie Dignan
Pen & ink on paper
Cobble Hill, B.C., Canada
www.changing-realities.com

Cover and book design by Katja Amyx
katja@katjaamyx.net

*To those we coach,
who daily inspire our work
and enrich our lives.*

This book is factually accurate,
except that all the names and identifying characteristics
of the individuals we discuss have been changed.

Contents

Preface

On one level we are all alike. We have waterproof skin, eat regularly, and stand upright to walk. We are assumed to be standard by advertising, advice columnists, and most medical science. We are encouraged to purchase what is advertised, heed the written counsel, and be vaccinated.

On another level, we are known to be completely individual. We have a unique DNA. Our family, pets, and crime investigators know we are original and different. Our social roles, business experiences, and debts cannot be exchanged for those of another. In turn we assure those we love they also are unique.

Between these poles of similarity and difference lies an important category. We have a consciousness that psychologists call an ego-state. The Enneagram describes nine distinct ego states that are so powerful they are often called personality styles. They are like the strong orientations we might have because of our nationality, race, or religion.

The Enneagram portrays the strengths and limitations of our inner habits of attention and response. It is a carefully observed account of the inner world from which people act. If someone does something we wouldn't do, we often ask, "What in the world do you think you're doing?" Their actions surprise us because their behavior would not flow from our inner world.

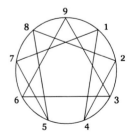

In one sense, our Enneagram style is a trance. Our habits of attention and response lead us to look at certain things. We usually don't see some categories of information. We describe ourselves and others as having "blind spots." The term is almost literally true. The deeper the trance, the more restricted the vision. We all know people in these trances: "Oh, I can't tell her that, there's no way she will hear it." If people act habitually from their response patterns we notice that, too. "Oh, George always gets furious if the coffee is lukewarm." We know from his rigidity ("always") and from his intensity ("furious") that George is in his trance. Lukewarm coffee means something important to him that it doesn't to some others.

When attention is too narrow and responses too habitual, we are captives of our worldview. In the trance of a worldview, we get into trouble—trouble that can range from being habitually late to flying into frothy rage when someone ignores us. One consistent thing about our Enneagram style is that it shows up everywhere: home, work, recreation, school. The same patterns that earned us a promotion also may cost us a marriage.

We refer to the limitations of an Enneagram style as a box and call our work out-of-box coaching. We focus on how to use knowledge of an Enneagram style to coach effectively. Because an Enneagram style includes a set of inner processes, we help people see those processes, what they leave out, and what they emphasize too much. Then we suggest ways to broaden their perception and create flexibility in their responses to what they do see.

Mary has kept case histories from her personal and business coaching career for many years. When she discovered the Enneagram she noticed with a psychologist's trained eye that the cases were fine examples of all nine styles. She contacted Clarence—Enneagram teacher, author, counselor, and newsletter editor. After she shared her case-collection we decided to write this book.

This is our report from the field: how we use the Enneagram, what works, and how we think it works. It will be useful to anyone whose role is to encourage others' development: coaches, managers, consultants, teachers, therapists, spiritual directors, and parents. Whether the Enneagram is new to you or familiar, our descriptions will flesh out your understanding of the nine styles. You can apply these techniques, insights, and suggestions to both business and personal situations. We've modeled our learning, teaching, and coaching process. We encourage you to join us.

Mary & Clarence

Untying the Knots

Tuning In to Inner Conflict

Mary's client, Walter Frazier, was an innovative, idealistic leader. He held high standards for himself, his employees, and the company, but he was losing people's respect because of the angry tirades he unleashed whenever he was disappointed with the quality of someone's work. Walter came to Mary only for help in managing his anger. It would have been easy enough to coach Walter on how to use anger-management techniques. But Mary's questions ran deeper: Why did he feel so much anger? How could she coach him to break out of the worldview that kept reinforcing his perfectionism? When she led him to this deeper level, he learned how to interrupt the inner patterns of processing information that made him angry. Walter became less harshly judgmental and his underlying anger began to dissipate. Mary was able to help him accomplish this shift because of the Enneagram's power as a coaching tool.

Most clients will acknowledge how important it is to act in accord with their internal needs and values. But you have probably discovered that they are often out of touch with their deepest motivations. Instead, most behave according to who they think they are, playing familiar roles and piling up trophies from their worldly successes. Often, the very characteristics that propelled them to reach personally important goals now get in their way. People like Walter who are idealistic and quality-minded standard-setters, for example, may find that their perfectionism and inability to delegate effectively prevent them from achieving their real goals.

When he hired Mary, Walter held a filtered view of how the world should work. Your clients, too, may come seeking help on how to make more money, quit feeling anxious, change to a more enjoyable job, or find a new boss/lover/spouse. We know a therapist who says that people come to therapy in order to make their neuroses work better. Coaching clients also may ask you how to shore up the

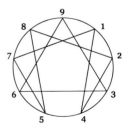

crumbling mortar of their personality styles when their usual coping strategies fail them. When you help people break free of their limited worldviews, you can give them more than they know to ask for. You take them beyond their immediate requests to get what they really want and often urgently need—a way to break "out of the box" of their habitual perspectives and reactions to the world.

We'll go into detail about nine different personality styles in this book, with cases that illustrate the gifts and foibles of each. Then we'll help you with some coaching tips, by style. We encourage you to study the premises of change outlined in Chapter Two and described more fully in the final chapter. Once your clients see the possibilities in what we call second-order or transformational change, they will gain far more than they would by simply changing their immediate problem behavior. You and your clients could superficially succeed by limiting your work to standard behavioral change, without being aware that both of you may have ignored or even unwittingly reinforced their more deeply rooted, unconscious patterns.

The Enneagram is a brilliant diagnostic tool to identify nine different ways of viewing the world, each of which has a common set of patterns. When you know these patterns and how to interrupt them, you will consistently see long-term, profound changes in your clients. For those who do not yet know the Enneagram, the following overview and nine brief case descriptions will help you begin to recognize the nine styles.[1] If you find yourself intrigued by one of these cases, you can go immediately to the chapter describing that style in greater detail.

The Nine Enneagram Styles

The Enneagram describes our gifts and attendant blind spots, ruts, and self-defeating tendencies that plague us at times. More important, it points to a central energy that is at the origin of these tendencies—an energy we tend to overuse. Our gifts can become liabilities and sometimes our downfall. A theater director who prides herself on spontaneity may try to run a production with a series of improvised decisions that create chaos. An executive whose competitiveness led to a promotion may find that morale problems caused by his style now threaten his hard-earned success. When our Enneagram coping skills aren't working well they cause stress. Under stress we tend to act out of our Enneagram distortions even more vigorously.

The Enneagram does more than describe nine personality styles. It points to a narrow focus of attention. Each style functions as a mild but profound trance,

---

[1] See our websites www.breakoutofthebox.com/enneagram.htm and www.enneagramcentral.com

focused on a few inward realities that lead to convictions about how the world works and how to deal with it. Here is the traditional Enneagram symbol, with brief descriptions of the habits or characteristics that each worldview and central energy generates:

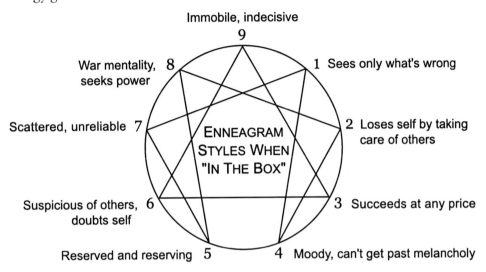

A flow of energy necessarily follows our narrow focus of attention. This energy supports a particular trance in a self-fulfilling way. Enneagram style Ones, for example, will habitually look for something wrong, and will then receive satisfaction from making a correction. This reinforces their worldview that they must strive for perfection. Reflect a minute on yourself. You know, with varying degrees of clarity, what makes your juices flow. You know that certain people, places, and events deplete you, whereas others—in the words of the street—get you pumped. We all are energized by our Enneagram style, by nine different ways of paying attention.

When we focus on a few inward realities and let the rest of the picture get a little fuzzy, we see the world in a certain, subjective way. You've heard about optimists and pessimists viewing the same glass of water as half full or half empty. Actually, any given glass of water can be interpreted nine different ways. For Fives, who live in a world of scarcity, it can be a resource to be hoarded. Twos, who try to meet their own needs through taking care of others, might see the glass of water as a possible bribe for someone who is thirsty. It could remind Sixes, whose self-doubt leads them to expect the worst, that they have to be careful not to spill things. These worldviews can get us in trouble. We develop a whole series of strategies based on the perceptions that we distort through our attention filters. What this means, of course, is that we go through life coping valiantly with a world we have made up.

We focus attention, expend energy, and create strategies to deal with our narrow view of the world. Consequently, we develop ways of thinking, feeling, interpreting, and ultimately acting that make sense in our worldview and continually reinforce and sustain it. You may have found other people's behavior strange; but in fact, their behavior is only strange because they're dealing with their world. We even talk that way. We ask, "What in the world were you doing? What could you have been thinking?" One clue in determining people's Enneagram style is evidence of a consistent pattern. Even when we think people are irrational, we can't help notice they are irrational in systematic ways. What may not make sense in your world always makes sense in theirs. A friendly word of caution: your world is not the real world either!

As you look through the following nine summaries, identify how each style's focus of attention shows up in the people described:

Style One

My toast would be, may our country be always successful, but whether successful or otherwise, always right.

John Quincy Adams

The gift of Ones is the ability to see and work toward perfection. This has narrowed their focus of attention so they often see only what is wrong, what needs fixing.

One Christmas, Clarence received a humorous e-mail with an unusual request to Santa Claus, asking permission to slap Martha Stewart's face! Martha Stewart is a One, and the joke was in response to her inner tamped down, low-key anger. This low-level anger of style One prompts them to keep a tight control over their emotions. You have seen this in Stewart's inability to gush. No matter what beautiful thing she displayed, she contented herself by saying only, "It's a good thing." The perfectionism of the One is driven by a fix-it kind of anger—not an inchoate rage but a rejection of something less than the ideal of what should be.

When Walter Frazier hired Mary, he was in charge of business expansion at a spin-off company of his corporation. The One's idealism showed up as he inspired his new team to bring in millions beyond projected revenue. However, he would burst out angrily at subordinates and become sarcastic with peers when disappointed in the quality of their work. "He can really nail you with his criticism," one person reported. "He blows people out of the water." Walter also had difficulty delegating responsibility to his team. "If you go in with a problem, however small, he dives into the details too thoroughly," complained a frustrated subordinate. Another suggested, "He needs to step back. Even with top-notch people he wants to be involved in everything. Nothing's ever good enough."

Style Two

The gift of Twos is the ability to anticipate and tend to someone else's needs. This narrowed focus of attention can cause them to lose themselves because they're so intent on taking care of others.

Caring for others without due respect for the self does not make a better world; unless we understand our own needs we cannot know the needs of others.

Mary Lou Wright

The Two's worldview is illustrated in quotes from a highly successful network marketing sales manual: "Helping someone else along the way helps us on our journey to the top." "You can get what you want when you help enough others get what they want." Giving to get is a delicate maneuver. On the high side, we all agree that to have a friend, you must be a friend. People in sales raise this exchange to an art form. They remember your birthday better than your family does. Twos' self-image of being helpful can be so strong that there is a great deal of pride in not acknowledging their own needs. On the low side, this can decay into seduction. They focus warmly on you, but if they're in the box, they aren't acting out of love; they're making an emotional investment. And if you don't reward that investment, they can engage in emotional blackmail.

Len Sands was in charge of customer service when his boss, Tom, asked him to work with Mary. "Len's fairly insecure," said Tom. "He has always required a lot of positive affirmation and recognition. And he's difficult to confront because he has such strong feelings. He gives the nonverbal message, 'You're hurting me, and I don't want to hear this.'" When operating out of their narrow worldview and trapped by the desire to please, Twos find it difficult to be direct, though you will see their emotions, even neediness, on their faces or in their body language. Because it's hard for Twos to admit their own needs openly, they often prefer to work behind the scenes. Len's peers described him as manipulative. He found a way to get what he wanted, with or without their cooperation. He had encouraged members of his team to switch roles several times because he wanted to broaden their perspective and deepen their experience. They felt he had pushed them too far, too fast but, like his boss, they found it hard to discuss this openly with Len. "He creates an environment of well-being," said one, "but the more you express opinions, the more difficult it is to get along with him."

Style Three

There's no deodorant like success.

Elizabeth Taylor

The gift of Threes is the drive to succeed in attaining a goal. This narrow focus of attention can become competitive striving that may rob them of their souls.

When Clarence's style Three friend ended her marriage after a number of years, she wrote her husband a "Dear John" letter, but wrote it as a letter of resignation from her role as his wife. The project was over! In-the-box Threes try to earn love by performance and often become workaholics, sometimes ruthless ones, in order to succeed. A deceit underlies this strategy: I may not be loved for myself, but others must love my success. Everyone loves a winner. As style Twos try to meet the needs of others, Threes try to meet the real or imagined expectations of others, especially when defined in a role. They measure success through the eyes of others.

Bill Danvers was being considered for the presidency of a small but highly profitable company that had been originally founded by the CEO, Darlene Rivers. "I'd like to retire and travel around the world with my husband," Darlene explained, "but I've put a lot of money in this business and I want to protect my investment. Bill knows how to sell and gets results. He's not really an entrepreneur but we're pretty stable by now, and would continue to be successful if he ran the company." However, Darlene knew through the grapevine that people who worked with Bill were not keen on a future in which they had to report to him. "I'm afraid I'll have a mutiny if I promote him," she said, and her concern was well founded. One of Bill's peers observed, "He's so intent on making a deal that I wonder if his decisions will serve the company in the long run. He's swift with numbers, but may not look at the bottom line because he knows he's judged only by revenues." Another peer added, "He's hung up on saying 'I' all the time. He only gets our input when he needs our expertise. He also tends to claim all the credit for deals, ignoring our work behind the scenes."

Style Four

There is no greater pain than to remember a happy time when one is in misery.

Dante

The gift of Fours is a passion for creativity, emotional depth, and a profound desire for authenticity. This narrow focus of attention brings up a fear of being ordinary.

James lives in a one-room, $360-a-month apartment. He scrimps and saves on food and clothing, but frequently attends the finest music concerts in town. Though brilliant and multi-talented, he works as a dishwasher for minimum wage, then

6

gives free lectures on Egyptian archeology. James is highly creative but sees himself unsuited for an ordinary life or job. Fours who remain blind to their Enneagram box get stuck in melancholy. They often feel different from others, which can be experienced either as having a unique perspective or as a flaw. Behind this worldview is a quality of longing: the child looking into the candy store, feeling that anything good is always unavailable.

Gail Gamble was being groomed to take over the top finance job for an international company. Their industry position was slipping and senior management was looking for innovative thinkers. "Traditionally we've had a uniform way of thinking," admitted the CEO, "and we need to change." He admired Gail. "She is very conceptual, intuitive, and visionary." A peer concurred: "She's definitely forward thinking, even unconstrained in what's possible for us." He added a concern that came to haunt Gail: "I realize that we've been strategy–deficient, but sometimes she's unrealistic about what we can really do." Gail had great ideas about how to make her ordinary organization extraordinary, but when she tried to get buy-in to her ideas she kept running into roadblocks. She dreamed of having a career that was less mundane. "My ideal job," she lamented, "would be to work for a company like Ben and Jerry's, where their culture reflects their values in a nontraditional way."

Style Five

The gift of Fives is the ability to conceptualize and to master knowledge. This narrow focus of attention can cause them to be emotionally remote and socially awkward.

People say that life is the thing, but I prefer reading.

Logan Smith

Steve, a merit scholar, loves computer role-playing games. His social life is so undemanding that each year at college, when his parents took him shopping for his school wardrobe, he only wanted three pairs of black pants and three white T-shirts and sweatshirts. His opinion? "Now everything I have goes with everything and I don't have to pay any attention." In-the-box Fives can live so completely in their heads that they wish to pay as little attention as possible to the physical side of life. Fives can be quite reserved. They are often intellectual and tend to hoard their emotions, time, energy, and thoughts as if there weren't enough to go around, instead of investing in life. These are your typical ivory tower characters.

Denise Harvey is a complex, intelligent woman who was brought in by the chairman of the board to turn a failing company around. "Her greatest asset is her mind," said the chairman. "She's an unparalleled strategic thinker in her field."

"But," he continued, "sometimes she makes comments that make other people seem dumb." Denise had brought in smart and experienced people to make up her team. They greatly respected her but found her stingy with appreciation. "Feedback doesn't come naturally to her. She has very high standards but never praises people," reported one of them. Denise was not well known below the senior management level. "She hates walking down the hall and talking to people," said one of her vice presidents. "I think it feels unnatural to her." However, Denise loved to debate. For her it was a way to connect with people and to refine her own ideas. To her staff, these debates were like mental duels. Commenting on this, one of her team members said, "She couches her thoughts in intellectual constructs and you never get the feeling beneath the statement, nor do you know whether she's taken your ideas into consideration."

Style Six

To live with fear and not be afraid is the final test of maturity.

Edward Weeks

The gift of Sixes is loyalty. This narrow focus of attention causes them to question their inner authority and to anxiously anticipate anything that could go wrong.

Sam expects the worst. He watches the news portion of the 700 Club TV program. There Pat Robertson, a style Six who thrives in expectation of apocalyptic disaster, assures him that the world is indeed much worse than anybody thought, and provides evidence of the pending calamity. Sam goes there for news, he tells us, so that he can "get the stuff the mainline media hides from us." In-the-box Sixes suspect that the world is not a safe place. The world does not feel safe to them because they feel powerless inside. They look to the group for security, rules, and norms, yet, paradoxically, are often the ones to challenge authority. Commonly referred to as fearful types, Sixes may be obviously anxious or self-doubting, but this unconscious dynamic is more often observed as a fear of fear. They cannot stand being afraid. Consequently, they focus on what could go wrong in order to take all the necessary precautions. They can only feel safe by covering all the bases.

Nancy Schwab, Director of Operations, had been a loyal supporter of her company through many years of industry changes. "She's a stand-up person," said her boss. "She has a logical approach to problem solving and can smell things out quickly." Her peers described Nancy as "the glue that holds people together" through times of stressful change. One co-worker credited Nancy for being "the consummate team player. She knows who needs to be involved." It drove Nancy crazy that her peers would agree when something was a problem, but in senior staff meetings they would just smile, nod, and not mention any problem. Nancy couldn't stand it. Suddenly she would blurt out her worries. Her boss's reaction? "It's a plus that she's candid, but she's too argumentative, too negative," he cautioned.

Style Seven

The gift of Sevens is positive, energetic, upbeat energy and the ability to generate ideas. This narrow focus of attention can cause them to be easily frustrated when things slow down.

Speaking of sins, the only thing I cannot resist is temptation.

Oscar Wilde

Hugh, an executive, was asking advice on how to juggle his schedule so he could find more time for his wife and children. Toward the end of the conversation he casually remarked that he was also considering running for state senator! In-the-box Sevens are gluttons for pleasure, variety, and novelty to the point of having little tolerance for boredom or discomfort of any kind. Since life has its ups and downs, being driven to be cheerful can leave this style a bit out of touch with the more negative portions of reality. Sevens habitually over-schedule and fill their lives too full of activity in order not to feel their inner fear. Usually fast-paced and upbeat, they seldom come for coaching until their coping patterns bring them public trouble.

Described by others in her organization as "fun to be around," Carol Burkhart was highly energetic, enthusiastic, and optimistic. She had a particular ability to get people excited about the organization's mission. In her first coaching session, she talked openly about herself and was easy to be with. She did most of the talking and told great stories. "I've turned this place around so quickly," she laughed, "I'm afraid we'll be accused of cooking the books!" Her engaging interpersonal openness helped her deal with customers, but created the impression she was a lightweight. For example, she did not watch the clock. Basking in her great results over the first quarter, she tended to mosey in to work when she felt like it, though she stayed as long as necessary. The people who reported to her appreciated this approach: "If everything's going a mile a minute she's in there; if things back off we'll have a relaxed atmosphere. Her predecessor was as serious as a heart attack every second." Her irregular work hours were a problem for her boss, though, because "she flies in the face of a culture that works from 6 AM to 10 PM. Her coming in later than others has been interpreted as not wanting to work that hard."

Style Eight

The greatest of all weakness is the fear of appearing weak.

Bossuet

The gift of Eights is a natural confidence and ability to take charge. With their narrow focus of attention, they claim power whether others like it or not.

Clarence coached the CEO of a small video production business. He told his client to be careful of intimidation, especially with one employee. Clarence said, "You know, you're a lot bigger than he is." Without a smile, the client answered, "I'm bigger than everybody." Eights feel they are in some way larger than life, and are driven to excess. If some is good, more is better, especially power. The thrill is in the hunt, however, so they are not necessarily satisfied with what they get, and can stir things up just to spice up a situation.

Tom Dafoe called Mary and said, "I'm about to be out-maneuvered by one of my key people. My financial guy, Sanford, is threatening to quit. I'd kick him out myself, but I've taken out a big loan to acquire a new business and I'll go bankrupt if he leaves now. He's been my right-hand man and I don't have time to find and train someone to replace him. Can you get him to tough it out?" When he first talked with Mary, Tom did not see his own role in scaring Sanford off. He wanted her to coach Sanford to not be "such a sissy" so he would not be intimidated. When Mary asked Sanford what it was like to work for Tom, he said, "He's incredibly generous if he takes you under his wing, but do not cross him."

Style Nine

Between two stools, one sits on the ground.

French proverb

The gift of Nines is in being calm, easy-going, and capable of understanding divergent opinions. This narrow focus of attention means they may avoid conflict, deadlines, or unsettling thoughts that could upset their sense of inner peace.

On C-Span one evening, an angry congressman said about Bill Clinton, a Nine, "I'm so damned tired of going up to the White House and listening to him agree with everybody for two hours!" Agreement is the Nine specialty. Nines can see all sides, agree with all sides, and then either achieve consensus or remain inactive, depending on their level of self-awareness. Anger is typically suppressed in this style, so while Nines can be energized, there is a basic lack of voltage. You cannot suppress anger without suppressing all feelings to some extent. It has been said of some Nines that they "make molehills out of mountains."

Beneath his calm exterior, Barry Foster typified the adage that still waters run deep. He was sincere and affectionate. One person commented, "He wears well over time." Barry's grasp of situations was typically global and complex. "I like to bounce ideas around with him," said a colleague, "because he can understand and appreciate a variety of viewpoints simultaneously." Barry often played the role of intermediary with colleagues who were having difficulty with each other. He was a great consensus builder. On the down side, Barry lacked assertiveness, so his boss convinced him he needed a coach: "You're too dependent on seeking others' views before you speak up. And you change your mind too easily." The most immediate problem was Barry's failure to deal effectively with two members of his team who were operating independently of departmental objectives. "There are a couple of people here who can 'work' him," reported an observer from another department. "He talks about confronting them, but he never does it. One of them in particular walks all over him every day."

Coaching with the Enneagram

Our vision is that you will see the value of working with these personality styles, not to stereotype or diminish people but to help your clients become more effective in their work and more whole as human beings. All nine styles, when unaware of the box they are in, protect their worldview at great cost to their full potential. With awareness of their underlying motives and openness to significant shifts in their perspective, the nine styles are also capable of great contributions and gifts to organizations, to relationships, and to society in general:

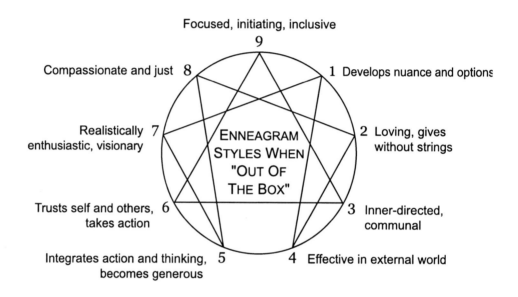

Imagine how effective your clients will become when you show them exactly how their view of the world is skewed and not shared by everyone, where their energy is being spent for good or ill, and, most important, how they daily dig the hole in which they labor.

Once you know your clients' Enneagram styles, you also know how they set their strategies in motion. An Enneagram style is not a static condition like being tall or brown-eyed; it is a series of inner and outer movements, something people do. The interruption of the strategy pattern is the exact location in which to exert leverage for change.

We mentioned earlier that clients often come with requests that, in effect, would only deepen their dysfunctional patterns. Threes, for example, want to work harder without feeling stressed. Sevens want to figure out how they can make it more fun to accomplish the nitty gritty details. Eights want to wield power without being intimidating. The Enneagram will add a brilliant diagnostic tool to your repertoire, one that will deepen the effects of techniques you already use. You will ask in each case: "What patterns of thinking, feeling, assuming, and doing are not working? And what do those patterns cost?"

Determining an Enneagram Style

This model describes motives. It tells us why we do what we do. Friends and co-workers can offer feedback, but easily observable behaviors could identify several styles. What drives the behavior is most important. It is best to take your clients through a process of discovery, focusing on the underlying dynamics that create patterns of behavior. You can help by asking questions that lead to awareness about their internal workings: values, beliefs, assumptions, and motivations. But the final decision is theirs.

COMMON TRAPS

Looking for 1-2 traits

Typing too quickly

Noticing behaviors instead of motives

Basing notion on 1 or 2 vivid examples

Not getting enough information

Too narrow a definition

In one situation, Mary was almost certain that a new client was a Four, but she was still gathering clues. When she suggested Four as a possibility, this woman said with great conviction, "No, you're wrong! I'm a One." The client spoke like a One: she saw things as either right or wrong, a pattern that stems from the One's drive for perfection.

If you use the Enneagram but choose not to teach the system, you will rely on your best guess based on your observations. Do not be overly confident, and do not despair if you have mistaken one style for another. You will learn as you go that typing is an art, not a science. It is difficult, subtle, and in many ways foreign to our usual way of thinking. Typing is an inference, not a linear conclusion. Be aware of these common traps:

- *Looking for one or two traits.* You know that Twos deny their own needs by focusing on the needs of others, so you might jump to the conclusion, "Oh, you bought such a thoughtful gift, you must be a Two." Or, given that Ones like to do things right and Sixes' self-doubt leads them to try to figure out group norms, you could prematurely decide, "You kept all the rules, you must be either a One or a Six."

13

- *Typing too quickly.* Speed typing is for keyboards. Enneagram typing is more like a detective looking for clues. A client says, "I'm always somewhat isolated, never part of the crowd." That is a hint this person might be a Four ("Am I alone because I'm flawed?"), or a Five ("I'll isolate myself so I won't have to expose my emotions"), or a Nine ("Will I alienate somebody by not following along?"), possibly even some other style. Follow the clues with questions.

- *Noticing behaviors instead of motives.* Both Eights (war mentality) and Threes (success at any price) are energetic, aggressive styles and both can be competitive. It takes careful observation, listening, and insight to discern signs of the Eight's motivations: "It's important to win against the other because it's not O.K. to be weak." Compare this to the Three's motivations: "It's important to look good and be the best because it's not O.K. to fail."

- *Basing your notion on one or two vivid examples and looking for a repeat.* Madonna and Mother Teresa are both Twos. Trust us, they are different. Mother Teresa exemplifies the truly unconditional giving of an exceptional human being. Madonna, in her legendary seductiveness, has mastered the art of giving to get.

- *Not getting enough information.* An Enneagram style is quite deep. At times, it does not show up at all. Wait until you have plenty of information before assuming you know someone's style. This doesn't mean you can't operate from a good working hypothesis. If someone says, "I think work should be fun, and people around here are far too serious," it's a good guess that this person might be a Seven. Ask questions, test out some assumptions. Just don't pour it in concrete until you have adequate information.

- *Having too narrow a definition of information.* Pay attention to the extended cues in the next discussion, including voice volume and tone, symbolic language, and patterns of behavior. For example, in-the-box Sevens tend to be con artists who will make efforts to get you to trust them. There is a lot of variation within the style, though, so broaden your definition of Sevens instead of assuming from this one observation that your client is a Seven.

To build a complete picture, collect the clues that reflect underlying motivations: their level and quality of energy, symbolic language and behavior, reactions under stress, communication style, and focus of attention.

Level and Quality of Energy

Remember that you are not looking solely at behavior; you are noticing which behaviors have more conviction, more psychic volume. Here are three examples with contrasting energy:

CLUES

Level and quality of energy

Symbolic language and behavior

Reactions under stress

Communication style

Focus of attention

- Eights are in-your-face people. When they bellow, they really roar. Sixes fight their own fear and self-doubt. When they raise their voices, you can often detect the fear behind the volume.

- Sevens seek variety and pleasure, so they will get bored with too much detail. When they clean a room they'll get most of the dirt. When Ones viciously attack every crumb and speck, they use a different energy: they are on a mission ("I have to get it perfect"). Be aware of these differences.

- Threes are driven to get results. When they say, "Let's do it!" you can sense that they are going to make something happen. Nines often go along with something because they're not sure what they want. When a Nine agrees that we need to take action, something may be missing. Not much juice.

Symbolic Language and Behavior

Remember to think and observe symbolically. Every Enneagram style other than your own is a world in which you may be a stranger. Each action makes sense in someone else's world, even if it does not in yours:

- A to-do list may be a four-minute mile for a Three ("I've got to get it done"), a confusion to a Nine ("I'm easily distracted because I'm not sure what my own priorities are"), an irritant to a Seven ("Good grief, can't I get someone else to do this?"), and is sometimes ignored by an Eight ("If it's not my way, it's the highway"). What does a to-do list symbolize for your clients?

- What do clothes symbolize? For a Five, dress may be protective coloration: "I want to keep my emotional distance, so I'm not going to wear something that brings attention to me." Clothes for a Four may be a statement: "I want to be unique, not dress like every person I meet on the street." For a Seven clothes might mean nothing at all. Sevens can be highly self-referential, not caring much about what other people think, so how they dress is not a big deal. For Twos, who relentlessly seek love and approval, the choice of clothing may be a directive from a spouse or mother.

15

Reactions Under Stress

People reveal their Enneagram styles over time and under stress. Watch for patterns there. Mary had a client who could not decide if she was an Eight or a Three. This woman was a very energetic, responsible person who typically did not involve her teammates before acting. Others in the organization were convinced she was an Eight because she seemed to need to be in charge, and she and Mary both agreed that was likely.

A year later, the company underwent an acquisition, heads rolled, and Mary's client barely came out on top. During the transition it became crystal clear she was a Three, not an Eight. Her focus on looking good became so acute that she was distressed to attend a board meeting in a suit whose skirt she felt was two inches too long! Her keeping others out of the loop had not been driven by control needs but rather by her need to be seen as the best so she would come out on top.

Communication Style

People of each Enneagram style have their own way of talking. These are tendencies, of course. They may not always characterize someone, but they will be there to some degree, and they tend to be particularly evident under stress:

1. Ones tend to talk in black and white and often sound over-controlled. You can see their restraint, even when they're feeling great emotion.

2. Twos will usually talk about others, not themselves. Even when you are their coach you will find them diverting attention to you. They also have more emotional volume than most styles. "That was the absolute best I've ever seen." "This change for me was HUGE!"

3. Threes often want to look good in order to succeed, so they tend to talk like the role they are playing. What words would a manager be expected to use, for example? A movie star? A politician?

4. Fours are sometimes lost in their own moods. They tend to have lamentation in their conversation and lots of feeling words. Events are recalled by their emotional reaction. They tend to dwell on the past.

5. Fives are likely not to talk, arising from their desire to keep a distance. But if asked an important question on a topic about which they know a lot, they can

go on far longer than you thought possible. This talk style has been described as giving a dissertation, and can seem academic, even condescending.

6. The conversation of Sixes often represents the group. A Six interrupted a meeting with something from his own agenda, and when challenged about its relevance replied petulantly, "But it's for the good of the group!" Sixes can also think with the group, which is harder to pick out because they change their thinking to match that of the group's.

7. Sevens are usually upbeat, energetic, positive people who love to talk. They derive their energy from their search for variety and pleasure. They like to entertain in conversation, often talking in pictures. Clarence, a Seven, describes our Enneagram style as the rope around the ring in which we fight most of our battles.

8. Eights tend to have loud voices and are not given to circumlocution. "It is my way and no other" reflects their strategy to take control and their dislike of showing weakness.

9. Nines may talk in sagas. It can take them five minutes to say it is raining. This stems from their taking all points of view, seeing everything as interconnected, and not being practiced in stating a position clearly.

Focus of Attention

Observe what your clients notice. Each style sorts for different things. Each notices some things first and other things later:

1. Ones notice what is wrong.

2. Twos notice people.

3. Threes notice what others expect.

4. Fours notice how they feel.

5. Fives notice information.

6. Sixes notice what can go wrong.

7. Sevens notice opportunity and action.

8. Eights notice who has what kind of power.

9. Nines appear not to notice, but the truth is they don't notice themselves.

Think in Pictures

Add these tips to the more extensive style descriptions in the upcoming chapters. Then consult Thomas Condon's Enneagram Movie & Video Guide and watch some movies of each style. Keep in mind the key areas to observe: Look for level and quality of energy, symbolic language and behavior, reactions under stress, communication style, and focus of attention. Here is a sampling:

1. Ones tamp down their emotions in the interest of duty. For a movie example, watch Emma Thompson in *Sense and Sensibility*, especially her early conversation about love with Kate Winslet.

2. Shirley MacLaine plays a Two well in *Postcards from the Edge* and again in *Terms of Endearment*. She completely focuses on someone else in both movies—presumably for their own good. In *Postcards from the Edge* she will not admit she wants to be the star she is trying to make of her daughter.

3. Out-of-the-box Threes have an internal life. In-the-box Threes try to earn love by achievement. Watch the love scene in *Jerry McGuire* when Tom Cruise goes to win his wife back and begins by telling her how tough the competition is and the achievement of his company.

4. Fours can get stuck in their own melancholy, often driven by envy arising from their self-perception of being flawed. Watch Salieri in *Amadeus* as he laments his ordinariness and envies the talent of Mozart. Or if your tastes are more lowbrow, watch *Batman Returns*. Danny DeVito as the Penguin is filled with hatred because he is defective, different, and not accepted by the townsfolk.

5. Fives can be distant, even cold, and need to integrate action and thinking. Watch James Spader in *sex, lies and videotape* as he mediates his desire for intimacy through interviewing women on videotape. Note his Spartan living, his exchange of secrets with Andi McDowell, and his desire for privacy and distance.

6. Woody Allen is famous for being a Six, the man to whom nothing good will or can happen, who is unable to trust himself and others. The world is out to get him and he is out to get himself in all his movies. If Sixes fight back against the scary world, they are called "counterphobic Sixes." Go see *Conspiracy Theory*, in which both stars are caricatures of this pattern.

7. When Sevens are healthy, they can look like *Patch Adams*, grounded but still funny, irreverent, and compassionate. When more scattered and too pleasure seeking, they can look like Barbra Streisand in *The Mirror Has Two Faces*. Almost every scene is about appetite, for either food or sex.

8. Michael Douglas, in the classic *Wall Street*, gives young Charlie Sheen advice. Listen to him explain how to be ruthless, relentless, and without friends. It is an in-the-box Eight's war manifesto. Russell Crowe gives a fine Eight performance in *L.A. Confidential*. If you want a brilliant female version of style Eight, watch Mary McDonnell in *Passionfish*. Look for evidence of growing compassion and justice.

9. Observe the way Nines can be lost to themselves and passive with others as Joanne Woodward talks to her husband in *Mr. and Mrs. Bridge*. This sleepy quality is associated with Nines' inability to structure their own lives. A more sinister Nine is Billy Bob Thornton in *Sling Blade*. Lest you think that easy-going Nines can only play one note, Karl has just been released from a mental institution where he was put away for homicide. He doesn't look at all angry throughout the movie, but...

Breaking Out of the Box

Some people become uneasy about personality typing, worrying that this is a box or label they are going to be stuck with, or one they refuse to be stuck with. We have news for you. We are all in boxes.

The Enneagram, like any diagnosis, identifies the box you're already in. That information is the first step out. Yes, people can change to some degree through insights and coaching in new skills: first-order change. But they can be transformed by reframing their basic assumptions, by seeing and operating within the world in a totally new way: second-order change.

In the next chapter we will show you what first- and second-order change look like, using Enneagram styles Three, Six, and Nine as examples. As you read, notice the potential of all three clients to step out of their boxes.

Breaking Out of the Box

Visiting the Guru

Once upon a time a young man asked a famous guru who was visiting town if he could become her student. The guru kindly asked, "Why do you want to become my student?" The young man poured out his troubles, explaining that his life was a mess. He said his house was a good example of how he just couldn't make his life work. The house had falling plaster, broken and dirty windows, an awful carpet, and even the doors and windows didn't work. The guru listened carefully and said, "I do not think you are ready to be my student, but I am going to give you a gift. Please return to your house." The young man left disappointed, but was cheered by the thought of a gift.

The next day a truck pulled up outside his ramshackle house and unloaded a beautiful couch. The young man was delighted. When the truckers asked him where he wanted it, he had them put it up against one of the worst walls in his living room. After they left he sat and looked at the couch with pleasure. But only for a while. He noticed how terrible the beautiful couch made his wall look, so he decided to clean up that wall. When he sat down to admire his work, he soon realized that the other walls looked terrible by comparison. So he decided to clean up the other walls. When he again admired what he'd done, he now realized that this room was in sharp contrast to the rest of the house. You can imagine how the story ends: From one room, he was moved to transform the whole downstairs, then the upstairs, then the outside of the house, the yard, the block—and eventually himself.

As a coach you will frequently be tempted to respond to a client's explicit request for change: "Help me organize the clutter in my house; get the job of my dreams; manage my finances; get along better with my spouse, my boss, my co-worker." You probably have well-tested interventions—time management techniques, templates for business plans, communication models—any one of which can

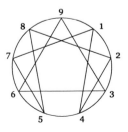

promise some success with your clients. Many of these need to be understood as quick fixes. There is nothing wrong with quick fixes in the short term. They can support and motivate your clients and cheer them on to further and more meaningful work.

However, you may reinforce some underlying dysfunctional patterns by helping your clients accomplish something that only looks like fundamental change. This is change of a sort, which we call first-order change. It solves a problem within a box or worldview without examining the parameters of the box. A first-order change addresses one of your client's symptoms, but leaves a more fundamental dynamic untouched.

Do not forego the chance to help clients achieve more profound change. If you only help them organize their home or office you may have lost the opportunity to explore the source of their clutter, how a cluttered office reflects their mental patterns, and how that same pattern appears in other areas of their lives. If you only work with them to improve one relationship, they may not see the underlying convictions and habits that affect all their relationships.

In and Out of the Box

We've used a number of personality assessments in our coaching practice that are great for measuring behavior. But they don't do what the guru did for her student—alter someone's perception of the whole world. We have found that small symbolic changes on the level of Enneagram style give clients a change in perspective similar to the effect the new couch had on the young man. This can have a deep and powerful impact on their lives and those whose lives they touch.

Small symbolic changes on the level of Enneagram style can have a deep and powerful impact on clients' lives.

We suggest that you encourage such *second-order* change in your clients: a fundamental shift. Second-order change can transform their inner experience so profoundly that they perceive their world quite differently and alter their behavior spontaneously. To bring about these deeper changes, you can ask your clients questions that lead them to:

- see how their patterns play out in ways that do not serve them well;
- break their habits, shake up the inner structure of self-defeating patterns;
- become open to new perspectives, willing, even eager, to face the unknown;
- create a specific vision of what is possible, one that brings them greater meaning and instills hope;

- develop and reinforce their ability, understanding, and willingness to make significant change in their lives.

For example, Clarence worked with Roy, an Enneagram Two, who felt trapped in his job. When in the box, Roy had subsumed his own needs to those of others, at work and at home. He had been unable to see the costs of that pattern, even though he was highly stressed. He suffered from sleeplessness and constant sciatic pain, but would not allow himself to take sleeping or pain medication. Because of what he perceived as the potential effect on his grown children, he would not consider leaving a marriage that had been unsatisfying for many years. With coaching, Roy learned to set limits on doing others' work and left to head a company providing a new service in his field. Had the coaching ended here, Roy would have seen saying "no" to excessive work demands and becoming head of a company as signaling success. But this alone would have been a first-order change.

As he gained awareness of his underlying Enneagram pattern, and challenged his automatic responses, Roy began to notice the effects of second-order change. He took a stand for his personal vision and purpose, and held himself accountable to live in integrity with his highest good. The seed planted during coaching allowed him to take better care of himself while still using his gift of compassion for others. He found that his taking care of his wife had contributed to a co-dependent relationship. When he finally asked for a divorce, they were both freed to heal, and his children understood and continued to love him.

With second-order change, a Two took better care of himself while still using his gift of compassion for others.

Mary's style Three client, Karen, was familiar with the Enneagram and open to exploring the effects of her coping strategies on her business and personal life. Karen's drive to achieve, typical of a Three, was now targeted to make her marriage the best. She had been blaming her husband, Jack (an Eight), for what she considered unacceptably angry verbal battles. He felt no recourse but to attack her verbally in order not to feel vulnerable.

Karen and Mary rehearsed ways to counter Jack's verbal attacks without escalating their fights. This alone could have resulted in first-order change. But because Karen also reframed her interaction with Jack in Enneagram terms, she was able to step out of the box that defined him as the problem. She began to see how they both contributed to their difficulties, especially how her relentless insistence on an efficient discussion with complete closure, the pattern of an in-the-box Three, felt like an attack to him.

Notice the two levels of change. As long as they focused on strategies within the particular box created by the interaction of their Enneagram styles (negotiation strategies for Karen, anger management methods for Jack) they would be stuck in the illusion of only two choices ("Will we fight when we feel controlled or will we have a calm discussion?"). They would struggle within the automatic patterns they continued to create. By stepping out of the box and noticing their patterns, they were able to have discussions about their process: "Let's stop and take stock of what we're doing here that's creating such pain. What could I as a Three and you as an Eight do that's different, that would break our patterns?"

In *The Invitation*, Oriah Mountain Dreamer writes, "It doesn't interest me who you know or how you came to be here. I want to know if you will stand in the center of the fire with me and not shrink back." We acknowledge that transformational change is not easy, that we must be willing to stand in the fire with our clients, and they with us. People helped by a coach's insights may realize their inner patterns but feel unmasked. This experience is unnerving and may raise other defenses. You can even anticipate that the ego, which controls the habitual coping pattern, will sometimes fight ferociously to resist such fundamental change. It is human nature not to face up to things about ourselves that are at odds with our carefully constructed worldviews.

Because clients may defend against changing even in the face of conscious determination, the way you provide help is vital. They will need your inspiration to believe in possibilities, and they will need to know that their inevitable discomfort can be transformed into energy for growth. Your unconditional positive regard and continued support will help them stay with the transformation process. As a good coach, you will lead your clients through whatever blocks have limited their potential.

First- and Second-Order Change

First-Order Change refers to behavioral change: learning new skills or capabilities that involve doing something better without necessarily examining or challenging underlying beliefs and assumptions. These are examples of first-order change only:

a. Bill Danvers, a style Three, became Mary's client because his peers saw him as going for the glory. In-the-box Threes are driven to succeed at any price. True to this worldview, Bill was in line to be president because of his spectacular sales results and because he'd taken all the credit, in spite of his teammates' behind the scenes support. Moreover, after agreeing with his team on negotiation parameters, he made deals with customers that overrode these agreements. In the excitement of the deal, Bill focused only on how good it would feel to close the sale. He could practically hear applause in his mind.

Because he wanted the approval of his peers to get his promotion, he agreed to tell customers his deals were tentative. He also learned collaboration skills to improve relations with his peers, and came across more as a team player. These behavioral tools might have earned sufficient respect to support his promotion, even if Bill used his newfound skills only to meet his career goals. He might have continued to see his peers as less accomplished than he. Worse, Mary could have unwittingly reinforced Bill's worldview of how important it is to look good.

With first-order change, a Three might meet his career goals but reinforce his worldview that it's important to look good.

b. Nancy Schwab's boss thought she was too negative and asked her to work with Clarence. Nancy is an Enneagram Six. Sixes want to protect against all negative possibilities in order to feel safe. From this worldview, it is quite natural to focus primarily on what can go wrong. Clarence coached Nancy to counter this tendency by using creative problem solving. Instead of saying, "That won't work because it will take too long," for example, she learned to incorporate her concerns into a solution statement: "I think that could solve our problem. Let's talk about how we can shorten the production time."

Nancy still had the worldview that the world is not safe and so looked for the negative contingencies, but she had a new skill. Her boss complemented her on sounding more positive and she was pleased to no longer be under the gun. At this point was the coaching successful? Nancy experienced a first-order change. However, she still lived in a world where she had to protect herself so she would feel safe. There was not yet a fundamental change.

With first-order change, a Six might sound less negative but still live in a world where she has to protect herself to feel safe.

c. As a style Nine, Barry Foster held and tried to harmonize all points of view. He hired Mary because his boss wanted him to confront two people reporting to Barry who would not collaborate with him. Barry had been trying to resolve the situation with some fairly abstract e-mails outlining his vision for the department. Newly promoted, he found that his preferred style was not working. The two players who wouldn't collaborate with him were used to operating independently and not about to change spontaneously. Furthermore, his boss, Malcolm, was tough, and clear about his dissatisfaction with Barry's easy-going demeanor. Malcolm wanted Barry to be "more authoritative, to take charge and bring those people into line."

Mary offered Barry some guidelines for confronting performance problems, and then showed him how to use relaxation and visualization techniques to increase his comfort level as he mentally rehearsed the impending confrontation. She and Barry might have felt they'd accomplished something significant if he became comfortable enough to actually get these two people with the program. Without examining and reframing his worldview, however, how much would Barry have changed? The transformational potential for Nines is to awaken, to release self-initiated energy, to focus on their own agendas. Look at what had happened with Barry. He worked with Mary because his boss was impatient with his consensus-seeking style. Mary offered a structure to help Barry deal with his problems. Where was Barry's agenda? How could Mary help him find it?

With first-order change, a Nine might confront performance problems but still seek structure from others.

Second-Order Change occurs when clients can see things in a radically different way and break the illusions inherent in a worldview. This change illuminates possibilities that exist outside their customary frame of reference. The fundamental reshaping of underlying patterns makes it possible for them to do what they have never done before. Second-order change enfolds first-order change, and also goes beyond it.

On the level of second-order change, people observe themselves and ask questions about their automatic responses: "What is going on here? How do I judge events, interpret them, and feel bound to respond to them in a certain way?" They begin to notice self-fulfilling and self-defeating habitual patterns that were below their previous level of awareness. They become less defensive and more open to significant change.

An understanding of the Enneagram can provide an illuminating road map for what to look for at the individual and interpersonal levels.

With second-order change, a Three breaks his pattern of competitiveness.

a. Bill Danvers, for example, began to notice how competitive he was and how he felt he must succeed no matter what it took. He then understood that his behavior was driven by his fixation as a Three to be recognized for his accomplishments. As he explored his own feelings and needs, he searched for an inner gyroscope that would guide him with more authenticity. He slowly became aware of messages he'd gotten that his worth depended on accomplishment. He recognized his longing to just be himself. Bill now saw that his focus on his own achievements often cost others their just recognition. In the past this reinforced his belief that he had to do everything himself in order to get results. Mary coached him to stay with the sensations he experienced[1] when he became impatient with someone (a first-order skill in a second-order context). He was gradually able to stop his habitual response when feelings of competitiveness and need for approval began to grip him.

b. Nancy Schwab noticed her general tendency as a Six to anticipate what could go wrong and to look for hidden agendas. She learned to see how that coping strategy stemmed from self-doubt and fed her sense of powerlessness. In addition to learning how to approach problems with solutions, she began to see how she created a dangerous world in which she always had to have her antennae fully extended. Her pattern of thinking left out what could go right. With some coaching from Clarence, she learned to notice how she filtered out the positive, in existing information and in possibilities. As she became more balanced in her risk assessment, she needed less and less to defend herself from her boss's criticism. She saw that she had been negative, and that her behavior invited and reinforced his response. Clarence suggested that when Nancy realized she was focusing only on the negative, she take out a piece of paper, write down all the negative possibilities in the left-hand column, and counter these with positive possibilities in the right-hand column (a first-order skill applied in a second-order context).

With second-order change, a Six breaks her pattern of creating a dangerous world.

c. At the level of second-order change, Mary coached Barry Foster to step out of the box of his Nine coping strategy. He learned that his shy and somewhat humble behavior with his staff was the result of a kind of lethargy or inner immobility. He forgot himself when he merged with other points of view. He began to see how his habitual behavior invited others (especially his boss) to speak up for him. This pattern reinforced the message he got early in life that no one was interested in what he had to say. While holding this new awareness, Barry learned assertiveness techniques (first-order skill, second-order context) and began to loosen up a bit. He started expressing opinions more openly and directly. At first he was anxious about causing conflict, but his new understanding shed light on why he felt anxious, so he spoke up anyway.

With second-order change, a Nine breaks his pattern of letting others speak for him.

Transformational Change is a matter of degree within second-order change. Once your clients have experienced a shift in their point of view, their habitual responses come into question. They will never be the same. Even if the habitual behavior comes up, they will experience it differently because they have now developed an observing self that recognizes the pattern. While they are likely to feel exhilarated during the process of change, they may also feel stunned, shocked, humiliated, disoriented, or even depressed.

---

[1]See *Focusing,* by Eugene Gendlin.

The anthropologist Victor White first used the term *liminality* (from the Latin *limen*, meaning *threshold*) to describe the space between two stages of growth and consciousness. Or, as we have heard: "Whenever one door closes another opens, but it's hell being in the hallway!" Jean Shinoda Bolen[2] refers to this in-between zone as a life passage, "a state in which we are neither who we used to be, nor who we are becoming." She reminds us that we are more vulnerable in these times of liminality, but also more "psychologically receptive and open to new growth."

Mary, a Nine, took a major step into that in-between zone in the spring of 1997. She knew that the transformation goal of a Nine is *active engagement,* and ended an Enneagram workshop with a deep commitment to stay aware of what she wanted and to ask for it. For a month she was excited and full of energy. Then she fell into a depression different from the familiar, transitory times of feeling a loss of energy. It took several months with her coach for Mary to be able to stay committed to setting boundaries instead of merging with others wishes, and to pursue her own agenda. She describes this as a "terrifying, amazing, and transforming roller-coaster ride."

Why would any of us resist such joy of self-discovery? William Bridges makes a key point about "what most people refer to unthinkingly as 'resistance to change.'"[3] Change takes place when something old stops and something new starts. We resist this transition because it requires that we let go of a former identity, even though it stands in the way of the desired change.

Transformation requires that we let go of a former identity and this can be an uncomfortable transition.

Those who work with the Enneagram will find themselves on the path of transformation. Your clients may balk and stumble, but with your wise partnership they can hold the course of a potentially uncomfortable transition while they break through the patterns that have been holding them hostage.

Transformational change does not move in arbitrary directions. It requires us to let go of specific patterns that have shrunk our world and distorted our vision, to move toward the strengths of our personality style. The nine generic Enneagram descriptions detail the gifts and liabilities of each. A sensitive coach who knows the Enneagram can help clients appreciate their gifts while building awareness of self-defeating motivations and consequent behaviors.

a. Bill, for example – the Three mentioned earlier – got in touch with his true feelings, and felt some shame at how he'd depended on recognition from others. He acknowledged to Mary that he'd always been impatient with feelings and group process, especially when they got in the way of the task at

[2] *Crossing to Avalon*
[3] *Surviving Corporate Transition*

hand. But he became more emotional than he bargained for. He'd convinced his team that he was collaborating, but still worked deals to his advantage—a slip back into his Enneagram coping strategy. He tried to resist thinking of himself as someone who looked for approval and who had ignored others in his quest for success. Only because Mary helped him maintain focus on the desired changes was he able to tolerate his transitional discomfort. With Mary's encouragement and reinforcement, he began to spontaneously access his feelings and to engage in true collaboration.

A Three begins to spontaneously access his feelings and to engage in true collaboration.

b. Nancy admitted to Clarence that she felt embarrassed to own up to her negative focus as a Six. She had always seen herself as a good contingency planner, almost psychic at times. She worried about her boss's criticism for days at a time, putting herself in a tailspin because the criticism hurt her feelings and damaged her self-image. She slipped back temporarily to the level of first-order change: she used the new techniques, but continued to accuse her boss of being unfair. Clarence knew that Nancy had to pull out of this tailspin if she was to experience an enduring transformational change. He encouraged her to keep balancing her negative expectations with positive ones, and she spontaneously began to notice both sides of the equation. This balance showed up naturally in her language and problem-solving capabilities. In this respect she was no longer the same person she had been. She now experienced herself and her world differently.

A Six balances negative expectations with positive ones and experiences her world differently.

c. Barry felt somewhat depressed when he identified himself as a Nine. He feared that the Enneagram confirmed his deepest fears that he was a wimp. He wanted to change, but still experienced himself the same old way. He rehearsed with Mary how to confront his problem staff members, but avoided actually setting up a meeting to do so. He then asked Mary to tell him how to overcome his own resistance to change. She gently but firmly left the choices up to him, and Barry moved ahead step by step in spite of feeling stuck. He discovered that he cared passionately enough about his department's mission to fight for it. As he continued to claim what was important to him and to stand up for his beliefs, he no longer needed to use techniques to diminish anxiety because he *felt* less anxious and more energetic.

A Nine claims what is important to him and stands up for his beliefs.

More on Reframing

We have mentioned that it is possible for a coach to unwittingly recommend strategies that could hinder a breakthrough by reinforcing the client's fixed point of view. Each Enneagram worldview is a narrow picture of reality. It is part of the coach's job to alter this illusory image by *reframing*: changing its context or description so it takes on new meaning. Here are some examples for the cases just reviewed:

Reframing means changing the context of a worldview so it takes on new meaning.

a. Teaching Bill collaboration skills for interacting with his team had two layers. Mary showed him how collaboration would increase his chances for success. (This is an example of matching the client's worldview in order to be credible.) It was important, however, that the content of the coaching implicitly reframe the meaning of success Mary told Bill his success would come through collaboration rather than competition. Here are some sample actions from a collaboration checklist she gave him that began to undermine his worldview as a Three that "I must be the best:"

_____ share personal information to create a common ground.

_____ give credit or recognition where warranted.

_____ work to develop teamwork and cooperation in the group.

_____ encourage exploration of differing viewpoints, attitudes, interests.

_____ cooperate across functions to achieve company objectives.

In working with Bill (or any Three), however, it was vital to short-circuit his habitual methods of achieving recognition. If Mary praised Bill for becoming more effective, even in following the collaboration guidelines, that could have blocked second-order change by reinforcing his achievement coping strategy—his search for approval outside of himself. Because he and Mary had developed a trusting, caring relationship (a necessary ingredient for transformational change), she was able to reflect on Bill's reactions in such a way that he experienced failure as a good thing (because it snuck him out of the box of having to succeed).

A Three reframes failure as a good thing.

b. Clarence gave Nancy a creative problem-solving technique that undermined her fixation on accusation as a Six. She had habitually looked for what could go wrong and why others were wrong. Focusing on solutions shifted her away from her habitual perspective. It enhanced the possibility of transformational change through self-empowerment. Clarence was explicit that this problem-solving technique was to help Nancy gain her own power and trust her own instincts, not to respond better to unwarranted criticism. If she had seen this as defending herself, that would affirm that the boss was too critical or unfair and reinforce her habitual powerlessness. Clarence reframed her blaming the boss as a way of keeping herself powerless and reinforcing her self-doubt. This helped her to let go of strategies that kept her in the role of helpless victim and to see opportunities for self-empowerment.

A Six reframes blaming the boss as a way she has kept herself powerless.

c. Mary had taught Barry how to be more assertive. This helped him speak up more readily for himself, instead of waiting to merge his views with those of others. He also heard himself when he was passive ("Well, uh, I don't know, maybe we could… well, what do you think?") or sometimes passive aggressive ("Do you really think this will work?"). He eventually stated his opinions more openly and directly ("This is what I think…"). It was important to frame Barry's adoption of this communication tool as a way to develop self-knowledge and choose what he wanted, not as a way to avoid conflict. As he became more assertive, Barry did, in fact, express annoyance and even anger more openly and directly. This solved his problems with his wayward team members (which his boss applauded), but did not go down so well when he communicated strong opinions to his boss, who tended to up the ante in direct confrontation. Barry sought support and encouragement from Mary, but she was careful not to provide all the structure. If Barry just followed her directions, this would reinforce his Nine fixation of self-forgetting and make transformational change more difficult.

A Nine reframes assertiveness as choosing what he wants vs. avoiding conflict.

Of course you could use other strategies and other ways of reframing than the ones cited in the three cases above. The quality of the coaching relationship and your coaching skills make all the difference. You can enfold many first-order strategies for change within an overarching vision of second-order change. You will guide your clients to experiment with fieldwork that breaks old patterns and brings about new ways of feeling and thinking. An outward change is helpful, but it is even more helpful when it triggers an inner change—a transformation. Thoughtful reframing at the second-order level of change, along with caring support, can provide the necessary reinforcement to fully integrate that change.

Transformational coaches suggest fieldwork that breaks old patterns and brings about new ways of thinking and feeling.

In addition, the coaching relationship itself is a mini-laboratory for breakthroughs. Whatever the inner dynamics that brought your clients to coaching, they will most assuredly act them out with you. And don't forget you have your own habits of attention. Always ask yourself if you are behaving in ways that help or hinder your clients' growth. Be aware that how you interact with your clients makes a big difference in their progress. For example:

a. Threes seek approval from outside themselves. They typically will list their accomplishments for you during each coaching meeting. Will you reinforce that in-the-box behavior by approving or will you help them see this habitual behavior as it occurs with you?

b. Sixes seek authority and then challenge it. Will you be caught in this pattern? Will you let them turn you into an authority or will you comment if you see the pattern and use what happens during coaching to encourage transformation?

c. Nines rely on others to provide structure. If you ask a probing question and find your Nine clients somewhat confused, will you jump in with a suggestion or will you be patient and encourage them to start anywhere—an arbitrary choice, a set of alternatives, or even a list of what they do not want to do?

Your clients will approach potential breakthroughs either as frightening ventures into the unknown or as potent explorations. How they move forward rests in the quality of your coaching. Transformational coaching requires that you: (1) be receptive, provide a safe harbor, listen deeply and empathically; and (2) take a stand and challenge their self-limitations. This is important especially when they (or you) are most discouraged.

Transformational coaches use their interactions with clients to listen deeply and challenge self-limitations.

Coaching like this requires devotion to your own transformation. You will improve your coaching as you learn about your Enneagram style. You can start to use your gifts more consciously and observe how your own patterns limit you and your clients. Then you can use whatever occurs in the coaching relationship as data for discussion.

While coaching a Two named John, for example, Mary faced him with his retreat from discussing a perceived criticism by her, even though he was clearly upset. He was still so tied to his pattern of focusing on her needs and feelings that he diverted attention from his own. After that session John wrote Mary an e-mail saying he felt she had betrayed his needs (a recurring theme for Twos). He wanted to stop coaching after the next session. Mary's first reaction was defensive: as a Nine she worried that she might have been too blunt, not kind enough to John. But she managed to stay centered, and not to take his attack personally. In his next coaching session, they were able to discuss the dynamic they had created and to explore how this same pattern showed up in John's other relationships. During this discussion Mary helped John express his needs openly (difficult for a Two). She gently pulled him back to his own feelings when he tried to move the conversation back to her. He subsequently decided to continue with Mary as his coach.

In the chapters to follow you will find a detailed case description and coaching analysis for each of the nine Enneagram styles. Each chapter includes coaching tips specific to that style, targeted to both first- and second-order change. Before entering that world of specifics, however, we invite you to keep in mind some general principles about transformational change.

A Couch Against The Wall

We began this chapter with the story of a young man who received a gift that changed him for a number of reasons.

Stories and other forms of right brain communication can change us in ways and on levels that we often do not understand. When we do understand how that kind of communication works, we have a better grasp of how to coach someone to make profound changes.

In the story, the beautiful couch was set up against a wall with which it clashed. Spontaneous change occurs when perceptions can no longer be integrated in one's worldview. Sometimes a few small, artistically placed changes can be transforming because these alterations clash so unmercifully with the client's outmoded worldview.

When the couch went up against the wall, the young man saw what he had never seen, and in a context with which he was intimately familiar. The couch changed the way he saw the wall and his house—and his life. We all deal with images of reality. People who say things like, "Well, the reality is…" or "Get real" don't understand that no one gets reality straight. No one "tells it like it is." So when you help change the way clients perceive things, they change the only reality anyone ever inhabits.

A few small, artistically placed changes can be transforming because these alterations clash with the client's outmoded worldview.

The couch on the wall reframed the young man's world by showing him that beauty could be present. The couch opened up a possibility; namely that his house and life could be attractive. That was news to him, conflicting with his worldview of despair and defeat.

Clients who suffer from their image of their world often act in accord with that image. Consequently, careful listening to clients has to come first. Every case is unique. What is their world like? It will not do you any good to simply bring a couch to your client. The guru did not just send out a gift; she listened carefully to the young man's story, learned his worldview, and then graciously altered it. She entered the young man's world, looked for his metaphors of life; his assumptions, beliefs, and illusions; then gently put one thing in his life that defeated his defeat. Good coach. If he had just been told to clean up his house, the young man might have done it, even done it well, but he would have kept his inner world belief that he was doomed to failure.

Clients are always kind enough to have a problem. That problem, or symptom, will be stated as an inability to do something they want to do or a desire to stop doing something they don't want to do. Their problems are rooted in their Enneagram style.[4] So don't look for solutions too quickly. First, you want to follow the symptom to its Enneagram taproot. Your clients will believe that their problem is impossible to solve, and it has always felt impossible. You have to have the courage to stand on the edge of this frightening world, see why their problem has seemed impossible, and then show them paths out. But you cannot lead them out unless you let them lead you in.

We are all used to objective, linear, analytic language—the language of the classroom—that goes by the name of reason. But that does not persuade or induce change. Sometimes it helps not to explain. The guru in the story did not. If she had sat down and explained why the young man had to change his worldview, nothing would have happened. The guru would have gained a reputation for wisdom and the young man might have come back to her, but his house would still be a mess.

Objective, linear, analytic language does not persuade or induce change. Transformational coaches encourage small symbolic changes that reframe a client's experience.

For real transformation, encourage small symbolic changes that reframe a client's experience. These may not seem logical. "A couch?" someone with a more left-brain approach might ask. "What's that supposed to do?" But look at what the wise guru accomplished with her symbolic gift.

We describe specific, right brain techniques for second-order change in the final chapter of this book. First, though, read the following case descriptions and coaching analyses of all nine Enneagram styles. When you learn the Enneagram, you will learn what couch to give to which client at what time.

---

[4] We know this is a big claim, but we will back it up repeatedly.

Chapter 3

Seventy Times Seven

"Edgar's done exactly what I asked him to do," said Paul Turow, CEO of the manufacturing company where Edgar Thurman worked, "so he's gotten my full support. But on the human side of it, he can't succeed if he doesn't change." Paul and the president of the company, Mark Kelly, had contacted Mary because Edgar's subordinates were close to mutiny. Edgar had been hired to repair quality standards in his division, but after a planning retreat with his team one of them had complained to Paul, "He basically told us everything we'd done was a pile of crap." Paul had his own take on that: "Edgar has a really strong, fixed position of what's right and wrong. I told him you don't tell a couple showing off their new baby that the child is ugly."

Mark Kelly added his assessment: "Edgar commands respect because he's intelligent and knowledgeable. He's broken records everywhere he's been and someone less aggressive might not have accomplished what needed to be done. He walked into a situation in which well-meaning people had scratched their heads for two years over problems they couldn't solve. He had a formidable task and timetable, and enormous pressure to show results. He brought about improvements almost unheard of in our industry." "But," he paused, "he needs to be careful not to shoot people out of the water."

Mary asked what Paul and Mark expected. Mark replied, "I don't want him to roll over just to get people to like him, and I want him to continue having strong systems." Paul nodded agreement, then added, "But he has to respect people in the process. Right now he doesn't know how to deal with the tension between efficiency and human relations. We can't afford to lose the people who are threatening to quit."

Both Paul and Mark warned Mary she would not find much support for Edgar among his peers. Paul explained: "He made some monumental changes without consultation. Everything he does has to be top-notch and he gauges everyone else

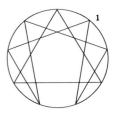

by his own standards." "Yeah," Mark sighed. "He wants to do the right thing but he comes off as intolerant and inflexible. He'll say 'That's the way it is.' It's very hard for him to admit he's wrong. He also needs to see there's more than one explanation for things."

When Mary interviewed Edgar's peers, they reluctantly agreed that he did outstanding work. They noticed the kind of creativity often found in style One—a constant effort to improve performance. "He's always thinking of ways to do things better, and when he's in charge of a project, it's perfect," observed Hank, a fellow vice president. But they also noticed a down side of style One—a belief there is only one right way to do things and a tendency to believe they are in full possession of that way. As Hank ruefully put it, "Unfortunately, he wants you to know he's right."

Sam, a third vice president, saw still another side of Edgar. He depicted Edgar's sense of humor as "a caustic, dry wit" that could descend into sarcasm and even condescension. "The other day he told me, 'That's a stupid idea. You should know better!'" Hank and Sam had tried and failed to give Edgar feedback: "He's incredibly sensitive to criticism." "I've tried any number of times to help him see the effect he's having on people, but it's hard to get through to him."

Despite the fact that some employees had threatened to quit if they had to work for Edgar, others appreciated the high standards he set and were proud of their recent quality improvements. One of his best performers said, "He gives good advice and he means well. He challenges our thinking, offers constructive criticism, and is quick to pass on credit to people who do their work well. The hard part is that he can give a real ass-chewing. He doesn't realize that his tone of voice is perceived as an attack. People feel hurt, blamed, even degraded sometimes."

Another capable manager said, "I think he has our best interests at heart so I don't see him as malicious. But you should see how he strafes and carpet-bombs people! He'll scold in a parental tone as if only he knows best, and he doesn't take time to listen. Instead he'll bark, 'That's unacceptable!' or 'Answer the question: Yes or no?' He doesn't do this every day, but when he does it's always triggered by someone not meeting his standard. He doesn't grade on the curve."

Edgar also kept a close watch on people who reported to him. One of his critics remarked, "He's such a perfectionist that he wants to make sure everything is covered. I think it's a control issue. He needs to know every infinite detail until I feel smothered. If you did ten things on a list of twelve and there were problems with the last two, that's where his focus would be, with no thanks for the ten things you did well."

Regardless of their standing with Edgar, his subordinates agreed on what needed change. It wasn't his performance; it was his style: "When you stick somebody's nose in failure that doesn't necessarily fix the problem." "When problems come up he needs to get the facts and involve people more in brainstorming solutions." "He needs to phrase things in a more constructive manner, convey what he wants by instructing or coaching, and use more positive motivation."

Initially, Edgar was wary of working with Mary. Mary knew that Ones can be self-critical, so she was not surprised when he voiced this concern: "I don't want to give the appearance that something's broken." He explained why his approach had been necessary: "I've always felt my job was to do the right thing for the company. When I came into this job, some staff members were incapable of doing the work without close supervision." He felt he was caught in a bind: "They asked me to come in and fix the problem and I did. Now they're complaining about the way I did it. Mark told me, 'Don't smother them,' but his standards are just as high as mine. We're heading into a period of far-reaching organizational change and we're in a tough market. We fight for our lives every day."

As Mary listened without comment, Edgar seemed to relax and soften a little, then said, "But maybe I've been riding herd on them a little too much. I've stepped back some, but if there are a thousand questions, I've wanted answers to all of them."

When Paul told Edgar to change his style of communicating, Edgar wrestled with how to do that and remain honest. His brow furrowed as he told Mary, "I'm not into this game of covering up things that aren't right. I always confront people when there are problems. I know I have the reputation of being ruthless, but one reason I've turned things around in several positions is that I gave people a choice: shape up or leave. I've rarely had to fire anyone. Either they improved their work or they left if they knew they couldn't do the job."

Mary asked Edgar where he got his high ideals. He answered that his mother had insisted he work hard. "She said, 'If you want to do anything, do it right.' She expected a lot and pushed me hard, but I looked up to her because she taught me a strong sense of right and wrong. I've always said that people should do their jobs in front of their mothers!"

Coaching Analysis

Coaching Edgar

Once he committed to being coached, Edgar was an eager student. However, the first feedback session with Mary promised to be a little tense. They planned to meet in an airport conference room. Mary prepared the feedback from interviews in such a way that Edgar would not feel either broken or needing to be fixed. Mary also wanted to establish a deeper working rapport so he would not become defensive. She reviewed her notes and carefully rephrased others' comments in descriptive, nonjudgmental terms. Then, she mentally rehearsed the meeting; picturing herself being calm and attentive, making sure he felt he was an equal partner, and drawing out his wry humor. She could not have planned what really happened.

Edgar arrived early, so he had a carafe of coffee, cups, and condiments waiting for Mary. After their first hello, she loosened the lid of the carafe and promptly spilled coffee on Edgar's notepad, narrowly missing his jacket sleeve. "Whoops," she said, trying to recover, "I thought you were supposed to be the one who's nervous." They both laughed with relief. Mary had made a public mistake and Edgar reassured her that she had done nothing wrong. He gallantly mopped up the mess, and was so at ease that he was surprisingly open to the feedback. The unplanned accident helped set a tone of comfort, humor, and partnership. During their months of coaching, Mary and Edgar worked effectively on several crucial issues.

The Pathological Critic

As they worked, Edgar began to see what his drive to perfection cost him and others. His mother's dictum, "If you want to do anything, do it right," had become more than a proverb, it had become a universal principle. At one point Mary commented, "So you have an internal critic that sometimes finds you wanting." "Yes," Edgar replied, "and I'd say it's a pathological critic because it operates more than sometimes. It beats me up constantly, and in turn I strike out at others."

As they progressed further, Edgar also learned to see mistakes as feedback. He created a new rule for himself, "There are no mistakes, only information."

As they progressed further, Edgar also learned to see mistakes as feedback. Mary explained that *feedback* is a neutral term borrowed from the science of tracking missiles. It simply answers the question, "Are we on target or not?" Edgar learned to value feedback as a clue to progress and a source of learning. For fieldwork, Mary asked Edgar to welcome a few less than perfect choices. That way he could constantly learn. He created a new rule for himself, "There are no mistakes, only information."

While Edgar learned to accept feedback as neutral, he also practiced how to give feedback effectively. Instead of making global, judgmental statements ("That's a stupid idea") he became more descriptive, specific, and focused on action ("You said we need to pour our profits into renovations to attract customers; I have a different idea about how to lure in more customers"). Over time, he learned to accept feedback without being defensive. He even invited it, agreed with what parts he could, probed for detail, then asked for suggestions.

Edgar made significant personal progress when he adopted the premises of appreciative feedback.[1] Mary explained: "Traditional feedback is problem centered. It attends only to what's wrong, what's not complete, and what's sub-standard. Appreciative feedback focuses on outcomes and resources. Everyone has to agree on (1) what will happen when individuals perform at their best, and (2) the resources needed to support that level of performance. Subsequent feedback is based on what's going well—on specific ways that people are moving toward the agreed-upon outcome."

He began to understand problems from their perspective instead of focusing on what they had not done. In response, they were able to come up with solutions they couldn't imagine when everyone was under fire.

Edgar was cautious at first because this approach sounded like being dishonest. Mary assured him he could be appreciative and positive while still keeping his integrity. She went on: "You can only fix things by not fixing them. You find what you look for. When you look for what's wrong you guarantee you will always find something to fix. When you use appreciative feedback you call for the best in people and accelerate the process of positive change." She also encouraged him to talk this way to himself, and predicted that when he appreciated his own improvements, however small, he would begin to muffle his internal critic. Instead of being pathologically punitive, he would more often see what was possible for himself.

Everyone Can Be Right
Mary reframed the meaning of being right: "In the past you identified being right as your way. You've turned people off when you insist they acknowledge you're right. Unwittingly you also diminished everyone's ability to solve problems creatively. They had to look to you for solutions instead of looking within themselves. You can help them solve problems in a way that integrates key assumptions, concerns, and objectives so that everyone gets to be right." Knowing Edgar's high standards, Mary carefully explained that this was different from compromise. She said, "The very notion of compromise assumes that right or wrong are the only two options. When you look beyond right/wrong to agree on a goal, you enlarge your vision to include new alternatives—many roads to one goal."

[1]David Cooperrider, *Appreciative Management and Leadership.*

Mary also helped Edgar learn how to engage in creative dialogue: to probe for understanding instead of trying to convince others that his ideas were better. He stopped criticizing people when they could not solve a problem. His new approach worked especially well with his division managers. He began to understand problems from their perspective instead of focusing on what they had not done. In response, they were able to come up with solutions they couldn't imagine when everyone was under fire.

A Parable

Mary asked Edgar for a situation that would be most likely to make him angry and critical. He said it would likely be the weekly meetings with the managers in which they compared their performance with their goals. If managers did not meet their goals he would typically feel anger rising from the pit of his stomach "like a heat wave." Mary suggested that the next time this happened, he pause for a moment and then ask for more information about the problem. At the same time, during this pause, he was to search for any other feelings that might lie behind his angry reaction.

Edgar did exactly what Mary suggested. At their next session he reported that he was shaken by what he discovered: "I asked some questions to keep this guy talking. While I listened, I heard a small voice inside me that said, 'I don't know how to fix this.' To bail myself out, I was about to make him be wrong." Because Edgar had listened to the managers' explanations without jumping to criticism, they could discuss possible solutions. Some of the managers told him later that their meeting "was the best they'd had in a long time."

Mary gave Edgar, a devout Baptist, Clarence's book, *Parables and the Enneagram*. He was eager to talk about the parable in Matthew 18:21, where Jesus tells Peter to forgive his brother seventy times seven: "It says in the book that if Ones can learn to forgive themselves and others, they develop the compassion necessary for real spiritual development. I've searched for years to understand why I felt the way I felt about myself and other people. Over the past month or so I've come to understand that I was never good enough. The weight of so much guilt was intolerable, so I laid it on others. Somehow that's lifting. I can accept others and myself as we are. That's something I haven't done so well in the past."

Coaching Style One

When you coach Ones, you'll discover they abide by principles and rules. They want guidelines. They will appreciate you being prompt and considerate. You will encourage and energize them if you matter-of-factly accept that they've alienated people while you acknowledge the importance of their ideals.

The proof of true love is to be unsparing in criticism.

Moliere
The Misanthrope
1666

Mary received an e-mail from Jesse about the possibility of being coached. Jesse wrote: "I'm in the midst of a career meltdown. Apparently I'm horrible to work with. I've been told I'm a perfectionist, demanding, and critical, even when I'm trying not to be. I'm totally unaware that I have that effect on people while it's happening. I feel stuck and don't know how to fix this. I've sought help from several people, but I don't want to keep trying what is patently not working. Is there any hope for me?"

This is a lovely invitation from a One. It may not seem like a great opportunity when Jesse writes that she is horrible to be around, nothing has worked, and she feels hopeless. But when she feels this much pain, she is most open to change, and will appreciate all the help she can get. Jesse's hopelessness was paradoxically Mary's cause for hope.

Mary read between the lines of Jesse's message. Obviously, Jesse was open and ready to be coached. She also needed to feel hope. She had tried to fix herself but that hadn't worked. Others had tried to fix her with equally dismal results. It was time to do something different.

Jesse, like many Ones, wanted to be good and help others be good, too. Ones are often surprised that their efforts to improve others are counterproductive. In their first coaching call, Jesse told Mary, "I don't want to hurt people." It distressed her to find out that people were so angry at her attempts to improve things that she had jeopardized her career. Why, with such good intent, would she have these negative consequences?

Mary encouraged Jesse with this response: "Indeed there is hope for you. When people judge you they reinforce your own habit of self-criticism, which is probably at the root of your distress. You need to experience some new behavior that will bring you approval so you can develop more confidence in your own mental health and good sense."

As they talked, Mary looked for signals typical of Ones: How controlled (over-controlled) do they sound? To what degree does their speech reveal rigid

41

assumptions about how things should be? How often do they say, "should"? Do they correct you? Can they enjoy or indulge in humor, as Edgar did when Mary spilled coffee at their first meeting? When reporting negative feedback do they rationalize, or do they at least tentatively accept it as Jesse did? ("Apparently I'm horrible to work with.")

In general, Ones need to observe and interrupt their key pattern of seeking only what's wrong. Your coaching will help them develop nuance and options.

Compares Reality to What Ought to Be

Pay attention to these four habits of in-the-box Ones:

Compares reality to what ought to be

Thinks in black and white

Defends with reaction formation

Becomes judgmental under pressure

Ones look at the world through a moral lens. They see the moral dimension of complex behavior with a clarity other styles can't match. Radio star and life-advice guru Laura Schlesinger ("Dr. Laura" to 20 million listeners) may not be your ideal of sweetness and light. She may trample on your feelings, but she has all those listeners because she offers a moral vision. She believes that she knows the one right moral answer to any question and energetically shares her certitude.

W. Edwards Deming influenced both Japanese and American businesses with his zeal for quality. His principle: "Zero Defects." Quality control was a moral imperative for this tireless teacher. He insisted that striving for perfection is always better than spending time, energy, money, and creativity on repair.

Ones know in their bones how things ought to be. When faced with what they consider someone's inferior work or dysfunctional systems they may react with visceral anger. Edgar described this anger as rising from the pit of his stomach "like a heat wave." Many Ones have a reforming streak, and their zeal can inspire action. Look at Ross Perot, John Ashcroft, or Ralph Nader in the USA or Nelson Mandela and Margaret Thatcher abroad. All have had a mission to make things right the way they see it.

Their idealism can lead them to want to improve themselves with enviable discipline. A One friend of Mary's has for many years risen an hour early each morning. She exercises for 20 minutes, meditates for 20 minutes, and then writes in her journal for 20 minutes.

Ones can often help others see the moral reward of a job well done. Their vision lifts mundane details to the level of virtuous striving. They don't lay bricks, they build cathedrals. In business, they excel at a task that many executives dread: having to evaluate performance. Evaluation comes naturally to them. They understand and value standards and, when out of the box, they apply them fairly. If they are in the box, they compare performance to an unreachable ideal.

People often misunderstand that Ones criticize out of love. When your mother corrected you and said, "I'm telling you this for your own good," she was doing what Ones do. Edgar's peers understood this intermittently: "He wants to do the right thing… in many ways he cares about us… he has our best interests at heart." Ones need to understand that criticism, however well intended, can wither self-esteem and kill enthusiasm.

Marsha came to see Clarence because she was furious with her workmates. She said they simply were not doing a good job. She wanted to feel less anger and she wanted them to do better work. Ones often have a heightened sense of responsibility, especially to reform people or situations, so Clarence asked what degree of responsibility she actually had for her co-workers. Marsha looked embarrassed. She stammered and finally blurted out that it was not really her role but she felt a moral obligation to correct them. Clarence asked how she currently tried to motivate them. Marsha paused, and then said that when they were slacking off, she reminded them repeatedly of the rules and what they were expected to do. But they did not seem to care as much as she did.

Clarence talked to Marsha's supervisor, who saw things a little differently. He said she had a reputation for arrogance and bossiness. She did her own job well, but snuffed out the morale of the rest of the department.

Clarence returned to Marsha and asked her for a noble motivation for correcting her fellow workers. She thought for a while, and then said she didn't want them to hurt the company or get into trouble. Clarence helped her to recognize that her noble intent had negative consequences.

Then Clarence switched focus from the visible consequences to her inner state. He asked if she criticized herself at times. Through tears she said she did all the time. Clarence then suggested that she keep a journal as fieldwork. Each day she was to note how her habit of criticism had prevented her from committing some moral fault—doing inferior work or being lazy or unkind, for example. This part of the exercise was to help her make friends with her critical voice.

By focusing on what was positive, Marsha started to weaken her habit of comparing herself and others to an ideal.

Next, Clarence asked her to give herself credit in her journal for how well she did things because of her internal vigilance. They discussed how it felt to appreciate herself instead of criticizing herself. The third step was for her to start recording all the things her fellow workers did that she could praise or appreciate.

By focusing on what was positive, Marsha started to weaken her habit of comparing herself and others to an ideal. She reported that her anger diminished

43

sharply when she discovered that her critical voice had blinded her to how hard people really worked. She was surprised at how much more seriously they began to take her observations, complimentary or critical, once she began to notice their good will and effort. She had the same hesitancy Edgar did. She feared she was not being honest unless she was being critical, but she gradually became aware that *she* made that painful and faulty equation.

Sometimes a One's ideals are aesthetic rather than moral. Miss Manners, a One, instructs the multitudes on social graces. Ones have a vision of the ideal and will spend heroic energy implementing and even sacrificing for it. They disdain those who talk about the bottom line and mean only profits. Their bottom line is excellence. Profits should not compromise ethics, integrity, or quality. Ones are not motivated by solutions they assess as easy, slick, or shady. They see these as short-term traps.

In order to reach an ideal, Ones may treat all rules as absolute and have trouble distinguishing between major and minor rules. They can be helped by learning to rank norms, rules, and obligations in order of their importance. All rules are not created equal; they are modified by context. Some rules conflict with others, so ask them why one is more important than another. For example, a physician might have the rule, "Always give the best care possible." Ask him to think of a circumstance in which that rule would either not apply or need to be balanced by another rule. The doctor might describe a situation in which the patient is terminally ill and has asked in writing that no extraordinary measures be taken. The family has agreed. Now a contrasting rule has priority: "When death is inevitable, it is humane to honor the patient's wishes."

If Ones worry about breaking a rule, have them describe the context, history, and the values associated with the rule. Then you can discuss circumstances under which a rule could be modified or even ignored. When they learn that the ideal is not expressed in every rule, they become more flexible and learn to discern. Ones often magnetically comply with routines and standards of external authority. You can help them claim their inner authority by suggesting that this rule may have been created in another time and context. Ask them, "Given the current circumstances, what do you think?"

You can even use their love of rules to instigate desired change. Ones often turn mere sayings into ironclad rules like Edgar did with his mother's axioms. A rule like "Never eat after 7:00 p.m., never leave a messy desk, never go to bed angry with your spouse" may govern their inner life thoroughly. Build on their attraction to pithy life guidelines by giving them proverbs or quotes that reframe their assumptions: "Life is painting a picture, not doing a sum" (Oliver Wendell Homes, Jr.). "Happiness is not a destination. It is a method of life" (Burton Hills). These sayings can modify a One's understanding of the ideal to which they compare themselves and others.

Ones find that learning to break some lesser rules can be amusing and even therapeutic. A staid One accountant performs as a clown on weekends in full makeup and silly shoes. A social worker dresses properly but has a Phyllis Diller hairdo, outlandishly bleached blonde and disheveled.

Ones find that learning to break some lesser rules can be amusing and even therapeutic.

Thinks in Black and White

In-the-box Ones have a black and white style of thinking. They have a clear notion of the way things ought to be and consider any other way completely wrong. This can apply to any task, rule, or even any attitude. If rigidly certain, they may have difficulty delegating even small tasks. So few people really *get* the perfect way to do things because so few share a passion for excellence. When Ones do delegate, because of their concern for quality, they may do it in such detail that they blur the distinction between *assigning* (telling people what to do and how to do it) and *delegating* (telling people what to do, then trusting them to figure out how).

On the other hand, some One managers may delegate with an ideal picture in mind, but fail to mention it to the employee. They set people up to fail because those ideal expectations will eventually surface. A request for a budget might mean a one-page summary to an employee, but the One might actually be expecting a detailed comprehensive computer printout. This can discourage employees when a lot of work has been done: "Well, why didn't you tell me that in the first place?" If they don't state their expectations clearly, in-the-box Ones will have license to find fault with what has been done: "I knew you couldn't handle that! I should have done it myself!" Ones need to learn to communicate their expectations from the beginning. Then, as the employee demonstrates ability, motivation, and understanding, they can support them.

In order to do a job perfectly, Ones may spend too much time on details and miss the larger picture. If the budget is due by Thursday and they feel they have to analyze every minute component, they may miss the deadline or feel it is unfair. They often are driven by the inner slogan, "There is always room for improvement." Perhaps there is, but there is not always time for improvement. If One clients constantly feel time pressure, help them see that all details are not of equal importance.

If they are too detailed in their instructions, they leave no room for creativity or initiative. If they check in on employees too often and fix problems themselves, they prevent their people from learning how to solve them. We have found that a short course in situational leadership works wonders with Ones: they learn to delegate based on the person's skills, motivation, and the nature of the task instead of simply judging performance as good or bad.

Ones may shrink complex situations down to one issue. For example, they may claim that all business problems have their source in laziness or irresponsibility. They do this to feel in control—to simplify things down to something they can deal with.

When you notice Ones assuming their position is the only right one, ask them to brainstorm three other possible options.

Their black and white thinking can be obvious when Ones judge complex situations by a single criterion. For example, they may expect to promote and be promoted on the basis of performance only. Meanwhile they could ignore their organization's political realities and resent it when others are promoted on the basis of charm, connections, or political savvy. Hillary Clinton, a One, promoted a health care plan and concluded her proposal with the phrase, "It's the right thing to do." While that single criterion may convince a One, it does not motivate people with other plans and priorities.

Ones may subordinate people to the demands of systems more than necessary, becoming harsh and inflexible. They may prefer to go by the book when bending some rules might be more humane and productive. When W. Edwards Deming said that 99 percent of business problems are systemic, he did not leave much room for personal differences. In a management role, Ones may allocate personnel or resources in such a way that feelings are hurt, but they will expect others to stuff their feelings as they ignore their own. They call this merely being objective but others may label it as cold or heartless.

When you notice Ones assuming their position is the only right one, ask them to brainstorm three other possible options. They may dislike brainstorming, but if you assign it, they will probably do it and loosen up a bit in the process. The technique has two parts—free association followed by evaluation—and you are looking for both. Your goal is to help them create options and nuances. When they cultivate their ability to create possibilities, they erode their habit of looking for the one right way. They often find this exercise refreshing, even though it may be foreign. After they have three options, distill the positive portions of each and ask if these elements can be combined. They might mix and match, do them in sequence, or find a common denominator.

Learning the common distinction between *effective* and *efficient* helps Ones since sometimes they can do the wrong task well. Mary had a One client who was writing a book with two co-authors. Each had written a third of the outlined chapters. They met for a week to review and edit their work to ensure a common voice. At 9:00 a.m. on Monday they each retreated to a separate room to work on a chapter. When they met at lunch, the two co-authors had produced volumes of work, many suggestions, and new ideas. In contrast, Mary's client had written, and rewritten, and rewritten one perfect page.

Defends with Reaction Formation

Reaction formation is the act of consciously criticizing what you unconsciously desire. Let's say you're driving along and you spot a sleek sports car. You begin to rant about the high prices of sports cars and how much money people waste on image. Inside, you may have a deep longing for just such a car. Ones may be unwilling to claim what they want because some desires threaten their self-image as a good person. They delete these desires by attacking them and telling themselves, "I don't want that. I want what I *should* want." A children's story illustrates how this works. Remember the fable of the fox and the grapes?

The fox longed to eat a luscious bunch of grapes hanging just out of his reach. He jumped, he ran and jumped, he jumped again, until he gave up in exhaustion. Then he muttered, "They were sour anyway." "Sour grapes" has become shorthand for devaluing what we know we *can't* have. Ones have a parallel attitude: they devalue what they think they *shouldn't* have.

Ones often inspire people with their idealism, but when they don't inspire, they can slip down a notch and begin to nag or criticize. When you find a One nagging, ask them about what they are criticizing: "Have you ever tried that?" "Have you ever wondered why they do that?" "What do you think they see in that?" "Under what conditions might their behavior/attitude be acceptable?"

For example, Joel, a One, was manager of a television station. He ran a tight ship and came to Clarence complaining he was being sabotaged by some of his camera crew. He fumed that he would send them out to do a story with strict instructions. He stressed to them that they should only do what he assigned, but instead, they often returned with expensive additional footage they liked—ignoring his instructions. Clarence's background is in media, so he watched their show for several weeks and found it excellent. He asked Joel about the technical quality of the work his employees did, and Joel grudgingly admitted it was fine. He kept coming back to the importance of their only doing what he assigned.

Noting the energy behind his complaint, Clarence asked Joel if he had ever been a cameraman. This question turned on a spigot because Joel had done a lot of camera work. He said he had always found camera work more enjoyable than his current job, but when he was a cameraman, he had always followed instructions, whereas this crew did not. They seemed to him to be in it more for their enjoyment When Clarence pushed for specifics Joel mentioned money again, but his energy was focused on their attitude toward detailed instructions.

Clarence asked Joel point blank if he envied them their job with all its travel, fun, and excitement while his lot was responsibility and conserving money. Joel seemed to get uncomfortable. He said that he thought they made a lot of money when you considered how much fun their job was. He also resented the strict accounting he had to give of their time as well as his own. Clarence asked if he would trade them jobs if he could. Joel frowned and said, "Who would want to climb back down the ladder?" Clarence told him the story of the sour grapes, and then asked him where he could find some good grapes. At first Joel couldn't think of any so Clarence asked him to picture his current job with enough difference so he could enjoy it more. "After all," he reminded Joel, "you create pictures professionally." With a little light prodding, Joel invented a new program designed to mentor young technicians that required him to go out in the field. He had found a virtuous way to claim his desires instead of reacting against them.

You can help Ones weaken their narrow focus on what they think they should do by making an "I want to do" list, a variation on a "to do" list.

You can help Ones weaken their narrow focus on what they think they should do by making an "I want to do" list, a variation on a "to do" list: In this exercise, Ones begin each day by asking, "What do I want to do today?" and writing down everything they can think of. This exercise may help them learn to claim their desires. It depends on the individual, but many Ones can profitably learn to enjoy sensual pleasures like good food and drink, or massage. Nature walks, music, or their favorite entertainment can help. Vacations are good for them because they can put Ones in a helpful double bind: it's their duty to relax and have fun.

Becomes Judgmental Under Pressure

When Ones compare reality to an ideal they tend to criticize rather than praise. In management positions, they don't think a perfect job deserves special praise; they expect it and see no reason to praise the ordinary. On the other hand, every mistake can seem like a moral lapse when Ones interpret all work in a moral light. Consequently, they don't excuse mistakes easily and often feel an urge to correct or in some cases punish. They can get picky, even nasty, about details that others might not notice.

To help them refrain from criticizing, teach Ones to give the kind of nonjudgmental and appreciative feedback that Mary taught Edgar to give. When they learn to give employees descriptive feedback instead of criticism, they lose their disapproving or punishing tone. They also empower their employees to do good work—what some Ones wish to achieve by punishing.

Like other Ones, Mary's client, Bruce, was uncomfortable with not being fully honest as he was learning how to give constructive feedback. With Mary's help, Bruce clarified his understanding of honesty ("direct, truthful, consistent, supportive") and dishonesty ("scheming, closed, devious, chameleon-like"). Then Mary gave him the following fieldwork: "Pick at least one situation this week to be a little dishonest according to your understanding." At the next session, Bruce proudly reported: "I decided to be slightly closed by withholding criticism from a guy who works for me. I told him some things, but not everything. The scheming part was to see if I could get him to do what I wanted him to do without criticizing him. He made the changes I wanted and seemed quite comfortable doing so. I had a good time choosing whether or not to look at something as good or bad. Now I'm seeing more good than bad, in others and myself."

Bruce added, "It was revealing to realize that by giving dishonesty such a categorically negative label I had closed myself off from some nuances of management. When I was a little bad according to my definition, I was a better manager. More broadly, I've realized how quickly I've judged others as being dishonest without taking the complexities of a situation into account. I'm learning not to label behavior so quickly."

Whenever you can, support a sense of humor in your One clients. It can be a sign of health and it mitigates judgment as well. Sometimes you can use humor yourself. You can comically exaggerate and distort a situation's dynamics until the One laughs and sees things in a different light.

It also helps to get Ones in touch with the consequences of being judgmental. For instance, Clarence had a critical workaholic One client to whom he told a familiar children's story—with an added twist—to help her see she was working too hard and being critical of those who weren't.

> Once upon a time there was an ant who worked hard all summer long. She was busy storing grain underground for the coming winter. Her friend, the

grasshopper, just sang and fiddled all summer. In the fall, the grasshopper came to the ant and asked for a bite to eat, but the ant told him sternly that he had wasted his whole summer so he deserved to die. The grasshopper went away hungry and died soon after. The ant went underground, ate all her grain, but also died from the stress of overwork. Worst of all, she died without ever hearing a decent piece of music or learning to dance.

When Ones are judgmental, their inner critical voice constantly scolds and judges them. Edgar heard his mother's voice commenting on every job: "You could have done this better. Why didn't you prepare more? You're wasting time." Ones can't silence this voice entirely, and you don't want them to. It keeps them out of trouble in a way they can come to appreciate. But, you might suggest that they use their imagination to install a volume control for that voice and just turn it down a bit.

Ones try so hard to be perfect that learning from mistakes can be difficult for them.

Ones try so hard to be perfect that learning from mistakes can be difficult for them. But they need to experience failure to learn. Mary told Edgar "If you had never failed, you would still not know how to walk." Clarence sometimes has Ones practice failure in safe territory. He suggests that they try to learn a new language for a week or so. He asks them to notice how often they have to fail in order to learn. If you use this approach, frame their study as a metaphorical practice. Remind Ones that some of the people they correct are in the same position as someone learning a new language.

Ones need to learn that following the rules does not automatically guarantee success. Even after Jesse had been coached for a while, and was able to influence others without provoking their defenses, she discovered her new skills did not work with everyone. For example, she planned to mail a birthday cake. She went to the post office and asked a postal clerk about the size, shape, and cost of mailing but he gave her the wrong information. So she guessed at what she needed to do.

When she brought the cake in to mail it, she discovered she had over-packed, and consequently overpriced, her package. Jesse asked to see the supervisor and explained that she had tried to get correct information, but the clerk had misinformed her. She added that the supervisor might want to instruct the clerk properly. Instead of thanking her, the supervisor said, "You asked him to price a hypothetical package? That's silly!" Jesse came to the coaching session asking, "What did I do wrong? I followed the rules, but he still attacked me."

Mary countered, "Who says you did anything wrong?"

"Well, it didn't work," Jesse replied in frustration.

"No, some people will be defensive no matter how well you communicate your wishes."

"But... but, where is the line?" Jesse asked plaintively.

"We all have different lines. There's no way to know for sure when you'll cross someone's line."

"But, but... how can I predict when it will work and when it won't?" Jesse was beginning to see the humor in her plea.

"You can't." By this time they both were laughing. Jesse realized that she was learning a big lesson. Sometimes there are no rules.

Albert Ellis' classic book on anger[2] is especially useful here. It directs Ones to examine their unwritten rules, which he calls "irrational beliefs." When people break these rules, Ones become angry. Phrases like, "She should not...!" "I can't stand it that...!" "How awful that...!" are phrases that flush out the particular irrational belief that justified the anger. Then Ones can examine the validity of their anger. This practice reveals implicit beliefs and invites a more appropriate emotional response to the actual situation.

For example, Mary's client, Wanda, was furious that her adult daughter had not called her when she was going to be late for a visit. "She should have called," Wanda fumed. "She's never going to become a responsible adult!" Mary pointed out that this was an irrational belief: "No one specific action proves or disproves maturity. People tend to meet their own needs and your daughter did not feel any need to call." Wanda paused and acknowledged it was her problem because it was her rule and expectation. "The truth is, I worry about her." So Mary coached her to tell her daughter ahead of time that she worries and ask her to call if she was going to be late. Asking for what she wanted replaced Wanda's tendency to criticize after her expectations were not met.

Their search for perfection may prompt Ones to ask for criticism and take it seriously. It's a form of love for them. Criticism expresses care. But while Ones want criticism, they also fear it. So when you tell them something they may consider negative, be specific, objective, and nonjudgmental. Mark and Paul had originally required Edgar to have a record of his coaching to be placed in his personnel file. Edgar was concerned that someone might see the file and consider him flawed. All three agreed on a one-page summary, to be approved by Edgar

While Ones want criticism, they also fear it. So when you tell them something they may consider negative, be specific, objective, and nonjudgmental.

[2]Anger: How to Live With and Without It

before it went on record. Mary carefully worded the summary, and then reviewed it with Edgar. Edgar objected to several words. Mary revised the summary. Edgar was finally satisfied it was exact and fair after the tenth rewrite!

The One's Vision: Shift from seeing only what's wrong to developing nuance and options

The work that Edgar and Mary did eventually broke most of the spell of his Enneagram trance. Comments in a six-month follow-up assessment show the kind of turnaround that is possible:

(From Paul and Mark): "Edgar's been totally transformed. He's 180 degrees from where he was. He empowers his people now. Even the ones who weren't used to being responsible have grown."

(From the two other vice presidents): "He routinely discusses business decisions that can affect us. He's easy to talk to. He's not defensive and welcomes feedback."

(From Edgar's employees, including some who were formerly ready to mutiny): "We enjoy the freedom to make decisions we never used to make. He's more interested in our opinions, he appreciates our efforts, and looks out for our interests." And, "He supports us now instead of criticizing. He's willing to help without taking over. His biggest plus is his new sense of humor. He's loosened up and will give and take a joke. He is now one of the best people I've ever worked for."

Chapter 4

Behind the Scenes

"I think it's important to live out my values, to focus on what's needed to take care of clients," Emily Dracker said. A 43-year-old single mother and former social worker, Emily was the CEO of an agency she had created to serve the severely mentally disabled. She hired Mary because she wanted coaching on how to persuade her peers to make changes in the mental health system. "I've always challenged how well we served the mentally ill," Emily explained. "Now that I'm running this agency, they see me as a threat because I ask, 'Why do we continue to let people who need help end up on the streets?'"

When Mary interviewed Emily's colleagues, she found that some liked the way Emily challenged the system but they all agreed she ruffled feathers. One agency director said, "She is honest and argues from her beliefs. But she places such high importance on clients' needs, I think she would manipulate the establishment to reach her goals." "She's very interpersonally oriented and genuine with her feelings," said another, "but she's slow to address things directly when they need to be addressed, not able to hold her own in an argument, sometimes too conciliatory. It's difficult to know where she's coming from because she can react emotionally." All agreed with these statements: "When things are not going her way she's manipulative." "Her agenda with resistance is always to get around it or to blow it up!"

Emily had convinced her staff that her indirect if not manipulative operating style was necessary. "When directors of other agencies start picking her vision apart," said one of her staunchest supporters, "she shows us ways to get her ideas carried out anyway, without outright sabotage."

People who worked for Emily saw how she satisfied their needs: "She's so caring." "She has a natural talent for feedback." "You could idolize her." "She's more of a friend than a boss and she's done so much for me." But trouble arose if employees tried to treat Emily as an equal rather than as a boss. If they pointed

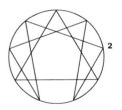

out her behavior that was at cross-purposes with teamwork, she would bristle and blame them for the problem. Emily also responded to their feedback with tears. She seemed to feel like a martyr: "I feel I cut off pieces of myself and feed them to people. I think they see me as Mom and want to take out all their anxieties on me. I've worked so hard to support them in spite of their failings. Maybe I've put too much faith in them. Sometimes they seem so childish!"

"I feel I cut off pieces of myself and feed them to people."

Many Twos are driven by an image of being a good mentor or caregiver. Emily had written a letter to members of her extended family announcing, "I am no longer taking care of people in this family," yet she often rescued a brother who was addicted to gambling. In the past he had been involved with organized crime and appealed to Emily to save his life—literally. He said she was "the only one in the family with enough money to pay my debt." In one coaching session Emily announced that her brother was in jail and needed bail. "I know this is an opportunity to act counter to my impulse," she said, "but it's really hard for me. I need to talk it through with you." Mary pointed out that as long as Emily took care of her brother, she subtly communicated that he could not take care of himself. She could only help him by not helping him. This observation shook up Emily's helping approach sufficiently to allow a different response. She told her brother she loved him but he would have to figure out how to get himself out of jail.

Twos like Emily create inner resentment because they find it so difficult to turn people down: "How can I make a breakthrough with the board chair so he realizes I'm doing absolutely all I can?" she plaintively asked, her eyes wide and glistening. "In my view I keep taking on more work with less staff. On my bad days I'm panic-stricken because I don't want to take it on and fail. But he gets me to do more and more by saying, 'There's no one else who can do it as well as you.' How do I keep myself from overload?"

The board chair offered a different slant: "She says she's overworked, but when I suggest dropping some projects to give her relief, she won't give them up!" A subordinate of Emily's further explained, "It's a double-edged sword because things fall between the cracks while she's trying to be everything to everybody."

On the positive side, Emily was described as charming, charismatic, bright, energetic, and "incredibly committed to mental health clients, really aggressive about going out there and finding out what we can do." One team member said, "She really cares about the mentally ill. Her mission comes out of the deepest sense of service." Another agreed: "This is true to a fault. I'm not sure she would even protect those of us who work for her if she perceived us to be in conflict with client needs."

Emily's interpersonal focus brought other strengths to her job as manager: "She has a wonderful capacity to empower people," praised one of her colleagues. "She took a group of misfits and malcontents, yet they've accomplished remarkable feats because they are committed to her. She values participation, shows them respect, keeps people informed, and shares decision-making. If she fails to delegate it's because she doesn't want to burden people." "Emily could be more hard-nosed," said another, "but she's good at giving people the opportunity to do something a little outside the normal course, and she fiercely defends her people outside the organization." "There's always a high level of pressure here," reported an employee who was up to his eyeballs with work, "but she can 'read' me when I'm stressed out; she does a lot of reality checking: 'Are you O.K.? Do you need help?'"

Emily created a strong sense of family, which inspired and energized her caseworkers. She also cultivated pride among them about the quantity and quality of their efforts, but she accomplished this at some cost to their relationships with social service workers in other organizations. Because Emily created tension with others in their professional community, an "us against the world" feeling prevailed in her organization. "She's the Lone Ranger when it comes to the rest of the world," said the head of another agency, "but she fosters dependence." Her staff corroborated this last point. "She's never happier than when someone says they can't get along without her," noted one of her caseworkers. "We're part of her gang," sighed another, "we'd be almost in tears if she left."

"She's never happier than when someone says they can't get along without her."

Coaching Analysis

Coaching Emily

To support Emily's shift from her helper image, Mary coached her to (1) clarify her boundaries, (2) counter her belief that she could take better care of others than they could themselves, and (3) recognize her own needs and assert them directly.

Boundaries

"The people who work for you appreciate your helpfulness," Mary told Emily. Then they reviewed the feedback that indicated Emily had been protective to the point of being parental: "They say you want to take care of things, give motherly advice, and change direction without consulting them." Mary suggested it was both good and bad news that others liked having Emily's help: "Because they feel supported by you, they don't hold grudges. But you give confusing messages. At times you want to be a friend, at other times you want to be the boss, but they haven't been able to confront you on this. Your boundaries are not clear." Together, they agreed that Emily would:

1. Distinguish between her personal needs and her values for leadership.

2. Separate her need to be loved from her role as a leader, and satisfy her personal needs outside of her leadership role.

3. Solicit and accept feedback about herself as a leader, instead of confusing the issue with personal, emotional reactions.

We coach all clients to observe their unconscious Enneagram patterns. Mary encouraged Emily to notice in particular how she merged with someone else's needs and forgot her own. When Emily could do this, she would see how her assumptions about others' needs kept her helping pattern alive.

Mary encouraged Emily to notice in particular how she merged with someone else's needs and forgot her own... how her assumptions about others' needs kept her helping pattern alive.

Once she could recognize her merging, Emily was to consciously take the perspective of the other person as if she were looking back at herself. This was different from her usual attempts to read minds because (1) it would help her separate her own body and emotions from the other person, and (2) the focus would now be on her, not on the other person. She would gradually learn to move back and forth between these perspectives until she could easily operate from or disengage from either of them. Her crossing of boundaries would now become a conscious choice.

No More Mind Reading

Mary pointed out how Emily assumed what others needed: "Others say you relate well with clients, but you think you can read and interpret their needs better than people who fund your projects." "Yes," Emily affirmed. "Not many people understand the mentally disabled the way I do. I have to educate everyone on what the consumers really need." Mary acknowledged Emily's fine-tuned receptors for the needs of others. But she also helped Emily see how this focus fed her Enneagram worldview. "For example," Mary offered, "you are overly concerned about your staff's need for healing. It is true that their work can be draining, and it's important in team meetings to attend to feelings as well as to the logistics of the work. But you focus too much on what you think they need instead of listening to what they want."

Emily knew she was empathic. She began to see how she moved from empathy into mind reading. Her mind reading was accurate at times, but not as often or to the degree she liked to believe. She believed her staff to be needy ("Sometimes they seem so childish!") and reinforced that belief by behaving maternally, which encouraged them to act like needy children. She learned to check out her assumptions in specific ways, to let her staff members define for themselves how they felt and what they needed.

It was important that her efforts not stop there. Emily gradually learned to be more self-disclosing. In particular, she became willing to talk about her own needs. She said to a staff member, for example, "It's hard for me to admit, but I do come off as a parent sometimes, because I get caught up in being helpful. I need to feel appreciated. So it will help me accept your criticisms if you tell me first what you appreciate about me as your manager."

Taking Leadership

Self-disclosure also became important with peers, who said Emily usually didn't express any of her own problems or ask for help. These colleagues went to her for help with relationship problems. They exploited her people skills by asking her to facilitate their directors' meetings. This had created some problems. The facilitator role fed her pride in being helpful, but it also kept her from developing equal or close relationships with her peers. With coaching, Emily became able to express and pursue what she wanted instead of attending to what others wanted. She saw how she was locked in the role of relationship guru with her peers, and how she focused conversations on the other person. She learned to disclose more of her work-related feelings, needs, and concerns. She even learned to ask for help. "This was a huge shift for me," she said.

Emily saw how she was locked in the role of relationship guru with her peers, and how she focused conversations on the other person. She learned to disclose more of her work-related feelings, needs, and concerns.

Her previous role with peers had reinforced Emily's need to be loved but held her back from taking leadership or getting direct credit for her ideas. "Your colleagues see you as bright, with an entrepreneurial instinct that's unusual in the mental health field," Mary told Emily. "You have shown leadership particularly in developing measurement criteria in a field traditionally sustained by soft data. But some are not fully aware of the quality of your ideas. You seem too ready to agree to other points of view or to back down from your own." Emily countered, "I have to be indirect to get things done the way I want. I always feel too easily taken in by others' needs in a direct confrontation, feeling there must be something wrong with my judgment. Then I figure out a way to do what I want behind the scenes." Mary helped her see the consequences of this undercover approach: "This indirect assertion makes you seem manipulative to your peers."

Echoing comments from her staff, Emily's peers said she had trouble giving candid feedback: "She lives in a world where she believes the best of everybody and seems to downplay any negative feedback." Mary bolstered Emily's confidence in her own ideas and opinions. She assured Emily that instead of "those little white lies," Emily could learn to tell her peers what she did not like. Mary suggested, "It's O.K. to share with them how difficult it is for you to give negative feedback. You can tell them you need the practice, and you want to be a real member of the team, not the relationship guru."

Emily had supported others so well that her colleagues had encouraged her to take that behind-the-scenes role. That met their needs. It took conscious effort for Emily to take credit for her own ideas, to assert herself more directly, and to make sure her own needs and problems became part of the mix. In spite of her personal skills, Emily did not form clean emotional relationship, as some comments by the group indicated: "Though she's friendly and sincere, there's always that sense of maintaining a certain reserve." "She doesn't seem to want to reveal herself, but rather to find out what she wants to know about me."

As Emily began to honor and acknowledge her own needs, she discovered her inexperience with the real intimacy built by sharing one's whole self. She learned to recognize and stay with her authentic needs. She realized that she had also been attracted to romantic relationships in which she felt needed, which forestalled intimacy. Her new focus affected her personal life as well as her professional life.

Coaching Style Two

Helping others, that's the main thing. The only way for us to help ourselves is to help others and to listen to each other's stories.

Elie Wiesel

Twos are highly relational. Match this focus as best as you can. Unless you also are a Two, accept that your emotional decibel level will probably be a bit lower than your client's. Be personal, emotionally present, and genuinely appreciative. Don't expect your logical strategies to be effective with these clients. If you jump in too quickly with analysis you may lose them. If you fail to listen deeply (their needs are well hidden) you'll miss some important clues. Even when you do discover unstated needs, share your personal emotions instead of merely a logical response. Twos respond better to *feel*back than to *feed*back.

In an e-mail inquiring about coaching, John described his friendship with a married woman, Gloria. "This woman," he wrote, "whom I adore, is set on self-destruct and I think I can save her. She thinks I can save her. I understand that I am exhibiting classic Two characteristics and despair that I can ever come to a place of equanimity about her. I'm so good at relationships in general, I can't figure out why I want to keep someone like Gloria in the wings to drive me crazy."

John admitted to Mary during their first coaching session, "I feel a sense of power and excitement when I'm able to seduce powerful, beautiful women like Gloria into being close to me. I impress them. In the strongest of these liaisons I often feel like the child, but take on the role of father. I flatter and make myself indispensable." Within a few sessions, John became aware of the long unmet needs these "dangerous liaisons" addressed. "As a child I desperately tried to please my mother and win her love I had a gagging awareness this week of reliving this in my attachment to Gloria. She, like my mother, is emotionally remote. I would do anything to get her attention, her appreciation, and her spontaneous expressions of affection. I feel tremendously sad about that."

Save any logical analysis with Twos until they become more self-aware and receptive to pattern information. Then guide them to self-discovery through caring and deep listening. Here's what John discovered: "Over the years I've tried to stockpile evidence that I'm okay, a good person. It takes much energy to guard and sustain that hoarded evidence. It keeps dissipating, seeping out and vaporizing, and I have to start all over again. I compile lists of who likes me, even who loves me. I plan carefully to use my energy wisely and surround myself with those who help restore my depleted self. But I burn it off like gasoline in high peak moments that leave me gasping as soon as the moment passes."

The following four sections spell out in detail what to look for as a coach and how to help Twos shift to giving without strings instead of losing themselves by taking care of others.

Gives to Get

Healthy Twos care for people unconditionally. They derive deep satisfaction from seeing and encouraging the development of others. In a business situation they typically give excellent customer service. Mary Kay Ash was an Enneagram style Two, as is the culture of her Mary Kay Cosmetics organization. She articulated the Two creed like this: "Outstanding sales depend on your ability to think from the customer's point of view and understand and respond to your customer's best interests." Ash elevated giving to get into a cosmic law: "All you send into the lives of others comes back into your own. If you give the very best you have in whatever you do, the best will come back to you in a boomerang effect."

Pay attention to these four habits of in-the-box Twos:

Gives to get

Puts people before objective standards

Always works through people

Suffers from identity problems

When out of the box, Twos become aware of their own needs. This awareness provides balance in their lives and allows them to give freely, without expecting return. If not quite so emotionally healthy, they tend to offer help and advice whether others want it or not.

Twos polarize between taking care of others and caring for themselves, as you saw in John's description of his feelings toward Gloria. They can repress their own feelings, even when they express a high level of emotion. In their distorted worldview, they don't have any needs, but others do. Emily's board chair was worried she would jeopardize the organization in her zeal to help others. Twos deny their own needs, project them onto others, and then meet those projected needs in others. They give the care to others they should give to themselves. When they do this, they have a sense of entitlement and can try to manipulate people. Emily's colleagues sensed this danger: "I think she would manipulate the establishment to reach her goals."

With an in-the-box Two, you may see some of the following patterns:

- *Invasiveness.* They help others who might prefer not to be helped. In this frame of mind they are do-gooders. They may manipulate with gifts to get something back that renders the gift meaningless. Unwanted gifts become a burden when Twos implicitly expect favors in return. In coaching Twos, it's important to watch for their dynamic of giving to others with an implicit expectation of getting something in return. You can ask them to describe their network and which of those people might owe them something. Or you can suggest a mock balance sheet where they put what they do for others on one side and on the other side record what they think they are owed in return. If you do this, make sure they register all forms of currency: emotional closeness, financial consideration, certain privileges of information or status, and the sternest currency of all—guilt. The more subtle the recompense, the more complete the balance sheet.

- *Seduction.* Twos can be seductive, and then turn suddenly on someone who does not meet their expectations. Monica Lewinsky is a notorious example. She had expectations based on a relationship, then turned and became aggressive when her expectations were not met. Madonna, the pop music star, built a $500 million dollar fortune on and is most known for her various forms of seduction, sex being one of them. The seduction that Twos use is an abuse of their considerable talent for knowing how to please people. If they are healthy, they are good friends. If unhealthy, others may have an uneasy feeling that a

In coaching Twos, it's important to watch for their dynamic of giving to others with an implicit expectation of getting something in return. You can ask them to describe their network and which of those people might owe them something... make sure they register all forms of currency...

gift—of attention, information, or affection—is tainted, and may feel seduced in one way or another.

- *Martyrdom.* They may make their needs known with difficulty. One of Clarence's Two clients runs a consulting firm. The client complained that he had counseled some adolescent daughters of friends of his and the parents did not even say, "Thank you." His disappointment was understandable until he added, "That's the fifth time this has happened this year!" He had given—and counted—more than 100 hours of counseling to these girls. Of course he felt abused. Twos often ache for approval, appreciation, and recognition but don't ask for or receive it. They tend to harbor feelings of betrayal when these efforts to be indispensable go unrewarded. John, mentioned earlier, had made it possible for Gloria and her husband to be part of a social group where he was the lynchpin. "I've learned a lot about my patterns," admitted John after a few coaching sessions, "but even though I ask nothing from her, I continue to feel disappointed and cheated. She thoroughly enjoys being in social situations with my friends, and me, but does nothing to reciprocate. I vacillate between being happy she's there and angry that she's so stingy. She always talks about ways she can 'help disadvantaged people' without any apparent awareness that there is at least one human being she could be kind to right here." When Twos complain that they're not appreciated, ask for a list of who should appreciate them and why. Then probe: "How aware are they that they owe you and why don't they know that?" The goal is to clarify their emotional expectations, especially those below their previous awareness level.

When Twos complain that they're not appreciated, ask for a list of who should appreciate them and why . . . . The goal is to clarify their emotional expectations.

- *Entitlement.* Leona Helmsley, who did jail time for tax evasion, built her fortune by making her hotels so attractive to people that her business flourished. The sense of entitlement that success can engender in a Two is probably behind her telltale remark to reporters, "Only little people pay taxes." Help your Two clients face and work through their anger at not being appreciated, not getting approval, and not receiving strong enough emotional responses. Self-awareness comes when they realize they are angry at having given themselves away.

You can address the pattern of giving to get by reframing the notion of help. Sometimes the most helpful thing Twos can do is to let people work something out for themselves, as this story illustrates:

Once upon a time a naturalist was carefully watching a big worm squeeze through a tiny pinhole in its sack. After many hours of struggle, a slender butterfly with powerful wings emerged and vigorously flew away. The second time the naturalist started his observation, he became impatient and made a thin cut in the sack so the worm got out in twenty minutes. But the worm emerged as a butterfly with weak wings and a heavy bottom. Without the exertion that pushed the juice up into the wings, the wings were flaccid and flabby. It couldn't fly. The naturalist's interference had crippled the creature.

Twos, especially in positions of authority, need to enlarge and alter what it means to really help someone. Even well meaning but misplaced help can keep people infantile, especially those who are weak by virtue of age, position, or competence.

You can address the pattern of giving to get by reframing the notion of help... Even well meaning but misplaced help can keep people infantile.

Twos somaticize easily and some control situations from a position of ill health, emotionally forcing others to do things for them. This follows Clarence's law: "What you do not get up front, you get out back." Poor health can be a form of blackmail. If Twos think they're being asked to work too hard, they might get sick. This gives them some time off and gets revenge on the responsible culprit by assigning guilt: "Look what you've done to me, now!" Emily did this when she complained, "How can I make a breakthrough with the board chairman so he realizes I'm absolutely doing all I can?" Some Twos break through by breaking down. Becoming ill is their only way of saying no.

When coaching a Two with health problems, it's often helpful to recommend assertiveness training, and to have them practice being assertive during coaching sessions. They especially need to learn how to say no. Clarence coached an executive who had a dream in which an angel wrote the word "no" in bright red lipstick on her white kitchen tablecloth. This Two did not have a clue about the dream's meaning until he teased, "What part of 'no' don't you understand?"

Perhaps because they are compulsive givers, Twos have the ability to give the perfect gift. They understand others so well; they know how to please them. Mary Kay Ash gave diamonds, fur coats, vacations, luxuries, and ultimately, Pink Cadillacs. She did this because she understood the symbolic power of the right gift. Money can be cold. We call it *cold* cash! Pink Cadillacs are warm. And deliciously, because of her buying power, she could give gifts worth more to the receivers than they cost her. You can learn much about a Two's network and strategy by asking what gifts they give. They may list only physical items. If so, ask them about time, access, advice, recommendations, or rule bending. Twos often give whatever is necessary to retain or strengthen relationships.

Sometimes this drive to keep the relationship at all costs is embedded in a corporate culture. Nordstrom's, the upscale department store, has a training video in which the story is recounted of a man who wanted his money back on faulty tires. Nordstrom's doesn't sell tires. The tires were sold by the company that owned that location before Nordstrom's took it over. The man got his money back. Why? Nordstrom's has built a sterling reputation for customer service, and this story was to illustrate how far they would go to make friends with someone who might, some day, be a customer. Only a Two or a Two culture would bend cultural expectations that far.

Under stress, all Enneagram styles become more pronounced. As they do, they strengthen their ego-patterns. As a coach, be aware that even if you create fieldwork together, Twos are apt to agree to whatever they think will get your approval. In the process they can dig their emotional rut deeper. It's most helpful if you make it clear that you are a partner, not the expert, so Twos can and should come up with their own fieldwork. Suggestions that run counter to their fixation might be an exception. For example, we often recommend periods of solitude for Twos. They will more easily find out who they are and what they want when alone. In the presence of others, they focus too tightly on the needs of everyone else. Solitude breaks their habit of seeking identity and approval from those around them, and relieves them of the pressure to affiliate so they can pay attention to themselves. They usually find this difficult, but it makes them aware of their habitual focus.

Because Twos know others' needs so well and are so eager to please, they are tempted to flatter. If they praise you excessively, look for the hook. John wrote this to Mary in one of his almost daily e-mails: "I spent some time at your web site this week. It is really a fine and informative and attractive piece of work. I read some of your poetry I hadn't read before. You have a wonderful mind, so in tune with your heart. Combined with your writing skills and the vast content of what you know relative to the functioning of human beings, you are a most gifted person." As much as these feelings were heartfelt, notice the high decibel level, the superlative praise. As a coach you need to be aware that this kind of flattery may mask a Two's hope that you will allow them to stay as they are and avoid change.

As a coach you need to be aware that flattery may mask a Two's hope that you will allow them to stay as they are and avoid change.

Conversely, because Twos give what they want for themselves, they thirst for praise. Mary encouraged John to use his desire for praise as a cue to explore his own needs. John discovered how difficult it was to break his pattern. He wrote: "I have never been able in the past to sustain such intense, primal feelings for any time at all without acting out in anger toward the person I felt had failed to appreciate all I'd given."

Because Twos need praise, they can feel humiliated by recrimination or scolding. The criticism doesn't have to be much. They notice any slight or oversight, even by emphasis. In one coaching session with John, Mary focused on a point she wanted to make instead of paying close attention to what John was feeling. John did not realize during the session that he felt rebuffed, but wrote afterwards that he wanted to terminate coaching after the next session. Mary apologized for pushing her point and helped him to ask her for what he needed. He recognized how he'd acted out his pattern with Mary, and decided to continue coaching. After a particularly tough week of his self-examination she wrote to him, "I want to acknowledge your work, your courage, and your strength. I believe you are absolutely right about the primal nature of what you are experiencing, and are now ready for and able to deal with. You are in the crucible. The alchemy is taking place." [1]

Because Twos give what they want for themselves, they thirst for praise... they can feel humiliated by recrimination or scolding. The criticism doesn't have to be much.

Puts People Before Objective Standards

Twos are people experts. They spend a lot of time cementing personal allegiance. They are keen judges of human nature and often surround themselves with people who will nourish them emotionally. They tend to seek and usually find personal commitment from a group. When they are out of the box, they want to be around competent and honest people. When in the box, their priority is to establish a bond between themselves and the people they want to influence. As someone who worked for Emily stated, "She's more of a friend than a boss and she's done so much for me." Twos sometimes hire people who emotionally satisfy them but are not competent to do the job they were hired for. If they continually help a low-performing employee, and content themselves with appreciation instead of developing the individual's capability, they may encourage incompetence.

For Twos, information is only as good as the people who filter it. They will, for example, often trust what a friend said rather than research a magazine, the Internet, or the library. These clients need crisp business plans in a business situation. Otherwise definitions, goals, and procedures will get sticky and emotional, and siphon off their attention. Objectivity is important. In a business situation Twos should rely heavily on their financial officers to give them an objective view of the company based on hard data.

In-the-box Twos are seldom the up-front stars. They prefer to be the power behind the scenes. They frequently have this by virtue of their relationship to those who have the titles and structural power, but others have the limelight.

[1] You will learn more in the last two chapters about the value of statements that pre-suppose a desired outcome. Notice that Mary's praise was for John's efforts to increase his self-awareness. She embedded her assumption that he will stay with his feelings and break free of his Enneagram patterns.

You can detect this element in John, who recognized that he felt a surge of power when associated with "powerful, beautiful women." Twos are the people who help others succeed, the support staff and supporting actors of the world. In business, they may try to climb the corporate ladder by attaching themselves to powerful people, expecting their own prominence by association. Put Twos with people and they will shine. Deprive them of people and they experience a power outage.

Coach Twos to clarify whether they are suited for the work they do. A client could well have become an accountant solely to please a boss who needed an accountant, despite the fact they have a little problem with arithmetic. This pattern showed up for Emily when she gave up her innovative leadership ideas to meet the needs of her peers for a relationship guru. Help Twos identify their efforts to please others, and how to access their own needs. They may find it painful to acknowledge their needs, and they will frequently report feeling selfish when they do, but they need to claim their needs if they are to step out of their box. While increasing his own self-awareness, John wrote, "Today I felt too weary to fill my own emptiness, too tired and disillusioned to believe anyone else could fill it either. I just let myself be empty. It was a relief to refrain from warding off the feeling of abandonment that comes from trying to be good enough to be loved."

Coach Twos to clarify whether they are suited for the work they do. A client could well have become an accountant solely to please a boss who needed an accountant.

Always Works Through People

Twos are the most interpersonal of all the styles, both in interest and in ability. Emotions are central. They constantly monitor the emotional climate, are frequently interpersonally shrewd, and never dismiss feelings. For Twos in business, emotions are an important component of their job, even if they lack words for their intense feelings. If there is no personal juice, in-the-box Twos find it hard to work. They may have little work ethic apart from relationships, because they tend to please people more than to fill job descriptions.

They can look more virtuous than they are when they cloak their activities with the mantle of love. No matter what the activity—manipulation, bossing, punishing, blackmail, or the purest of friendships—they do it in the name of love. Emily had entangled one of her key managers so tightly into her web of friendship that the manager (a loyal Six) wouldn't consider another job he was offered, even though it would have enhanced his long-term career prospects.

Twos can have a seductive manner that may be misunderstood or understood only too well. As leaders they can give followers the impression that each is a favorite. In personal relationships this self-giving will sometimes be sexual. Emily

65

felt that she had been giving and not receiving in her personal life as well as in her business relationships ("I feel I cut off pieces of myself and feed them to people"). Gradually she began to understand that seduction was her part of the sexual dance that left her feeling used and used up.

Twos can create instability in a corporation by their intense personal focus, as Emily did in her organization. If the personal relationship changes, so do all the rules and structures that depend on it. If the Two is at all fickle, this can raise havoc. Clarence gave an Enneagram seminar to 80 people in a large corporation. The Two organizer called each of the attendees by their first name. The entire operation depended on her personal network. If she were to leave, she would leave no real formal structure.

In coaching Twos, push for objective uniform standards that apply to friend and foe alike. Help them focus on goals they can achieve on their own and not through someone else.

If business is the overt agenda, but some form of interpersonal relationship is the covert agenda, honest communication and effective action become difficult. Twos who do business only through people can create confusion like Emily did with her staff. They didn't know whether Emily was the boss or a friend. In coaching Twos, push for objective uniform standards that apply to friend and foe alike. Help them focus on goals they can achieve on their own and not through someone else.

Co-dependency can be a trap for Twos. The desire to help might be a hidden desire to live through someone else—an elaborate emotional investment policy. Someone else's problem becomes their mission in life. The phrase "Get a life!" has a poignant relevance for some Twos. They need to learn to distinguish among dependence, independence, and interdependence.

Twos often negotiate badly when the relationship is so important they give away financial, moral, or social content. They may not charge enough when selling or working because they want to stay friends. Or they will break moral codes because they want to please someone. "I'll do whatever I have to in order to keep our friendship/love/relationship." There is a high side to this emotional priority. An out-of-the-box Two can forgive easily and keep friends others might lose because they carry a grudge.

Suffers from Identity Problems

In-the-box Twos may lack inner self-definition; they may substitute the wishes of another: "I am who you want me to be." They want to work where they feel valued by someone they think is important. Without approval, they wither like plants without water. They need to learn to see themselves as they really are, not as they are reflected through the reactions of the people they consider important.

Blunt feedback is gold for them, but they will have a hard time getting it for several reasons. First, they frequently surround themselves with those who will tailor their feedback to make them feel good. That tailoring may be part of an unspoken understanding. Second, that unspoken understanding comes about and is reinforced because Twos respond to feedback with defensive emotion, as Emily did. People may back down from a Two's reactions out of discomfort with such intensity of feeling. We know a senior level executive described as "holding others emotional hostage." Nobody knew how to deal with him when he expressed his hurt with widened eyes and drawn-down mouth. This can play out in the coaching relationship, as well. If you haven't donned kid gloves when confronting your Two clients, you will need to be astute about managing their emotional responses.

These clients may experience betrayal of self in order to affiliate with others, including you. Soap operas are a daily Two drama and a favorite line is, "What a fool I have been!" When Twos come to you with some form of betrayal as their presenting thorn, look for identity problems as one likely cause. We often discover that the betrayal is self-inflicted. If Twos can assimilate that insight, they have the power to interrupt the pattern. A good leading path is to ascertain what Twos have ignored that would have told them something was rotten. On the flip side, you can ask what they focused on that led them to miss the warning signs.

Even during coaching, Twos may attend to your needs instead of their own. They will try to please you even when it goes counter to their own preferences. When you catch them betraying their needs, repeat back what you observed in the interaction. You can often follow this string to the identity issue. This is what happened in the interaction between John and Mary mentioned earlier. John felt rebuffed by Mary's lack of attention to his feelings. He wanted to please Mary, so did not challenge her interpretation, and ignored what he was feeling. In their next session, Mary said, "I could tell that you didn't buy my interpretation in the last session but you went along with it." John replied, "It seemed really important to you to see it that way." Mary asked, "What stopped you from challenging me?" After a long pause John admitted, "I guess I didn't want to disappoint you." "Then what happened after the session?" Mary probed. John said, "I felt betrayed by you, that you didn't really care about what I was feeling."

Twos may succumb to cultural images, unable to distinguish their feelings and values from those of the culture or group. Media advertisements are most eager to define Twos as the users of their products, especially when those products promise to define you: "You can always tell a _____ man."

These clients may experience betrayal of self in order to affiliate with others... When you catch them betraying their needs, repeat back what you observed in the interaction. You can often follow this string to the identity issue.

When Twos betray themselves, they complain about anger, sometimes with tears. Like Emily, they don't see how they contribute to their overwork. They don't see how they invite invasion of their time, space, finances, and sometimes their bodies. A weak identity can cause boundary problems. Watch the careful lines Mary Kay Ash walked as she advised her salespeople: "To really listen, you must find out about the other person. Listening tells you what the other persons' wants and needs are, as well as the way they want to be treated. Listen to learn." This intense personal attention is for the sake of sales, but it doesn't look that way. Healthy Twos intuitively translate this kind of advice correctly. Other Twos think they understand it, but they set up ambiguous emotional expectations. Many Enneagram styles would choke on that synthesis of business and personal relationships. Are you making friends or making sales? Twos might smoothly answer, "Both."

The Two's Vision: Shift from losing self by taking care of others to loving and giving without strings

Transformation is a continuous process. We describe it as stepping out of the box. But when people step out of one box, they face another—one larger, perhaps more open and allowing more freedom of choice.

So be patient with yourself and with your clients. Their progress will wax and wane as the waves of an incoming tide roll in and out, but always in the direction of the shore. In one of his last contacts with Mary, John wrote: "I've learned a lot, but I don't feel transformed yet. I do feel much more at peace with who I am right now. There are still many rough edges but they make for an interesting personality contour. Yesterday was great. People came to my country place and everyone loved it and want to come back. I enjoyed watching Gloria but while she was the star attraction for me, I never left my own body or deserted my other friends."

Chapter 5

The Show Must Go On

When Mary was asked to coach Ted Swanson, she received a favorable report about him from his boss, Greg: "Ted has a sharp edge. He likes a strong definition of things. Early in our relationship he called a couple of times asking to be included in meetings. I was a little annoyed at his persistence, but other than that we hit it off right away. He's really personable with me, his political instincts are great, and he respects my role. I'm surprised he doesn't work better with people in his department. For example, I've heard that he takes credit for any suggestion they make. Also, he's very competitive with his key peer, Mark. He doesn't see Mark's group as being equal to its task. It seems important to Ted to know where he stands with me even though I'm always positive about his work. He tackled a major reorganization job, working through all the bureaucratic red tape, and achieved it in a very aggressive time frame. He keeps his eye on the deliverables."

Ted's peer, Mark, was concerned about Ted's lack of teamwork. "He's open to my opinion if he thinks I'm right, and I've never seen him get angry. But he holds up competitiveness as a virtue. It's easy to get in his doghouse but tough to get out. Not everyone trusts him, and I'm not exactly sure why. I marvel at how personable he is. People seem either to bond with him or polarize against him. I think his ambition gets in the way of relationships. He seems arrogant, and acts like he's superior to others He gives this impression partially by being opinionated, and partially by wanting you to know how much he's doing. He'd do better to let his work speak for itself and not always have to show how important it is. While he's focused on self-learning, I'm not convinced he could acknowledge a mistake and learn from it. He keeps Greg happy, but I've noticed he doesn't make his lower performers feel good about themselves. He doesn't take the time to give them the kind of 'feeding' they need."

When Mary met Ted, he looked sharp—good-looking, fashionably dressed, physically fit, and energetic. He spoke with a rapid-fire delivery. He reminded Mary of Tom Cruise, with his cocky charm. When she asked about his strengths and development areas he came right to the point. "I only have two speeds: Full ahead and stop! What drives me is making a difference, whatever the job is. I look at bottom-line indicators of success or failure more than most people. I'm strong on implementation, especially in managing multiple tasks. But I expect people to take too much on themselves and I'm weak in working with non-motivated employees. My style is to push and push to a certain point and then give up on them. I know I'm perceived as wanting to change things too fast. I don't think I'm disciplined enough in motivating my staff. I tend to gravitate toward the ones who learn quickly."

Ted began to understand how driven he'd been by his need to always be the best. His outward success was a counterpoint to his somewhat barren inner life.

There seemed to be no end to Ted's energy. In addition to his many professional commitments, he was the star of a community volleyball team. Learning from Mary about the Enneagram Three, he began to understand how driven he'd been by his need to always be the best. Ted's outward success was a counterpoint to his somewhat barren inner life. He suggested, "This may explain why I've always been drawn to the parable from the Book of Matthew about a house built on sand."[1] He saw that success had not filled his heart. For example, even though he had been a superior athlete in high school and college he discounted this by saying he had "a room full of empty trophies."

When asked about his feelings, Ted characteristically spoke about his role. Mary asked him how he felt about his boss. He responded, "My main concern is how Greg reacts at the moment to something I suggest. I filter through what he says to me so I can get his support for what I'm doing without turning him off." Mary repeated his response so Ted could see that his answer was not about feelings. "I'm not used to looking at myself," he admitted. "And when I'm asked about feelings, I don't know what to say." He reflected further, "When we came home from a party a couple of weeks ago my wife asked, 'Weren't you annoyed about what so-and-so said?' And honestly, I had no reaction at all, even when she pointed out the guy had been overbearing. I was more focused on how I could interest him in a business deal."

His best-performing employees were high on Ted. "He seeks excellence in everything," applauded Jerry, "though some people think he goes too far. I don't agree with that, but then, I like the pace he sets. He lays out objective goals, is results-oriented, and gives me good feedback about my performance. He gets frustrated when he doesn't get the results he wants, and perhaps he doesn't give some people enough direction. He's outgoing, easy to get to know and to talk to on a lot of subjects, but I don't know what motivates him. Because I like him so much

---

[1] *The rain came down, the streams rose, and the winds blew and beat against that house, and it fell with a great crash.* Matthew 7:27.

I tend to think, 'There isn't any hidden motive here, he's just impatient,' but there are some people who suspect he does things out of his desire to be the best."

"He's a bundle of energy," noted Darlene, "which is not a fault because he never seems worn out or frazzled. I can keep up with him, but even with me he'll sometimes grab something from my hand. He thinks so fast, if you beat around the bush he'll start asking questions because he wants to cut to the chase. So a lot of people have trouble communicating with him because they're not able to express a problem succinctly. Also, I don't think he has a very balanced personal life."

Ted's lower-performing employees felt a pinch. Steve, in particular, was definitely at the bottom of the totem pole: "I rarely get time with him," he complained, "and when I do, the phone rings and he picks it up, as if he'd rather be somewhere else. I feel like a dusty encyclopedia, kept around because of my technical experience, but out of the loop on most things. He has a problem building the team he needs to support him. I think we see each other more as competitors than teammates. He's created an atmosphere where people think, 'If I can do something that makes me look better than you, I'll do it.'"

Ted has a problem building the team he needs to support him. I think we see each other more as competitors than teammates.

Barbara was one of the out-group who wished for more direction: "I don't know if I'll ever get to his level of enthusiasm. This grieves me to the extent that he thinks we all should be this way. We're at odds if we don't have that 'fire in the belly.' We're often confused about what he wants accomplished, yet if we fall short of expectations it's our fault. I think he should reward people more for their performance, but when I brought this up to him he said, 'I don't believe in giving awards to people just for showing up!'"

Coaching Analysis

Coaching Ted

Mary used two key interventions with Ted. The first was to change the meaning of looking good. She told him, "You're too good at what you do—too smart, too quick, too likely to impress people with your results. The company will never support your progress unless you build collaborative relationships with your peers and find out what motivates your lower-performing subordinates. You'll be successful when you share credit with others." What would have felt like failure in Ted's old worldview (sharing credit instead of competing for it) was now reframed as success.

The second intervention was subtle and required that Mary pay close attention to her relationship with Ted. Threes can quickly complete a project if it is couched in concrete, achievable terms. You fall into a trap if you stroke these clients for doing what you, the coach, suggest, because you unwittingly reinforce their pervasive coping strategy—succeed at everything. Ted smiled when Mary said, "I'm not going to give you any feedback about the results you get from our work. I'll only tell you how it feels to know and work with you as a human being." They both understood that this could transform Ted. Knowing his Enneagram style had helped him notice his drive for results and how he depended on approval. Ted said, "This may be the first time in my life that anyone has cared for me regardless of what I accomplish."

Working without praise was foreign to Ted, but after a while he became comfortable enough to just laugh if Mary forgot and praised him or he slipped and tried to show off. He understood more deeply that neither he nor others had known who was really home, because he had been so busy shaping people's responses by saying, "look at me, look at me."

Collaboration as a Virtue

Ted admitted that he had held competition to be a virtue, and began to see how this prevented collaboration within his team. As a result of coaching he put a priority on performance management, primarily to build capability and morale among his lower-performing employees. Mirroring Mary's process with him, he began to hold regular one-on-one meetings with everyone who reported to him, collaborating with them to create their own development plans. He collaborated in two ways:

- He gave each of his employees a book on the Enneagram and talked about the gifts and blind spots of his own style. Then he helped them incorporate the similarities and differences of his and their styles into their developmental work.

- He used a collaboration assessment tool in which employees rated him at the same time he rated them. After discussing the assessment results, Ted and his employees created development plans that included expectations for a true partnership. Ted's regular one-on-one meetings began to include feedback based on the plans they had created. They monitored their boss/subordinate relationship to ensure that they were collaborating as agreed.

To increase collaboration in Ted's department, Mary and Ted designed a team workshop with these key objectives

- Team members will see that we can make a bigger difference by collaborating than by competing, both within the team and with other departments.

- Ted will demonstrate that collaboration is vitally important by his words and his behavior.

- The team will become self-renewing. We will keep our eyes on a shared vision, observe the patterns we create, and take mutual accountability for problems.

Ted and Mary created team activities to explore their dynamics as individuals and as a group. They looked for evidence of competitive attitudes and behaviors, and learned collaborative models and methods. They planned how to collaborate better with other departments, as well.

During the evening between the two days of the workshop, Mary and Ted set up a volleyball game. After about 30 minutes of normal play, they asked the team to figure out rules that would make the game collaborative.[2] There was a long moment of confused looks. Then team members good-naturedly went about inventing non-competitive volleyball. They laughed and cheered, but at no one's expense. They did not taunt or make joking put-downs. The next morning, they figured out how to apply what they learned in the game to their work with each other and with other departments.

The most dramatic breakthrough came when Ted agreed to use Mary as a process observer. Part of her role was to call time whenever someone made a competitive remark. She would write the remark on a flip chart, ask the group to identify the belief behind the statement, and then help them construct a statement that reflected a collaborative belief. The first time she called Ted on a competitive remark the group reacted with stunned silence. It was invaluable to see him openly accept his failure to collaborate, to acknowledge how deeply rooted these patterns can be, and to experiment in public with new ways to communicate. Those who had criticized him for being on an ego trip did a total about-face. To experience this public exposure without trying to cover himself changed Ted dramatically.

It was invaluable to see Ted openly accept his failure to collaborate, to acknowledge how deeply rooted these patterns can be, and to experiment in public with new ways to communicate.

Sometimes clients will come to a coach fully ready to break out of their box. This may be less likely with Threes than with other Enneagram styles. Their coping strategy tends to bring such external success that they typically don't feel any need for change. A crisis—a major illness, a divorce, or a business failure, for example—can trigger a breakthrough for any client, but this is especially true for Threes. Ted had faced and survived cancer a few years before he worked with Mary. His illness had slowed him down enough to deepen his inner life. Also,

---

[2] Ted and Mary prepared by reviewing Terry Orlick's *Cooperative Sports & Games Book.*

he was now aware that continuing to compete could create a crisis. He knew he needed to build better teamwork with his own team and his peers, so he was more open to change. He trusted Mary and was unusually willing to admit his own relationship failures.

Coaching Style Three

A cynic might suggest as the motto of modern life this simple legend – "Just as good as the real."

Charles Warner

Develop rapport with Threes by matching their worldview. Make the terms of your agreement clear, set goals, and use your time well with all clients, but especially with Threes. Otherwise, they will not be willing to invest real time and energy. Be concrete and succinct in your observations. Do not wander. Focus your conversation. Ask them, "How will you know that coaching worked? What are your criteria?"

A transformational shift for Threes occurs when they weaken their belief that success is everything and failure is never acceptable. Once you establish trust, you will find opportunities to show them how their competitive striving can rob them of their souls.

Second-order change is never easy. This is especially true for Threes. They will be willing to change some behavior, particularly to fix things quickly. However, unless they have had a critical event in their lives, as Ted did, they are not as likely to be interested in going deeper. In-the-box Threes typically are not introspective, but events that represent failure can prompt them to do some soul-searching. They do have emotions, but tend to suppress them in order to get to work. Consequently, emotional work can be unfamiliar. Getting them to look at their values, for example, may not be as appealing as it is to some other Enneagram styles. You can get there, but it's a delicate operation.

Mary described collaboration—a departure from Ted's habitual competitive approach—as a way to succeed and move ahead in the organization. This new understanding reframed his usual notion of success and put Ted in a helpful double bind. If Ted continued to compete with his teammates, he would fail. If he helped others perform better, he would succeed. In this good-willed subterfuge, Mary matched Ted's worldview while she introduced a process that would break him free from it.

The next four sections explore how you can coach Threes to grow from trying to succeed at any price to becoming communal and inner-directed.

Derives Feelings From an Image

Inwardly living the roles they play, Threes tend to derive their self-worth from how well they think they play their roles. They can become image-conscious, valuing how they look over how they really feel. They often evaluate themselves on how perfectly they can match their roles and mistakenly believe others will do the same. They can base their personal worth on outside approval for their *performance*. The word performance describes a Three's striving. It means to do something well and to do something for an audience.

Threes have a subterranean confusion between image and reality. They tend to believe, "I am who I appear to be." This preoccupation with appearance can make them depend heavily on recognition. Threes will work extremely hard for certificates, awards, ribbons, medals, or tokens of some kind. Ted's striving for recognition prompted Greg's observation, "It seems important to Ted to know where he stands with me," and Mark's suggestion, "He'd do better to let his work speak for itself and not always have to show how important it is." In-the-box Threes may reward appearance almost as much as reality, and punish anyone who doesn't make them look good. The slower or less productive people reporting to Ted, who might make him look bad, felt punished when he gave them less time and attention.

Threes may use their roles to claim more glory than is rightfully theirs, using "I" when "we" would be fairer and more accurate. Ted was criticized for taking credit for his team's work. In business this temptation to take undeserved credit is especially acute when Threes report to those above them. One style Three boss would not release a department report if an individual's name was listed as author. If no one was named specifically, she could take all the credit. This is the opposite of good management practice, which is to credit people publicly and criticize their mistakes privately. Out-of-the-box Threes, of course, shrewdly mete out recognition as a motivational tool. When inwardly secure, they will share the spotlight as Ted eventually did. As they learn to share credit, they strengthen teamwork.

Coach Threes to enjoy the people in their lives, at home and at work. Their feelings can be so bound up with their roles and image that they ignore relationships outside of them. They can get so task-oriented that they run over, forget, or abuse others. They may not do these things on purpose, but our Enneagram style can be our compulsion, that which we do without conscious intent. As a transformational coach, the first step is always to help your clients become neutral observers of their own patterns.

Pay attention to these four habits of in-the-box Threes

Derives feelings from an image

Fulfills expectations of system

Thinks of self in mechanistic terms

Polarizes between success and failure

In one coaching call, a Three client told Mary she had asked her husband to take video footage in the middle of a casual party, but he refused, saying he wanted to spend time with their guests. "Normally, I would have pushed back until he did it," she said, "but because of our coaching I realized that having a video record of the party was an image thing, so I focused on what was going on with me. It was hard. I felt very uncomfortable. But what came up for me were issues of self-worth. Before, I would have gone off on him and it would have escalated into a fight. Instead, I learned something about myself. I also let myself just enjoy the party. That's a significant change for me."

With tongue in cheek, another Three announced to Mary that he attributed the acting out of his habits to his "Evil Twin." To help Threes let go of judging themselves for not always looking good, you might suggest that they think of several situations where their image-seeking pattern shows up. Then ask, "At what point did the Evil Twin take over? What happened right before that? What consistent patterns do you see among these situations?" You may have to coach them to search for what feelings lay behind these patterns.

You may have to coach Threes to search for the feelings behind their patterns. When you notice them speaking in image terms, help them pick the emotion that lies behind the image.

We have asked Threes to search for these feelings by experimenting with a feelings vocabulary. When you notice them speaking in image terms, ask them to review their feelings vocabulary and pick the emotion that lies behind the image. For instance, a Three might say, "He showed me up in front of my boss." You could distinguish between feeling mad, sad, glad, or bad and ask which category most closely fits the sensations he felt. For example, if he says, "mad," then help him sort out what kind of anger he is feeling. Is it mere frustration or is it a reaction to perceived injustice or is the anger a cover for feeling inadequate? Many Threes need help to find their true inner concerns and the feelings that go with them.

Fulfills Expectations of System

"Just do it!" is not only a slogan, it's the Three's prime directive. They're oriented to activity, they prefer being proactive, and they typically don't take a lot of time for reflection or self-questioning. Instead, they tend to buy into the system and work overtime to play their role in it. They become the stars and often make any system work better. In the case of business, the system makes profits and Threes are all for that. Typically they are not innovative thinkers or risk-takers, preferring to stay in the mainstream because taking a risk makes success less predictable.

Threes usually work harder than anyone else, and they also focus clearly on priorities, strategies, and goals—their own or the system's. They know how to manage their time to accomplish tasks, projects, and goals, and to reap the rewards. Life and work can be synonymous. But when they operate from their Enneagram worldview, they don't achieve the success in life they really want—what inspirational writers call bliss.

Instead, Threes can let someone or something outside themselves define success: the country, the corporation, the team, the community and/or its representatives. In those contexts, the tasks define success. If their job is to make a profit, then profit means success. They will feel blindsided if assigned the task of profit and then criticized for morale problems, unless morale maintenance was clearly spelled out as part of their job description. They work best where the markers of success are clear, and they set personal goals and meet them. In a study of 1933 Princeton University graduates, only two had clearly defined written and updated goals and objectives, and these two made more money than all the rest of the class combined. Princeton advertised a forthcoming book these two wrote as one on how and why to set goals and objectives. Had they known the Enneagram, they probably could have called their book, *Why Threes Tend to Make More Money.*

All the Enneagram styles except Threes coincide (at the low end of their potential) with a standard identified psychological disturbance. But being a workaholic in the U.S. is not seen as neurotic; it is more often called professional excellence and rewarded with lots of money. To understand the down side of workaholism, we recommend Chapter Two of Robert Kaplan's book, *Beyond Ambition.* He describes how "expansive executives" can be too focused on winning, unnecessarily competitive, lacking in perspective, unrealistically ambitious, controlling or even exploitive, and too hungry for rewards. Three can be a hard driving, results-oriented, high energy, and high performance style.

As their coach you can help Threes learn that speed kills. Many exist on adrenaline, caffeine, and shallow breathing. Ask them to find ways to slow down: "Don't hurry up and finish life so you can die. Slow up so you can live." See that they take some time for pleasure, reflection, and emotional indulgences like family, friends, and cultural richness. Help them take a long-term view of things to integrate people, spirituality, and emotional values into their lives. A long-term approach will ultimately make them more productive without the fallout that usually accompanies overwork. Coach them to choose their work, to look at tasks and ask, "Is this one for me, do I really want to do this?" Help them see that choice is not the result of freedom. It creates freedom.

See that they take some time for pleasure, reflection, and emotional indulgences. It is especially helpful for them to explore their own values.

It is especially helpful for Threes to explore their own values. Clarence's client Scott loved being with his young sons, but did not have much time for them because he had a key role in many professional organizations. After a month of coaching he reviewed a list of values and set clear priorities for more authenticity, love, and connection in his life. When he implemented these priorities, he took a backstage role in every organization except the one supporting education for inner city children. With his freed-up time, he began to play more with his sons, to join his wife at their Little League games, and to take more interest in their schoolwork.

Thinks of Self in Mechanistic Terms

Threes often hire a coach because of stress or health-related issues. They may not come to you about their Enneagram habits but about the problems their habits cause. They do not see that stress occurs naturally because of their lifestyle. Clarence asked a Three client for a metaphor to describe himself. He said he saw himself as a race car. If you can drive a car for 100,000 miles, you should be able to drive your body for 100,000 miles! Another client said to someone who worked for him, "You're the engine that makes your department run." And the woman mentioned in Chapter One who resigned from her role as wife told Clarence, "The next husband I marry is not going to be a fixer-upper!" These mechanical metaphors are telltale.

Plants and people alike grow slowly by just moving toward the light. We are not machines, but in-the-box Threes may think they are.

In the Threeish culture of North America, we talk about people being maladjusted. One adjusts carburetors or thermostats. One does not adjust roses. Like roses, people are organic. We use the term burnout to describe emotional fatigue, but cats or birds or carrots don't burn out. Engines do. The experience of stress from being pushed beyond comfort levels usually comes from an outside stimulus, not from the impetus of inner growth. Plants and people alike grow slowly by just moving toward the light. We are not machines, but in-the-box Threes may think they are.

You might have Threes take a hard look at how much time they spend working. Ironically, they are less productive when they work too hard. One of Mary's Three clients grieved the losses that his success had caused him. When he turned fifty, he sold the corporation he had built, left everything and went to Africa with the Peace Corps. When he returned, his entire focus was to build relationships with his extended family, and treat himself to the pleasure of learning for learning's sake. As he describes it, he has become "a student of life."

Polarizes Between Success and Failure

The importance of success is accompanied by a fear of failure, often unrecognized by others but a driving force of Threes. In-the-box Threes work tirelessly because they do not have inner permission to fail. They assume they will and can do whatever it takes to succeed.

Threes have a strong commitment to competence. They value it in themselves and insist on it in others. Competence is defined as the ability to get the job done: whether that be technical, social, political, or artistic. Competence relates to results. It is not only a talent; it is the ability to use that talent to succeed.

They might love sales competitions, keep close tabs on their competitors, and tend to evaluate themselves in terms of what others are achieving. They frequently succumb to the game of one-upmanship. The notion of competition is inherently polarized because if one has to win, the other has to lose. We are so polarized between winning and losing as a society that one way we describe cooperation is by the phrase win-win.

The deepest problem many Threes face is their definition of success. When they are in the box, they not only try too hard to succeed and avoid failure, they allow others to define success and failure for them. Sometimes the other is a person— "Do I make as much money as she does?" Other times it is a standard—"How high did I score on a standardized test?" or "Where do I stand in relation to the national average?" Some companies establish Employee of the Month programs. While this system may motivate one person who wins, it often discourages everyone else. People who set up this system expect each employee to try harder because they believe competition is good. This assumes that employees find the ratings fair, that everyone has an equal chance, and that recognition from the outside means a great deal. These assumptions are transparently shaky, but they make sense to in-the-box Threes.

Threes not only try too hard to succeed and avoid failure, they allow others to define success and failure for them.

Threes can thrive or wither on comparisons of office space, location, invitations to parties, or access to the boss. These comparisons establish their sense of worth and carry a value that would amaze others. Every field has some version of "who's hot and who's not." Who cares? Threes care fervidly. The Three boss mentioned earlier, who wanted credit for department reports, learned of an upcoming project which she assumed would be another feather in her cap. Then at a meeting of all the key players it became apparent that this innovative proposal was something for which she couldn't claim credit. In her worldview if they won, she lost. She blew up and told everyone she had not agreed to this and stopped the project.

Help your Three clients observe their use of sporting metaphors (stepping up, punting, going for the gold). Sporting metaphors often foster competition.

79

Competition is divisive because it creates winners and losers, success and failure. Threes love it because it acts out their inner script. Their implicit expectation is that they will work hard and win and people will love them for their success. Competitive Threes focus tightly on the kind of results they can take to the bank. The down side, if the focus is too tight, is that they don't develop parts of themselves that are crucial but can't be pressed into competition. Being a good spouse, parent, or friend might fall into this category.

Help Threes see that when they compete, they focus on the other person. When they don't compete, they can focus on their own strengths, weaknesses, needs, and loves. Tell them: "Don't be afraid to fail. Give yourself permission to try some things that might not work." Don't reframe it with nice sayings like, "Failure is not failure if you learn from it," or, "Failure is always temporary." It's not a rule of life that we should not or cannot fail. Sometimes people will fail, and they have every right to fail even if they don't learn much. Failure is merely one consequence of trying.

The Center for Creative Leadership has published some interesting research on the lessons of experience that predict leadership success. One is the opportunity to learn from failure. You can help Threes probe their inner life until they come to terms with their fear of failure. One client described herself as "pathologically self-confident." She explained, "There's a fine line between defining failure as success and learning from failure. For example, I'll recognize some sort of failure, then engage in a lot of fancy thinking in the guise of analyzing what could have been done better or differently, then turn it into some sort of learning experience. It's not so much a distinction between a failure and a lesson learned that's the problem; it's the shifting so quickly over to the lesson learned. I've become aware that there's a little pathology in this."

One of the lessons of experience of successful leaders is the opportunity to learn from failure. You can help Threes probe their inner life until they come to terms with their fear of failure.

The Three's Vision: Shift from succeeding at any price to becoming communal and inner-directed

Transformed Threes collaborate and nourish teamwork. In organizations or groups they connect as human beings, not productive machines. They are in touch with their feelings and their key values. Their resulting authenticity reflects what really matters and they relax their focus on appearances.

Mary contacted Ted several years after completing their coaching work. She knew that he had recently achieved a top-level position in his organization and was pleased to note that he did not emphasize his outward success. Instead he spoke with quiet peace about his inner life: "I am happier than I've ever been. You know, when you reconnect with your core values and take the time to live them, it changes your outlook on many, many things."

A Different Angle

Chapter

6

"I'm an Enneagram Four. I interpret things differently from most people," wrote Teresa Panatelli in her first e-mail to Mary. "I've become disenchanted with my job. I feel I'm innovative, but my co-workers don't know what to do with my ideas. Can you help me break them out of the box?"

Mary responded to this request with a quotation from Plato's allegory of the cave[1] where Socrates speaks symbolically of the human predicament: Human beings have been living in an underground cave since childhood, their legs and necks chained so that they can only see in front of them. Behind them is a fire, and between them and the fire a raised stage with marionette players working puppets. To them, the truth is nothing but "the shadows of the images."

"Plato suggested," Mary wrote, "that if released from our caves, we may still be unable to trust the world outside, believing instead that the shadows of our perceptions are true. Those who try to lead others to the light are not likely to succeed. Some companies thrive on innovation. But most people approach a problem within the same paradigm that spawned it. They look for solutions that continue the current way of doing things."

"You describe yourself," Mary continued, "as innovative, someone who wants to do things outside the normal paradigm. You may see these people as unimaginative, stuck, and resistant to change. But when a person or corporation operates in a certain way, it feels wrong, even dangerous, to do things differently. It's important for you to accept that you threaten the status quo."

Teresa liked Mary's use of metaphor and hired her as a coach. At their first face to face meeting Teresa began by talking about her life-long ability to perceive the familiar from a unique perspective: "In my earlier career as a photographer, I photographed things no one else could see. A segment of the side of a building, a part of the body, a view of a tree that shows a pattern but is not identifiable in the usual way."

4

[1] Book VII of *The Republic*.

Tera, as she preferred to be called, was being groomed to take over the top human resources job for an international corporation. But she was intensely dissatisfied with the organization's culture, which she saw as traditional and unoriginal: "I'm creative, open, and expressive. Some people ask me into a conversation because they know I'll come at it from a totally different angle. My boss has told me I drive the policy people crazy, but I consider that a compliment."

People trusted Tera with their confidences and found her to be genuine and candid. This was a particular strength in her relationships with line managers who said they were used to being "bullshitted" by human resource representatives. Because she held their trust, Tera had been able to accomplish changes that benefited employees without their bosses feeling cornered or unjustly accused. Several people she'd helped described her as "genuine, sincere, empathic, friendly, and candid." She also understood the business and had a sense of urgency that others respected.

"She has a tendency to live in stages of gray and discontent." "She gets frustrated when things go wrong and despairs and agonizes."

On the down side, people who worked for Tera said she sometimes seemed unapproachable. They would see her furrowed brow, fear she was in a bad mood, and avoid her. Tera's boss added that she gave up on several projects when the going got tough: "Sometimes she's just too moody." Others mentioned Tera's negative emotionality: "She has a tendency to live in stages of gray and discontent." "She gets frustrated when things go wrong and despairs and agonizes."

Tera acknowledged that sometimes she wallowed in her own feelings: "I really care about people but that just feeds my moodiness. A guy came to talk with me recently because he got demoted, and it reminded me how organizations thrive on blame instead of recognizing people's strengths. If the job they were hired for has changed, the company should offer them another position. I buy into the 'vale of tears' theory. I think life is extraordinarily hard. I've always had compassion for others but it also comes from personal tragedy. Like Thornton Wilder I think that life is random and unpredictable and you try, sometimes desperately, to control what you can." Tera then recited the ending of Wilder's book, *The Bridge of San Luis Rey:* "But soon we shall die and all memory of those five will have left the earth, and we ourselves shall be loved for a while and forgotten."

Tera's ability to see things from a unique perspective also led her to wonder why she rarely saw the world as others did. She questioned her own reality—was she unique or was she flawed? "As I've gotten older and accepted my own flaws, I have mellowed somewhat," she acknowledged. But questioning her uniqueness continued to haunt her, and on her bad days she would give up when one of her innovative ideas met with resistance. Instead of fighting for her point of view, Tera would sink into a defeated gloom.

She admitted that her occasional melancholy could be compelling, like pushing a tongue against a loose or aching tooth. Tera's "existential angst," as she called it, was expressed through a redemptive sorrow for the world (another of her favorite books was Victor Frankl's *Man's Search for Meaning*). When she focused on what was missing in her organization, she touched the tooth of her sorrow, so her pain rarely went away.

Coaching Analysis

Coaching Tera

In conversations with Tera's colleagues, Mary found some who liked Tera's comfort with new and innovative approaches. She shared their feedback with Tera: "They respect your ability to speak your mind without being adversarial. They see you as persuasive, yet also skilled at drawing people out. Most notably, through your passion for excellence, you act as a beacon for others. And when you hang in with a project you get exciting results." Mary also told Tera that her boss saw her potential and her failure to exploit it fully: "He said you need to challenge the status quo, focus on what can be done about it, accept your part in it, be accountable for dealing with the friction that occurs, and work at changing other people's positions."

"You need to challenge the status quo, focus on what can be done about it, accept your part in it, be accountable for dealing with the friction that occurs, and work at changing other people's positions."

Mary's coaching strategy for Tera took two key directions: 1) helping her to maintain her unique perspective without holding herself apart from others, and 2) finding creative ways for Tera to use resistance as a source of energy for change.

Leading From the Couch

Mary began the coaching process by emphasizing how Tera inadvertently broadcast her moodiness: "You tend to focus almost exclusively on how things could be, then seem depressed when things don't change. Co-workers have noticed your moodiness. They say things like: 'What may be a big problem to her can seem minor to others.' 'She has these personality swings and I wonder if it's something I've done.'"

"One person described you," Mary continued, "as 'an outsider,' in part because you come from a different background. But you also create this perception by conveying that you'd rather be somewhere else." Tera was only a little surprised that her dissatisfaction made observable waves, and acknowledged the truth of comments like, "She has a good job with a good future, but I don't think she's ever really satisfied."

Mary knew that Tera studied leadership by reading biographies of people she admired. Abraham Lincoln had problems with melancholy, so Mary asked Tera to read a biography of him, adding the suggestion, "You will discover the solution to your problem somewhere in his history." The assumption behind such an ambiguous assignment is that clients know how to solve their problems and will find out while searching for the answer. Mary trusted that whatever Tera found noteworthy or memorable would help lead her toward a solution.

When they next met, Mary asked Tera what in Lincoln's biography had seemed most relevant to her. Tera said, "I was struck by the fact that even when Lincoln was at his most melancholy, lying on the couch in his office, he continued to meet with people and conduct his presidential duties." Mary soundly reinforced this observation and encouraged Tera to think of all the ways she could apply it to her general work habits and specific situations.

"I've just realized that my tendency to seek greener grass is also a gift. I can see possibilities others don't see. That's why they want my 'new slant' on things when they're stuck."

Next Mary asked Tera to write about her personal history as a spiritual journey. She was to note the strengths and resources she had drawn upon to get her this far and to summarize in detail what she had learned from the hard times. One outcome of this exercise was that Tera began to see her so-called flaws in a more positive light. She said, for example, "I've just realized that my tendency to seek greener grass is also a gift. I can see possibilities others don't see. That's why they want my 'new slant' on things when they're stuck."

A New View of Resistance

At times, Tera had been so preoccupied with feeling rejected that, despite her natural empathy, she couldn't "feel" for others. Passionate about change, she had relied on her ability to persuade others that change was necessary. As the coaching continued, Tera began to see that she could apply her deep capacity for empathy to understanding why others feared change. "If they don't buy in to your ideas right away," Mary pointed out, "that's a cue that they're either threatened in some way—which to them is legitimate, or trying to maintain something they value—which is also legitimate."

Mary helped her create a new personal vision that balanced Tera's habit of imagining how things could be better with appreciation for the realities of organizational life.

Tera learned to see the "defenders of the faith" as sources of important information. She realized she needed to climb into the box with them so they could all find a way out together. By listening carefully she could allay concerns about threats to job security, autonomy, or sense of competence; and show how the changes were congruent with their core values. She also recognized the negative self-fulfilling aspects of chronically wishing "If only we could..." Mary helped her create a new personal vision that balanced Tera's habit of imagining how things could be better with appreciation for the realities of organizational life.

Coaching Style Four

Fours usually don't have goal setting as their first priority. You will establish more rapport when you witness their pain, show your empathy, honor their unique way of seeing things, and focus your questions on how they feel.

Phil O'Reilly, a young graduate student, wanted to find more productive ways to organize his dissertation. He felt he had to overcome what he called his "negative personality traits." Mary sensed quickly that he might be a Four. Phil began by lamenting how out of it he felt compared to faculty and even the other graduate students. They seemed to conform so easily to all the guidelines. While he could have focused on his opportunity to shed new light on traditional topics, he described instead how dejected he felt from trying to meet department expectations. Like many Fours, he had repeated his sad story for so long, he couldn't imagine feeling any other way.

If you, as a coach, have a personal situation that parallels a Four's dilemma, share it. It can be a simple common experience or a story that subtly embeds a possible solution. Mary had suffered through her own dissertation, so she affirmed the difficulties Phil must be enduring. This made his reactions feel more acceptable: "Others have suffered through these things." She embedded a possible solution, too: "Yes, working with my dissertation committee was dreadful. They wanted a statistical study and I wanted to draw theory from a series of case studies. The only way I survived was to form a dissertation support group."

Mary told Phil that Fours are often able to see things in a new light, so they are understandably frustrated when others can't see what they see. This frustration is made worse when they realize their insights would eliminate solving the same old problems over and over. Phil was surprised to hear these positive aspects of his Enneagram style. Mary knew, however, not to share these positive aspects until after she had reflected on his feelings. Fours often feel that no one understands their pain.

Your knowledge of the Four's patterns will guide you to coach them from being moody and unable to get past their melancholy to being effective in the external world.

The first step, we believe, is to embrace sadness, emptiness, and despair as powerful teachers of life's most profound lessons.

John E. Nelson and Andrea Nelson
Editors
Prologue to *Sacred Sorrows*

Considers Inner Reality More Important Than External Reality

Pay attention to these four habits of in-the-box Fours:

Considers inner reality more important than external reality

Sorts for what's not there

Sees self as defective

Defends with introjection

Feelings rank first in a Four's world. This emotional intensity can be contagious. While Fives might try to motivate by giving information, and Ones would tend to appeal to rectitude and propriety, Fours appeal through and to emotions. Feelings are as important as hard data. Even in corporate cubicles, you may find Fours encouraging and rewarding feeling states as much as action. When they have a powerful personal vision, they can engage the passions of the workforce so the project becomes a cause greater than the individual. The appeal is to the soul—to depth, to inner resources seldom accessed. Spontaneous generosity becomes the order of the day. An entire department can become passionately engaged.

Soul is not about intellectual brilliance, though Fours can be extremely bright. Soul is about depth, emotional intensity, personal integrity, and vision. Of course, even these values can have a down side. If a Four's vision is too personal or idiosyncratic, then others can't identify with it and become reluctant to engage. Their withdrawal drags the work down, perhaps even the work of the entire department. Routine work can become difficult in the presence of Fours, because they expect you to do more than just show up. They expect passion. Their managerial style is concerned about depth and commitment more than profit, acceptability, or the system. David Whyte, in *The Heart Aroused,* writes the following:

> Adaptability and native creativity on the part of the workforce come through the door only with their passions. Their passions come only with their souls. Their souls love the hidden springs boiling and welling at the center of existence more than they love the company.

Whyte's book, with his impassioned message to corporations, is intended to influence the business world to embrace poetic values.[2]

If a Four's vision is too personal or idiosyncratic, then others can't identify with it and become reluctant to engage.

In matters of taste and creative design, feelings reign, no doubt, but in other parts of the creative process, feelings can and must be muted. Fours may search out those whose feelings match their own most closely, and not attend enough to the talent and energy needed for the task. In many business settings, Fours report they feel they are actors playing a role. Their external business role is mundane, ordinary, and bland. All the while, their feelings, in sharp contrast, are in riotous turmoil. They split their feelings from their external action. No harm in that, unless they spend too much time searching for support for those feelings. If they are leaders, they may spend time, energy, and attention eliciting and rewarding emotional congruence instead of deploring what they were hired to do.

---

[2] An Eight client gave Mary two tickets to join him and his wife at one of Whyte's weekend retreats. She observed with respect that the Eight and other business people openly wept as the poet "aroused" their hearts.

When coaching Fours, it is important throughout the session to allow time and emotional space for them to ventilate, regardless of what else you discover. Understand their subjective position. You don't have to grant objective reality to it. They themselves may not consider it anything but their subjective opinion, but they will cherish it every bit as much as statistical evidence. They often feel misunderstood in a business office, but their work setting may not be the proper place to expect understanding of their deep wells of feeling. They can legitimately expect people to cooperate, but it may be unrealistic, even unfair, to expect emotional gratification.

When coaching Fours, it is important to allow time and emotional space for them to ventilate. Understand their subjective position.

Fours may come for coaching because they feel their relationships are not authentic, profound, or satisfying enough. These concerns touch their hearts because their lives tend to be structured by a web of relationships. Mary's client, Rolf, was in despair because Peter, his boss, seemed unwilling to share his feelings. Rolf's descriptions suggested Peter might be an Enneagram Three who was not aware of his impact on others. Rolf came looking for a strategy to deal with Peter, who wanted to move forward quickly with a new mission statement. Rolf had convinced Peter to approve a management retreat designed to flush out hidden resentments in the staff before they could create a meaningful mission statement. Peter had agreed that Rolf would facilitate the discussion. But during the retreat Peter competed for airtime, was impatient with staff members' negative feelings, and, most of all, was disappointed because they didn't complete the mission statement. Rolf was crushed.

Mary knew it was vital to search for the meaning behind Rolf's emotional response. He felt inferior ("I'm not as good as Peter is, because I'm too emotional, too touchy-feely"). As Mary and Rolf discussed his feelings, he became aware of a childhood message that his passion was a flaw. So when he felt passion, he felt inferior. When Mary walked him through the meaning of his reaction, he was able to see his gift for empathy more clearly. This gift had enabled him, for example, to surface the staff's hidden resentments. Further exploration brought his core value of authenticity to light. When he understood that, he saw why he felt drained in a work situation in which "there's a façade in place." So he let go of his focus on how bad he felt, and learned to find emotional support in places other than feeling states. A few Enneagram insights helped him see the variety of ways people show support. For example, Fives habitually show their emotions through intellectual debate and Ones show their passion for excellence by good work, but they don't gush a lot about it.

Sometimes you can help Fours bring a deep passion forward to champion a project they believe in. Clarence coached a Four who was unhappy with an organization that had hired her as a consultant. This organization represented a large percent of her income, but she didn't like being involved in the internal politics. This consulting work was quite different from her long-standing dream to create an innovative film project. She had been blocked by worries about income if she started the film project. Clarence helped her define her personal mission. With his support, she trimmed the time with the company that brought her income and conserved her energy. Then she found an arts foundation to fund the development of her dream.

It's wise to probe for which feelings of a Four are real. Ask questions like, "Where are you in your body?" or "Get in touch with your emotional center." You will discover that their melancholy has a sweetness underlying it that links them either to the past or to the future. Bring them back into the present with questions like, "What is happening now?" and "How are you feeling now?"

Their melancholy has a sweetness underlying it that links them either to the past or to the future. Bring them back into the present.

Fours can be highly creative. Ask for their solutions. The search for solutions encourages them to move their focus off their response and on to the real problem. They often surface highly individualized discoveries. Mary gave Tera the fieldwork to find her answers by reading a Lincoln biography. When she did, it gave Tera the freedom to make her own sense of it. Fours often value aesthetic endeavor. You can frame the limitations of a difficult situation as the medium in which they are to make a work of art.

Fours can be drawn to drama and excitement. They may appreciate negative intensity more than serenity. In times of peace, coach them to leave well enough alone. Even in times of turbulence, they can learn to face it without drowning in their accompanying emotional flood. This quote from the letters of a Zen master inspired one of Mary's clients: "You have to be in yourself 100 percent, and you simply go forward. You don't have to know anything. Just put one foot in front of the other.'" She needed his permission to stay calm. Previously, when faced with a problem, she would rev up her emotional intensity.

Because Fours lead so emotionally, their inner storms can capsize an entire crew. We recommend the series by David Reynolds, *Constructive Living*. He offers helpful tips on how to keep working despite inner turmoil. The title of his book, *Thirsty, Swimming in the Lake*, is an apt metaphor. Fours may fail to face their problem, even though they have ample resources here and now.

90

Sorts For What's Not There

Looking for what is missing can lead to unique views. Fours frequently envision possibilities others are blind to. But they tend to assume that pointing out possibilities is sufficient for others to say, 'Let's go!' When this doesn't happen, when they encounter resistance, sometimes they plunge into despair. You can illustrate this pattern with an analogy. When Americans tried to introduce farming innovations to third world countries, their first efforts failed because they didn't consider the force of tradition. "You will have better crops," was not motivating for traditional farmers, who had ancestors to consider, festivals to keep, and other rich cultural traditions to honor. Fours might imagine they are anthropologists exploring a foreign culture and consider the caliber of respect they need to show when examining the barriers to their new ideas. From this perspective they can see how carefully they need to respect the organization's culture, to learn the language and customs of the "natives." Looking for what is missing can cause Fours to undervalue what is present. Mary told Tera, "Only when you learn what the world looks like to others will you see opportunities to help them change. You might even find it is sufficient to improve what is already being done."

Fours frequently envision possibilities others are blind to, but looking for what is missing can cause them to undervalue what is present.

Fours may ask for help with an immediate problem, like getting someone to adopt an innovative idea. If you keep the focus that narrow, you may only redecorate their perceptual cave. Help them realize how they accent the difference between their ideas and those of others. Tera's real growth came when she began to see how her focus on difference alienated the people she was courting and brought about the very resistance she feared. This recognition was a second-order change.

The Four's focus on what is missing does have a big bright side. Fours are rarely guilty of the kind of groupthink that keeps a team from seeing its own process. When Tera learned to distinguish between necessary change and the compulsion to change things, she was able to contribute her fresh point of view more effectively. Fours can keep a system from slowly dying of untested and outdated assumptions.

People with this Enneagram style long for something they feel deeply that they're missing. When they have this longing, they also feel a strong sense of entitlement. They have a personal Garden of Eden, romanticizing a past time when life was perfect. If you alert them to this preoccupation, they tend to soften their dramatic inner turmoil. You can help this shift to the present by focusing on their strengths and resources, as Mary did when she had Tera review her life as a spiritual journey. You can also reframe their longing as a desire for growth and transcendence.

Fours achieve balance when they identify areas of satisfaction. Help them cultivate a sense of gratitude.

Fours achieve balance when they identify areas of satisfaction. Help them cultivate a sense of gratitude. They become more positive as they develop possibilities in their current situation.

Fours tend to identify with the underdog, because their habitual pattern is to position themselves as cosmic underdogs. They feel alienated, so they ally with others who are unpopular, defective, or somehow marginal. Their belief in their own defectiveness can preclude efforts at popularity. They tell themselves that if they were popular it would be because nobody is astute or cares enough to notice their flaws. From this vantage point of rejecting and being rejected, Fours bond with other outcasts. In a business situation, that habit can lead them to nurture those having trouble and ignore those who may be responsible for much of the company's success.

Sees Self as Defective

Fours easily feel alienated if they can't find opportunity to express their subjective vision. Of course, we all have our private convictions, but in-the-box Fours have little else. More emotionally intense than other Enneagram styles, they risk sinking into despondency when they meet with resistance to their private passionate convictions. When their subjective convictions clash with conventional, standard expectations, something has to give. In-the-box Fours withdraw into moodiness and lose their energy to fight for what they believe.

Rolf did this when he faced Peter's criticism. He felt inferior and withdrew, unable to assert his subjective position. When this dynamic occurs, a coach hears sad stories from Fours. Starting from an implicit posture of being defective, they lament, "Everybody else is normal. I'm not. I don't fit in." Their urge to be different complicates this and sustains their alienated worldview: "I suppose I am different, but difference makes me special. I suffer because of this, but my suffering makes me more authentic."

Disagreement or criticism can be difficult for Fours, because they may experience criticism as total rejection, reinforcing their conviction that they are defective. If this happens they may lose their energy or may even resort to sabotage. Failing to pursue a project that meets with resistance, as Tera did, is a form of sabotage. She withheld the fresh vision that could have saved the day. When critics prevail and Fours sink into despondency, they slip into a telltale speech pattern that begins, "If only..." "If only television had a forum for good taste." "If only we had adequate funding." Criticism can be understood as a neutral suggestion on how things might be improved, a goal Fours can appreciate.

Fours cope better when they recognize their tendency to swallow criticisms whole and smear their entire inner landscape with them. Many Fours have a unique perspective, which itself brings pressure for change. They must expect to receive criticism when this happens, so it is important they understand criticism as an effort to improve matters, not an attack on them personally. Change combats the familiar, and the familiar often has deep roots. Encourage Fours not to defend themselves against criticism, but instead to ask for as much detail and explanation as possible. This process interferes with their habit of self-depreciation and short-circuits their defense system that can lead to a downward spiral.

Fours combine the subjective and objective in ways that bring them peak achievement or lead them to disaster. Begin with "taste." Taste is subjective. The old legal maxim, *De gustibus non disputandum est,* says, "You can't litigate (or argue) about taste," precisely because taste is subjective. This maxim does not apply to Fours. They thrive on disputes about taste because that is how they combine their private passion and public assertion. Fours tend to be of the opinion that, "If you cannot see the beauty in this (work, art, fashion, idea) then you lack taste." The catch is, of course, that taste, being subjective, is self-defined. Fours can sway a group by their dedication to good taste, or they can become idiosyncratic and indulgent. If Fours value taste but lack discernment, they find that hard to admit and will still try to install their private vision on public ground.

All Enneagram styles have a generic either/or assumption.[3] Fours believe *either* they can be accepted *or* they can be their real (defective) self. To sustain this belief, they often try to pre-empt rejection by rejecting anyone they think may criticize (reject) them. Whereas another style might see criticism as a rejection of an idea, Fours see it as a rejection of their passion, perhaps their very self. Just hearing that others feel differently can trigger feeling they are among Philistines with little or no taste.

All Enneagram styles have a generic either/or assumption. Fours believe either they can be accepted or they can be their real (defective) self.

They may be hypercritical in their scorn for mediocrity. In a period of feeling rejected, Rolf expressed his contempt for Peter: "He thinks he's such a great leader, but he's pitiful. I think he's got a screw loose where work relationships are concerned." You can help a client like this notice an implicit arrogance: "I'm more authentic, sensitive, and aesthetic than you are." They will need your help to see the arrogance because the pre-emptive criticism feels like inferiority—a defense against being rejected.

Fours' passionate certitude about what they believe is not blind. It is confidence in the subjective. They value their personal vision higher than cultural norms,

[3] See Chapter Thirteen for the either/or assumptions of all nine Enneagram styles.

traditional ways, or industry standards. Their emphasis is on the unique, the elite, and the special. Clarence's client, Alberto, served on several art academy boards. He commented on one, "I've stayed with them because the chair comes from an artistic background and has high aesthetic standards. The changes I'm interested in making are with the quality of the program, and she holds those values as well. I've resigned from another board that doesn't share those values." Objective corroboration of refined taste and artistic value is hard to come by and is deeply appreciated.

We suggest meeting Fours at their strength for unique and innovative ideas. Metaphors work especially well to access Fours' personal gold.

We suggest meeting Fours at their strength for unique and innovative ideas. They may reject the tried and true out of hand but surprise you with their personal, unique solutions. In coaching Phil, the graduate student blocked on his dissertation, Mary led him to discover how much energy he wasted by trying to meet the expectations of his academic advisors. He blocked his innate creativity instead of using his gifts to gain the support of the committee. As Mary encouraged him to claim his soul, he shifted his attention from the support that was missing to what he could do:

- He became more aware that he could synthesize and build bridges across separate and somewhat mutually exclusive academic disciplines. This awareness guided his research, which had been bogging him down. He learned to appreciate and claim his unique perspective.

- Using mind mapping, he learned to diagram conceptual categories in circles, then to look for links without forcing a linear outline. He let the ideas create their own structure.

- He had been challenging himself to write a polished piece on the first try. He worked past his writer's block using a creative problem solving technique, to write a first draft without judgment and then to rewrite.

Metaphors work especially well to access Fours' personal gold. With Phil, Mary used a train station metaphor. She suggested that attempting to bridge two academic disciplines was like trying to go between two railroad stations, one of which would only accept blue cars, the other only red ones. "If you believe the blue car can add something, but it isn't accepted at the red station," she suggested, "then you may need to paint the blue car red. Once you get into the red station, it will be easier to show its added value." Phil was inspired by this metaphor to create a way to bridge disciplinary barriers between departments.

Fours may accept some of your ideas, as when Phil used Mary's suggestion to use mind mapping, but they will often do even better with their own solutions. Given emotional permission, they will come up with highly individualized discoveries. If you suggest a metaphor, they will develop their own quest. Sometimes an ambiguous assignment frees them, like the one Mary gave Tera to discover a solution somewhere in Lincoln's history.

If you offer suggestions that have worked for others, even other Fours, you may find they will put their own spin on it. Mary suggested mind mapping to a Four who was having trouble setting priorities to carry out her mission statement. She told Mary, "I couldn't do the mind mapping. It didn't flow for me. But it reminded me of something that does work for me: to sit down with a clean pad of paper and a sharpened pencil. We had talked last week about each strategy being part of a whole, and now things are falling into place. I made a list of what I had to do and then rearranged the tasks in order. I'm starting to prioritize everything I do."

Fours may feel despair and display great dramatic pain about things you consider trivial. Depending on your Enneagram style, you may need to develop more sensitivity here. Anyone can suffer depression at times, but many Fours report life-long depression, often with a history of medication or medical attention. If you've never been clinically depressed, you will deepen your coaching skills with Fours if you learn about depression. The book *Sacred Sorrows* is a good place to start. Its essays describe symptoms, treatment, personal stories, and—most important for transformation—how some aspects of depression can be framed as part of a spiritual journey. We have seen Fours learn from their darker moods by helping them understand their melancholy in a sacred light.

You will deepen your coaching skills if you learn about depression. We have seen Fours learn from their darker moods by helping them understand their melancholy in a sacred light.

If their depression is not severe, you may detect a subterranean enjoyment in their laments. Listen for a certain bragging undertone when they massage their pain as Tera did when she lamented her organization's culture. Encourage Fours to observe how they polish and shape their laments for maximum effect. They may discover a cycle of longing/getting/rejecting. Mary suggested to Tera: "When you notice yourself saying, 'I've been wasting my productive years in the wrong place,' step back and say, 'Ah, that's the box where I compulsively focus on myself as an outsider, a misfit.' When you feel disenchanted, step back and say, 'Ah, how interesting. I'm in the box again, playing out my worldview that the grass must be greener somewhere else.'"

Because they feel so alienated, Fours tend to think they are the only ones with their pattern-problems. They are often helped out of their presumed isolation by reading lives of Fours or novels with strong Four characters like *Madame Bovary, Sense and Sensibility,* or *Anna Karenina.* France, a culture with some Four characteristics, has produced a number of classic Four stories. *Beauty and the Beast, Cyrano de Bergerac,* and *The Hunchback of Notre Dame* all feature defective, lovable heroes.

Defends with Introjection

To introject is to carry an image of a person or ideal within yourself and judge yourself, usually negatively, in comparison with it. This habit in Fours gives them a negative identity: "Michael is perfect, I am the person who is not perfect, not Michael." Even though they value authenticity, they try to achieve it by comparison: "I should be like my father and I'm not." Fours can induce their own depression and low self esteem by comparing themselves to unrealistic ideals. "If I can't be like my idol, then I am a failure. Not even, "I have failed," but "I am a failure." They carry this image of the person they admire inside themselves as a constant reference point. They may not be consciously aware of this process, but it can show up in a search for implicit standards that lurk in their background: "A good student gets A's even without much effort." We have also seen the dynamic reversed. A Four told Mary she felt shame about her bouts of temper "because I don't want to be the harridan my mother was."

Fours can induce their own depression and low self esteem by comparing themselves to unrealistic ideals. So when dealing with their discouragement, try to find the point of comparison.

By comparing themselves to the perfect person or ideal, Fours make themselves feel significant, and—if in the box—miserable. After all, misery feels better than being merely ordinary. Better a mutant peacock than a barnyard chicken. The ideal that inspires them, judges them. So when dealing with their discouragement, try to find the point of comparison. Their introjected comparison may be a mere possibility, not a reality. Sometimes when they lament their inadequacy, simply, ask, "Compared to…?" Leave them the choice of inserting a what or a whom.

Their focus on the perfection of the ideal to which they compare themselves also leads to a great emphasis on integrity. The ideal is always present to them as a goal, a measuring stick, and a personal criterion. The ideal, not political or financial reality, is how they evaluate their work and the work of those in their orbit. Their personal vision is the point of departure for their own efforts and they demand allegiance to this vision from the group. Fours in leadership positions will not mind at all that their vision is unusual, even dramatically different from much of the field. From the Four's point of view, the group's work is to express that personal vision of theirs.

This personal perfectionism relates to style One in the insistence on quality. But the difference is that Ones hold everyone to an objective standard that all recognize, such as a law or policy or canon of excellence. Fours keep the standard, but the standard is subjective. Their private canons of good taste and elite aspirations are now considered universal standards. In self-aware Fours, this perfectionism becomes a visionary ideal and can energize an entire group. The group can create and carry important projects and make significant breakthroughs. In a more in-the-box Four, the subjective norm can get quirky and idiosyncratic. The vision may be difficult to communicate because of its subjectivity or it may simply not appeal to others. Fours may have difficulty recognizing when this personal vision is not appropriate for all. When this happens, their whims and annoyances, often derived from this introjected ideal, become the standards by which work is judged. Those who can't accept or understand the vision begin to walk on eggs wondering what is expected of them. On the high side, when Four leaders have a subjective ideal that compels others, even if it is introjected from someone else, they profoundly energize the group or organization.

The link between the private passion of a Four and the public execution of that passion is frequently symbolic. Being one's ideal is never entirely possible, but being like the ideal in one significant area may be. You can see this dynamic among all those who have ideals beyond themselves. How many small boys used to wear Michael Jordan jerseys? They couldn't play like he can, but they could wear his jersey, a symbol of his excellence. So Fours may do certain things in exactly the way they think their ideal would want them done.

Symbols have the power to reach both the cognitive and emotional levels that a compelling vision must have. Fours frequently read symbols as easily as others read the alphabet. Clarence worked for a corporation that hired a consultant with a PhD in computer science and an MBA. So everyone wondered why she, bristling with left-brain credentials, spent the whole first day at the place reading the environment. She read the walls and the memos on them, the cartoons, the carpet, the plants, and apparently calibrated the volume, frequency, and timbre of conversations. She did this because she is a Four and has a great ability to decipher symbols. The environment yielded a type of information that books and hard drives could not.

The peril of this gift of symbolic sensitivity is that small things can have an impact beyond their intent. A smaller office than expected, a social slight, or a forgotten milestone can become a source of intense emotional pain. One of Mary's clients said she was "angry from day one" because the office she was given "smelled like a ferret's." When Fours are thrown off by a symbol, everyone tiptoes around trying to deal with a mood whose origin they can't fathom.

Tera was immediately drawn to Mary's quote from Plato as a symbolic parallel to her situation. Mary was able to draw on Tera's rich, multiform symbolic ability to shift her perspective in a way not possible using only logic. Mary knew better than to "talk her out" of her problem.

Fours often speak of the black hole of their emotions. The coach has to find a way to enter into that black hole. Symbols are one way. Anecdotes that contain symbolic suggestions are powerful. C.G. Jung is reported to have dreamed that he was drowning in a vat of human waste and calling out for rescue to his therapist, who stood above. "Help me out," he cried. Instead of taking his outstretched hand the therapist pushed Jung's head down into the liquid, saying, "Through, not out." "Is that how it feels when you stumble into your black hole?" you might ask as you reflect on this story with a Four. "You're crying, 'Get me out of this vat of shit!' But your way is through, not out."

Fours often speak of the black hole of their emotions. The coach has to find a way to enter into that black hole. Anecdotes that contain symbolic suggestions are powerful.

You may notice Fours going for million dollar sweeps. Their vision is so inwardly compelling, they eagerly bet the farm or firm on it. Help them assimilate the hard data, the external realities, before they make a decision based on passion. Homework is not as emotionally fulfilling as polishing a vision, but you might suggest it is like a birth process: a lot of pain and mostly labor. In Mary Karr's poem, *The Worm-Farmer's Lament,* she describes workers grunting up the next hill in the hope they could reach a clearing "gold with sunflowers" where everyone could sink "knee-deep in a humming splendor."

The Four's Vision: Shift from being moody and unable to get past melancholy to being effective in the outer world

Fours move toward transformation when they become aware they have enough of what they need. Instead of dreaming about a better place, "knee-deep in humming splendor," they learn to live in the moment and appreciate what they have. When they develop this focus and the serenity that comes with it, they can support their passionate ideas regardless of their mood. They realize that resistance to change is natural, and honor it as a source of energy instead of being blocked by frustration. With this energy harnessed, they can help others see possibilities beyond the familiar.

Three months after their last contact, Tera called Mary with great excitement about a new project. She was to lead a cross-functional task force. Their goal was to design and implement an innovative structural re-design she had conceived and sold to the organization. A true Four, she quoted the poet Rilke to describe the significance of her shift in perspective: "He writes, 'I love the dark hours of my being,' but he also knows there is room in him for 'a second huge and timeless life.'"

Remote Control

Forty-three-year old Lyle Clayburn was the information technology director for an international banking company. In his first coaching session with Mary, he sat behind his desk with his hands in his lap, his intelligent face offering few clues to his feelings. His body type and general appearance gave the impression of a curious teddy bear. His button-down shirt with small checks of indeterminate color was slightly mismatched to the rest of his clothes. His red suspenders belonged on a farmer but they did manage to hold up his wrinkled khaki pants. A quotation framed on the wall behind him read:

There's only one success: To be able to spend your life in your own way.

—Christopher Morley

When Mary commented on the quotation, Lyle responded, "I always thought of myself as the strong, silent type who didn't need anybody in any way. It was only after my wife died last year that I admitted to myself how much I count on my family. When I took this job with all its problems, I came to realize that other people's help and support are necessary. They'd probably feel good if I told them this—I regret that I didn't talk more with my wife—but I don't want to lose control of my emotions. My boss told me, 'You have to be the rock for those people.' But there are too many of them. I can't deal with all of them. I do keep my office door open, and I tell people they should feel free to come in—one at a time."

The view from the top reinforced Lyle's problematic self-assessment. What Lyle saw as his personal problem, his boss, Spencer, saw as a company problem. Spencer worried aloud to Mary about it. He said he was disappointed with Lyle's inability to resolve the issues in his division more quickly: "He's bright and knowledgeable; he expresses himself well, and he has top-notch technical expertise. I could tell he was feeling the effects of his wife's death even though he never said so. So I thought this promotion would be the perfect way to help him refocus his energy. I told him this would be an opportunity to test his management skills in a more

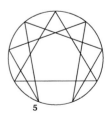

complex situation than he'd been used to. He has to pull together a team of seven that includes several highly dependable managers and two under-performers. Now if I wonder if he can handle the job, with all these issues I keep hearing about."

Spencer said Lyle's peers were concerned as well. "He doesn't use the other directors as resources enough. They say that when they send him e-mails they only hope for a response, and when he does respond, his messages are cryptic. We expected him to have a learning curve, but my boss is putting pressure on me to speed things up. It's not happening," Spencer fretted. "We're hearing all kinds of complaints from some big customers, and morale is slipping." He added, "I appreciate his abilities and feel sorry for the guy. I know we've put him in a bind and I want you to see if you can help him."

Mary felt as if she'd taken a wrong turn into a "Mission Impossible" movie. Spencer had moved Lyle from a technical job for which he was superbly equipped into a job with a sharply different set of demands, many of them social, for which he was ill-equipped. Lyle was introverted, independent, and preferred to work alone. As an Enneagram Five, he had been put in a situation from Hell: a job requiring that he closely coordinate a team and interact frequently with both subordinates and peers. It didn't help that Lyle was already suffering personal stress and working for someone who was under his own pressure from senior management.

The three other directors on Spencer's management team added specific complaints. "Lyle lives in his own world," said Peggy. "I have to chase him down for information in order to do my job. The biggest problem is that we all depend on e-mail to communicate because we travel so much. There can be a seven to ten-day delay in getting responses from him." Bill noted, "He misses team meetings when we're all here, even meetings that are key to his area. Or he'll show up late and leave early." Larry added, "While he's in meetings he rarely talks. He appears to listen to what people have to say, but he never gives anything back so you don't know what he took in or whether he goes along with it. He can seem cooperative and then go off and do things his own way, even if he's agreed otherwise."

"Lyle lives in his own world. I have to chase him down for information in order to do my job."

"While he's in meetings he rarely talks."

Not all their comments were negative. They respected Lyle's keen mind. "He's awesomely bright," said Bill, "perhaps the most intelligent person I've ever met." Larry agreed: "Few can keep up with him. You work on a project for a week and he absorbs it in a day. He eats it up; it's scary how well he remembers things." Peggy noted that Lyle's intelligence had a down side: "He may not be aware when people don't understand his instructions. He's two steps ahead and this may make it hard to delegate."

The people who reported to Lyle agreed he failed to delegate and saw this as a control issue. "He rations our contact with customers," said one of his more experienced managers. "He isn't trying to steal anybody's thunder, but he's so determined to understand the problems we've got that he takes calls from customers he could direct to one of us." When he did delegate, Lyle seemed to assume that others operated the same way he did—by figuring out everything on their own. His team felt abandoned: "He's been specific about his values, so when we make a decision we know if he'll think it's smart. But he doesn't seem to think we need direction at all."

His team felt abandoned: "He's been specific about his values, so when we make a decision we know if he'll think it's smart. But he doesn't seem to think we need direction at all."

His staff's feedback had already prodded Lyle to communicate more effectively: "He's getting better. We're so separate geographically that we're liable to work at cross-purposes. Now he's scheduled a regular videoconference once a week with all regions. He cancels them half the time. Still, it's a major accomplishment for him to schedule some at all. It's an opportunity to hear what everybody is doing." One staff member highlighted a key issue: "Lyle goes to individuals and handles things one-on-one. This works counter to our team operation and creates a huge potential for problems. We see some of them already in our poor service reports."

All of his subordinates complained that Lyle created an in-group/out-group dynamic. How well they liked Lyle depended on which group they felt they were in. Here's how Patty—one of Spenser's "under-performers"—described it: "Lyle's got three teams. Members of his first team are confidants—people who fill his needs and share his viewpoints. Norb belongs because of his political savvy. Fran, who's in tune with people's needs, serves as Lyle's conscience. There's the second team—good, solid, get-the-job-done people who won't cause embarrassment or trouble but who disagree to some extent with the way Lyle runs things. I belong to the third team. Lyle considers us unessential so he doesn't include us much. He's all but told me he thinks I'm brain-dead."

Coaching Analysis

Coaching Lyle

Mary began the feedback session with Lyle by outlining four problem areas: he hoarded information, he tended to debate, he isolated himself, and he had limited social skills. These are common for Enneagram style Five.

Hoarding Information

Mary focused first on Lyle's habit of hoarding information, which often led to cryptic and inconsistent communication with peers. As an example, she reminded him that he had agreed to fill in the Myers-Briggs Type Indicator (MBTI) and return it to her several days before a scheduled meeting. The day before the meeting, she called to ask if he'd mailed it. He had not. He sent it by overnight mail but this still forced Mary to prepare for their meeting at the last minute. This incident paralleled situations Lyle's co-workers had reported. He would agree to something, but withhold the information unless pressed for it.

At first Lyle didn't seem to realize it was not enough that he know something. The whole team had to know. He valued information for himself, but had to overcome his reluctance to share it with others. He made things worse because he didn't know how to tell people when other priorities made it difficult for him to give them what they needed. Mary coached Lyle to communicate in a way that considered everyone's work demands. For example, she encouraged him to ask for the reasons behind a request so he could weigh its importance against other priorities and then respond honestly. Practicing with the MBTI incident, Mary suggested that Lyle say, "Help me understand why it's important to have that information before our next meeting. I have two major projects due in the next week that I have to give top priority. How much time will you need to prepare once you receive the MBTI information?" With this interaction as a model, Lyle began to exchange the necessary information and support with his peers. After learning how their project objectives overlapped with his, he created a system that encouraged communication between his staff and theirs.

Lyle began to exchange the necessary information and support with his peers.

Debating Habit

Lyle brought his team together for a problem-solving workshop on supplier relations that Mary facilitated. After some initial conversation it became clear that his team disagreed among themselves on how to negotiate contracts with suppliers. Some members believed in the tough negotiating style that succeeded in the past. Others felt they should begin to treat suppliers as partners, which would make them honor their contracts more faithfully. The old-liners reacted to this with scorn, describing it as "warm and fuzzy" and "caving in." Those who advocated change accused the old-liners of having a "fixed mind-set" and "being "in a rut."

Ordinarily, Lyle would have encouraged debate about the two approaches, which in the past usually had led to *either/or outcomes*. Lyle had based his prior decisions on whomever he thought won a debate. One group would leave thinking they had been ignored and/or defeated. Mary showed Lyle and his team how to clarify common objectives and create innovative solutions by searching for *both/and* options ("How can we *both* build new supplier relationships *and* maintain our record of enforceable contracts?")

Isolation

As he worked with Mary, Lyle began to observe how he habitually isolated himself. He realized that his secretive and somewhat cynical style of relating was holding him back. He saw how he would be hampered personally and in his work if he failed to break those habits. He began to reach out more, to be more compassionate, and to support others more generously.

To serve his development goals, Lyle and Mary created a questionnaire to give him feedback on his progress through time. His team assessed him on the following behaviors anonymously every six months for a year and a half:

Communication

1. Probes others' points of view.
2. Seeks clarification of others' nonverbal communication.
3. Reflects back what others have said/seem to be feeling.
4. Discloses own feelings openly and directly.
5. Fully explores differing opinions.
6. Summarizes or seeks summary of agreements.
7. Makes it clear if he needs time to think through others' input.

Coaching

8. Makes performance expectations clear.
9. Gives balanced, specific, descriptive feedback.
10. Affirms positive efforts.
11. Delegates in ways that foster responsibility and accountability.

Teamwork

12. Seeks agreement on team vision.

13. Structures roles to support envisioned teamwork.

14. Coaches team to make meetings effective:

    a. Shares information

    b. Solves problems creatively

    c. Manages conflict

    d. Makes decisions

15. Debriefs team interactions at each meeting.

Over time he became less isolated and more of an active manager with the people who reported to him.

Lyle and Mary used the team's feedback as a focus for their coaching. Over time he became less isolated and more of an active manager with the people who reported to him.

Social Skills

Lyle's previous year had been difficult. Besides having problems with his new job, he grieved for his wife, Anne. He missed her companionship at home and her contribution to his social role at work. She had been outgoing and kept conversation going when they were with others. As a company executive, he now had to attend many business and social events where he was uncomfortable without the support of his wife and her social charm.

Lyle had trouble with light conversation, so Mary suggested he practice small talk on the plane in his frequent travels. He said he usually buried his head in paperwork during flights so he wouldn't have to talk to anyone. "From now on," she said, "talk to people next to you on planes. It's perfectly safe, because you don't ever have to see them again." Aghast, he muttered, "I wouldn't know what to say." Mary persevered: "You're a good observer. All you have to do is notice what they're reading, how they're dressed, whether they seem nervous about flying, any clues to their lines of work, and ask a question that invites them to talk. Think of it as adding to your stockpile of information," she urged, appealing to his acknowledged love of information. "Take it slowly, and if they give cues that they don't want to talk, let it go. You'll be intrigued by how well they respond to you. As you develop comfort with these casual conversations, you'll more easily engage people on other social occasions."

Coaching Style Five

When Mary's client, Jane, first contacted her, Mary was charmed by a visual clue to the Five's low profile style. Jane's e-mail inquiry for more information was written in eight-point type:

Cogito ergo sum. I think, therefore I am.

Rene Descartes

> What is the going rate for an expert coach such as you? What are the logistics of this?
> How do I pay my money? Do you take MasterCard, or shall I drop you a check?

Fives will be particularly likely make sure of your expertise before they hire you. You'll do well to reassure them right away by speaking their language. Mary overcame her reluctance to use Jane's word, "expert," in quoting her fees and wrote, "My fees compare quite favorably to those of other experts."

Fives polarize between retreating into their heads and taking external action. You can expect these clients to know their style already or to learn it quickly. Fives have little trouble understanding their issues but they have trouble taking action. They want to be able to break free of their patterns, as Jane so capably observed: "My being an Enneagram Five has served me well in the past but I tend to overwhelm myself with book learning and not make any practical progress."

These clients will progress most when they observe how they act out their style personally. They grow when they interrupt their habitual patterns and begin to move from thought to action. As they take action, they become more confident and comfortable in social interactions.

Fives use time and space as boundaries to give themselves privacy and safety, so give them time to think things through. They like schedules. Give them advance notice when you intend to bring up issues they might find uncomfortable. Give them space also. They may prefer a desk between you and them. You might sit just a bit farther apart from Fives than you would other clients. They may learn easily by phone and even prefer phone coaching to face-to-face meetings. This medium helps them create whatever emotional space they need, to avoid what they might consider unwanted emotional invasion.

As they experiment with their fieldwork, support them with specific feedback. They value feedback as they value all information and are likely to take action only when certain they are well informed. When you give them feedback, you make them more secure.

Even though they cherish privacy, Fives can come to a level of trust where they take emotional risks. With trust established, they may even be playful. For example, Jane had been one of the most knowledgeable people in a field where advancing technology had made it impossible to know everything. But as she worked to keep up with the technology, she missed the political dimension. She didn't know about the people involved in projects—names, positions, needs—which caused problems in situations where the political dimension was important.

Mary asked Jane, "What stops you from asking questions about the players when you need that information?"

"I don't want to appear stupid for having forgotten."

"Will you do something far out if I suggest it?"

"Yes," Jane answered, with an act of trust.

"The next time this comes up, try really hard to appear stupid!"

Jane and Mary both laughed at Mary's suggestion. Laughter is one of those right-brain breakthrough signals.[1] During their next coaching call Jane said, "I found myself feeling stupid. I simply noticed it and said, 'Oh, I'm feeling stupid' and decided to make it happen more. That was great! It was empowering to actually cause it. I realized that I can't know everything all the time."

When you coach Fives effectively, they will become less reserved and reserving, more generous, and will integrate their thinking with action.

Fears Being Overwhelmed by Others

Pay attention to these four habits of in-the-box Fives:

Fears being overwhelmed by others

Believes there's not enough information to take action

Fears self-revelation

Compartmentalizes people, thoughts, activities

Fives can be the most independent of all the Enneagram styles. They may seem emotionally distant and almost callous, but this attitude is a defense against emotional interactions they fear will be more than they can handle. In business, this preference for emotional distance can lead them to surround themselves with other highly capable people who need little or no emotional reinforcement. They are reluctant to share their feelings either at home or at work for fear of being emotionally inadequate.

Fives create distance—social, physical, or temporal. They think emotions may cloud their thinking, and they pride themselves on clear thought. They dislike emotional confrontation and prefer to think apart from it. Their tendency to withdraw can be emotionally distancing to others, but also allows Fives more objectivity. Regardless of the emotional turbulence of a situation, when they

---

[1] Don't be discouraged if it takes a while to be this free with your Five clients. Trust doesn't come easily for them as a rule. Jane was quite self-aware when she began her work with Mary.

remove themselves temporarily they are usually better able to respond to problems in a balanced way. They can see all parts of a conflict or problem more dispassionately. They act out of this perspective, not out of the feelings of the moment.

The Five style can be expressed metaphorically by a modern electronic gadget: the remote control. All ego styles are methods of control, but what distinguishes Fives is their desire for control from afar. They may prefer to communicate by e-mail rather than discuss matters in an office or over suitable beverage. E-mail gives them time to think before they answer (if they answer at all). It provides hard data, and usually has little or no emotional content. It also can be private, unlike conversation at a meeting. E-mail usually bypasses social chitchat about sports, family, or weather.

Fives may seem emotionally distant and almost callous, but this attitude is a defense against emotional interactions they fear will be more than they can handle.

When Clarence gave an Enneagram retreat to a group of executives, the Five CEO instructed his group ahead of time that he was not to be interviewed or asked to meet any employees, as he had been on a previous retreat. His company held him in high esteem; he was well liked by practically everyone, and he was personable one-to-one. But he did not like casual social interaction. Some Fives will have a few close friends who are extremely important to them and they communicate well in that context. But small talk and spontaneous dealings with people they don't know well often bothers them. Managers with this style may work admirably well with small groups, but may have trouble elsewhere.

All ego styles are methods of control, but what distinguishes Fives is their desire for control from afar.

Because Fives prefer to work alone or in small groups, they may choose professions such as research chemistry, computer technology, or engineering. But promotions in these environments to management positions—where most of the problems are people problems—are often given to the best technician. This is frequently a recipe for trouble for Fives. If they pay attention only to the technical side of their job, the emotional component may sink them.

When asked for a metaphor of his life, Lyle said, "I am a battery and people drain me." Fives want privacy because thinking energizes them. If they don't have privacy, the demands of social interaction drain them. They need to be aware of who and what drains them so they can allot some private time to recharge. They also need to acknowledge legitimate claims on their time and energy. Their emotional health hinges on this balance between thinking and (inter) acting.

Sales people are sometimes trained to go to homes with "No Soliciting" signs because these often signal that the owner has difficulty saying no. Fives actually have a difficult time saying no to social demands. They say a general "no" so they don't have to say specific ones. They set up extra clear boundaries precisely because they fear they will not be able to defend them.

In-the-box Fives often stay distant from their own emotions by living in their heads. When they *live* their ideas, they don't experience their emotions. This focus on ideas and muted awareness of feeling can give the impression of serene objectivity and sometimes even arrogance.

In business settings Fives may avoid team members who thrive on relationships, considering them as emotionally needy. In-the-box Fives are coolly independent and expect self-reliance from others. They don't consider handholding as part of their job. If employees come in distraught and upset, Fives are inclined to give them information on where to get help.

Acknowledge their legitimate needs for space and privacy, but encourage them to keep others fully informed.

When working with Five clients, acknowledge their legitimate needs for space and privacy, but encourage them to keep others fully informed. If they are physically leaving the premises, suggest that they let people know how they can be reached in a crisis — e-mail, cell phone number — anything so people don't feel abandoned.

One Five was feeling trapped, torn between fulfilling his work commitments and retreating to his private space. He thirsted for pursuits like reading, meditation, or exploring the Internet (none of these helped him make a living, which he resented). "Are you familiar with Dali?" asked Mary. "I admire Dali—I have several books of his paintings," he responded. "Then put a picture of one of his melting clocks on your desk where you can see it every day. Something interesting will happen." He took Mary up on her suggestion and discovered that having the Dali clock reproduction on his desk melted his resentment at the time he spent working. He had feared he would spend all his precious time at work, leaving no time to himself. He had been hoarding his private time as if he could never save enough. Gradually, his sense of time became more fluid and he became more present to his work. This in turn allowed him to be fully present when enjoying his private pursuits.

Suggest that they ask for silence when they need it, so it isn't misinterpreted. "I need time to think" is both truthful and respectful.

This Enneagram style likes silence more than most. Suggest that they ask for it when they need it, so it isn't misinterpreted. "I need time to think" is both truthful and respectful. The husband of a Five was annoyed that when he'd ask her a question there would be such a long silence he'd think she hadn't heard or was ignoring him. "Oh," she assured him, "I'm thinking it through." They agreed that

110

she'd fill these silences with an occasional, "Uhhh…" to let him know she was still thinking!

When talking to Fives, use words like "interesting," "intriguing" and "curious." You can use their familiar language to open them to new understanding. This matches their worldview in which information is valuable while it leads them to a richer world of experience.

If they find it hard to share time or affection but voraciously seek information, you might use water as a healing metaphor. Suggest they put a picture of a body of water in a prominent place where they spend a lot of time: "Water needs both input and output to stay fresh. You may concentrate on input and forget the output. Everybody, even a body of water, needs both to stay fresh."

Fives may not be in touch with their feelings, even though they might talk about them. Sometimes they have the words but won't feel what is going on within themselves. As they mature, long-buried feelings may erupt, and they will need help to accept and integrate them.

As they mature, long-buried feelings may erupt, and they will need help to accept and integrate them.

They may report that closeness and the corresponding involvement feel like a loss. Reframe involvement as a gain, as Mary did when she suggested to Lyle that he have polite conversations on airplanes: "You'll be intrigued by how well they respond to you." She reinforced this embedded positive expectation with another one: "As you develop comfort with these casual conversations, you'll more easily engage people on other social occasions."

For some Fives, emotional distance and privacy feel safe but can also feel like a prison. Many teachers use the image of a castle to describe this style. A moat may surround the castle and only the Five can raise or lower the drawbridge. Castles have thick walls and deep chambers, where one can become lonely, however secure. Listen for such metaphors in their language and help reframe them. If a Five speaks with pleasure of her ivory tower or castle, work with that metaphor. Suggest that she could let down her hair like Rapunzel, or pry loose the lock to a chest of jewels that represents withheld feelings. Perhaps she can throw open the wooden door to let light into dark and musty corners.

As your Five clients begin to claim their own feelings, they will find it easier to share those feelings. Help them discover passions that can connect them to others. For example, a Five wanted to regain the romantic quality of his early relationship with his wife. Upon learning that he had written poetry in college and that he was passionate about music, Mary asked him to write a poem about music and bring it to their next session: "Rather than telling me about your passion for music," she requested, "write it in such a way that I feel your passion for music." When he was able to create poetry about music, he would more easily discover the poetry of his relationship to his wife.

Believes There's Not Enough Information to Take Action

Fives often find taking action difficult because they need more information. "More" is undefined for them, and that unspecified need can paralyze them. They want ample time to think things over, gather information, relate the big picture to all the details, and deliberate. *Deliberate* describes their process perfectly because it means both to take time and to do something on purpose. Fives may plan too carefully. They don't think they can succeed by accident or immediate intuition. They seldom fly by the seat of their pants. Their deliberate pace can cause bottlenecks when quick decisions are needed. While others may want quick decisions, especially on details, Fives consider details worth more than a snap decision. For them, all details deserve scrutiny.

They fear they don't have the complete picture. They crave predictability. There are so many steps to make ideas clear that they can't just turn on a dime. Five managers prefer detailed budgets and critical paths for all projects, no matter how small. Andy, a Five, approached Mark, a Seven, on a Wednesday morning in May. He asked if Mark could teach a class for him at a nearby college. Mark looked a bit worried and said, "Not tonight, but I can on Thursday or Friday." Andy's face went blank for a moment, and then he replied, "I was planning for mid-October." Sevens thrive on spontaneity; Fives avoid it when possible.

Because they prefer careful, detailed, long-range planning, Fives relish schedules. This mentality carries over into day-by-day business management. Fives do not want people to bounce into their office unannounced, bringing problems with them. They want to know ahead of time when the person is coming, what the problem is, and what supporting data describes the problem. They will usually welcome as much detail as possible. Those who come in with this information will get a hearing, a warm welcome, and sage advice. Well, usually a warm welcome.

If Fives agree to a social engagement, they may want to know exactly who is coming, the ambiance, the time frame, and any pertinent social agenda. Some may script their phone calls seeking the same assurance—no surprises. They usually insist that all meetings have a clear, detailed agenda. The smart team member will warn them ahead of time before bringing new information to an agenda.

As managers, Fives may rely on only one kind of information. Their need for objective clarity may override any sensitivity to social repercussions. They can demolish a colleague's position publicly, unaware of causing embarrassment. This approach leaves out information of another order: fear, anger, fatigue, confusion—the whole range of human emotions. Lyle's original preference was for debate because logic was everything. Emotions had no place. He had to learn how to include others openly in conversation and how to seek mutually satisfying solutions. He began to see that he was doing more than exchanging information; he was also motivating people and deepening relationships.

When coaching this style, help them become aware that they risk appearing arrogant because of their bank of more and better information. In meetings or when solving problems, encourage them to ask for feedback, for opinions, and even for more information before they give their input. Then, when they respond, they can summarize everyone's thoughts, not just give their own information. Jane, the client who wrote Mary in eight-point type, reported, "Your suggestion was to look for things I don't understand and ask questions about them. I noticed that I resisted asking other people to clarify things, but I did it anyway and it didn't destroy my ego. I felt more connected to the people I was talking to and they seemed to feel more acknowledged for what they knew. In the past my ego had been saying, 'I'm the only one who can know something.' I felt better for giving them the gift of their being able to shine."

Help them become aware that they risk appearing arrogant. Encourage them to ask for feedback, for opinions, and even for more information before they give their input.

Clients with this Enneagram style won't mind if you challenge their ideas, as long as you substantiate your opinion with hard data and logic. They may be threatened by new information if it clashes with their existing synthesis. Early in your coaching process, try to link new information with what they already know. Later you can use dissonant information to interrupt their Enneagram patterns. Insight is not usually enough to bring about second-order change. But sometimes with Fives it is, because they live their ideas. New ideas can bring new life.

Fears Self-Revelation

Fives' desire for privacy has another component—fear of self-revelation. They tend to hoard all information, especially that about themselves. Sometimes they don't distinguish between who they are and what they know. They can believe with Descartes, "I think, therefore I am," and then conclude, "I am what I think." When they over-identify with their thoughts, they may withhold information necessary for their team. Nancy's comment about Lyle reflected this reluctance: "I have to chase him down for information in order to do my job." Co-workers can hesitate to ask for what should have been rightfully theirs by virtue of their task. The Five's need for privacy becomes one more obstacle to teamwork.

Pay attention to their wardrobe. Fives can make the worst-dressed list. In the first chapter, we mentioned the student who bought three pairs of black pants and three white t-shirts and sweatshirts each year for college. "Everything goes with everything," he said triumphantly. He did not understand that a colorless wardrobe was a shield. Nobody could tell anything about him from his clothes because they were always the same.

Fives can make the worst-dressed list. They can learn to appreciate texture and color and style as a way to improve their relationship with their bodies.

Another Five's team members all mentioned the knit ties "that he wears until they're balled up." "He's not a GQ-type person," one of them explained. "But it's expected in his role, where first impressions count. I know he wants to retain his individuality, but his shirts are sometimes wrinkled or stained, he has half a dozen nondescript suits, and he just doesn't care about it!" This isn't a superficial matter of appearance or good taste. Fives can learn to appreciate texture and color and style as a way to improve their relationship with their bodies.

They usually profit from some bodywork. They can tend to see their bodies only as a way to keep their heads off the ground, and they often fail to use their bodies for self-expression. When they work out, they experience their bodies more vividly and weaken their habit of identifying only with what they think.

Reinforce their efforts to reach out to others with as much warmth as they can.

Many Fives are truly shy. Their shyness blocks their expression of affection. Even when they care about someone, it usually doesn't show. People may find it difficult to interpret their restrained demonstration of affection or approval. Reinforce their efforts to reach out to others with as much warmth as they can. Reassure them that you know how difficult they may find these efforts. For example, as Mary and a Five client were walking out of his office one June day, he turned to his secretary and said, "Make sure you schedule appointments now with Mary for the next few months. I'll be away from the office a lot during the summer, and I want to continue to meet regularly." When they next met, Mary said, "When you asked your secretary to schedule me several meetings ahead, that was your way of saying you find our time together valuable, wasn't it?" Shyly he looked away and muttered, "Yes." "And it's hard for you to say it directly to me even now," she continued. "Yes," he agreed, and then sighed, "Why is that so difficult for me? My wife and daughter have begged me for years to show more emotion."

Fives may consider that their real world is their mental, private one. They can have many pastimes as a defense against external reality, such as playing video games, reading, or surfing the Internet. We heard of one who said he wanted to read every book ever written! While they truly enjoy these private pleasures and get re-energized from them, Fives need to learn to expand, be active in the world, and not use these practices as a retreat from action.

Fives need to learn to expand, be active in the world, and not use mental pastimes as a retreat from action.

Realize that beneath their desire for knowledge is a desire to know and love themselves. "I feel more confident and more present in my life," said Jane after half a dozen coaching sessions. "I have more depth instead of just being in my head. I still have all these things I want to learn, but I'm engaged in so many different levels in my life. I'm letting go of a structure that has provided me with stability in the past. The image that comes to mind is that now instead of walking it's more like I'm flying. I've been edging toward this as we've worked together, but now I feel it rather than just think it."

Compartmentalizes People, Thoughts, Activities

Just as Fives know how to fit parts into a whole, they can also separate the whole into parts. In-the-box Fives do just that—they compartmentalize their lives. Each part is distinct and separate from the other. Several long-time friends of a Five may not know each other and may never meet. That way nobody knows everything about him because each knows only one part. We knew a Five, married and mother of a son, who carried on a love affair for more than twenty years, until her lover (who was also married) died. They kept a small apartment in a suburb not likely to be frequented by others who knew them. They lived a life together totally separate from their married lives.

Cubicles may have been invented by a Five. Comic strip hero, Dilbert, is a Five and his native environment is the cubicle. The cubicle creates the illusion of privacy. It's also a good metaphor for how Fives compartmentalize people, thoughts, and actions. Everything has its own cubicle. Dilbert hates to have the wrong (stupid) people in his cubicle, especially the boss.

In a management setting, Fives need to compensate for this tendency to fragment by disseminating information to everyone who needs to know it. A tendency to separate units of a work team, with only the Five knowing the complete picture, can cause serious problems. Fives may consciously want to keep everyone in the loop, and then unconsciously sabotage communication. They may arrange the flow of information so that only they have it all. Everyone else's portion may be rationed and their view kept partial.

Fives may manifest this tendency to compartmentalize by having different groups report to them, but then not share one group's information with the rest of the team. Sometimes they create an information hierarchy based on who knows what. Lyle favored Norb for his political know-how and Fran for her people skills, both of which he lacked.

Sensitive Fives compartmentalize even within themselves as a defense against certain feelings, sometimes against their depths. In the middle of the night, a Five's wife found him sitting in the kitchen. His father was scheduled for surgery the next day and, as a physician, he knew the inherent dangers. But when his wife asked him what was going on he mumbled, "I don't know, I just can't sleep." She consoled him with, "You're probably worried about your Dad." He burst into tears.

The Five's Vision: Shift from being reserved and reserving to integrating thought with action

When self-aware and free of their habitual patterns, Fives retreat less into their minds and move more into action. Lyle felt so energized by his newfound comfort in connecting with people when traveling that he was happy to try sharpening his social skills with people at work.

During a follow-up call to Mary he described a "Far Side" cartoon. "It reminded me of myself," he laughed. "This plane is full of strange looking goons, one of whom is sitting with an empty seat beside him, saying to himself, 'Thank God nobody weird is going to sit next to me.' And coming down the aisle toward the empty seat, of course, is the most bizarre being you could imagine!" His conclusion: "It's fascinating what you can learn from people on airplanes!"

Chapter 8

A Package of Contradictions

Pete Stratford, the CEO of a public utilities company, was planning a significant shift in strategy. He wanted his team to function "like a finely-tuned instrument" so they would be effective leaders and move the company forward. Mary coached Pete and all three vice presidents on his team, starting first with Jean Jones. This is Jean's story.

"My father was dominant, short-tempered, and controlling," Jean told Mary. "My mother was caring, traditional—totally focused on her kids, her husband, her home—and she was always fearful: afraid of an accident, of something bad happening, always talking about who's sick, who's dying. They were both strict, and although I was a good kid, they wouldn't trust me. Even today, my mother asks unbelievable questions about my health." As Jean spoke her posture was taut. She leaned forward slightly, crossing and re-crossing her legs, jiggling whichever foot was on top.

Five feet, four inches tall, with short dark hair and a slender build, Jean had a bird-like quality. Her brown eyes darted and her head moved quickly as she spoke. Her mental quickness bordered on the psychic; as they delved into the Enneagram, Jean was often one step ahead of Mary, quickly seeing how the patterns of the Six style showed up in her life. When Mary described another Six who often "wore his emotions on his sleeve," Jean nodded and said, "I think I'm too open. I've heard Pete describe others somewhat deprecatingly by saying they go 'straight from their gut to their mouth,' and I think that's how he sees me." Jean was both cursed and blessed by having a brilliant and visionary advocate in Pete. Measured against him, she came off merely as an implementer but, as Mary drew her out, it was obvious that Jean was bright and curious herself.

Like many Sixes, Jean was overly responsive to others' opinions and tended to underplay her talents. When asked what she wanted from coaching she replied, "Pete told me I need to be more creative, more strategic, less focused on the

6

down-side. I don't always show him my curiosity, because I don't want to appear stupid. Rather than ask a question, I'll go look it up myself. My teammates probably don't see my creativity because often when I have an idea I assume everybody has already had it. Then somebody else will bring up the same idea and people will love it and I'll kick myself for holding back." When Mary commented that she seemed pretty smart, Jean still hedged: "I'm really learning and changing, but I hide how hard I have to work at it."

"I'd like to be more centered, more at peace with myself so I don't react every twenty minutes to something one of my teammates says!"

When Mary probed for desired personal changes, Jean replied, "I'd like to be more centered, more at peace with myself so I don't react every twenty minutes to something one of my teammates says!" For example, Jean resented Pete for being "stingy with praise," and she bristled at suggestions from Tom, another vice president, describing him as "meddling." Jean's response to Joe, the other vice president, was also strong but so positive it bordered on dependency. She constantly sought his support, which contributed to an us-versus-them dynamic that sometimes split the group into two camps.

After getting Jean's input, Mary interviewed Pete. As Jean predicted, he was critical of the way she "blurts things out." Despite Jean's worries, however, Pete was enthusiastic about her potential: "She's a great human being. She's honest and forthright, with good common sense. That's gotten her a long way, but she needs to be more sophisticated in using her analytical skills. This doesn't necessarily mean getting an Executive MBA, but it does mean finding a way to fill some skill gaps. I asked her to improve her strategic thinking six months ago and she still hasn't responded."

The other vice presidents, Tom and Joe, also described Jean as bright and capable, with "a lot of emotions pumping." "She brings great energy and excitement to the group and puts in long hours to reach her goals," said Tom. They especially applauded Jean's management skills: "She motivates people. She understands the little things that make a difference, and she treats her people with respect," Tom explained. "She also charms her way across company lines," Joe added. "She appreciates the interlocking roles in the company, so she promotes interdepartmental discussions, copies others on e-mail, and reminds her staff to include others."

"She has this concern for 'danger out there,' yet she can come across like a bungee jumper."

Tom agreed when Joe characterized Jean as, "a package of contradictions." "She is thoroughly professional," he expanded, "but she worries too much about what people think of her. She has this concern for 'danger out there,' yet she can come across like a bungee jumper." This paradox in Jean affected her decision-making: "She can act impulsively," Joe added, "but is as likely to list all the reasons why we

118

can't do something. She will even say, 'I guarantee this will fail!'" Tom assumed that Jean "wants to do well and be right, yet has serious doubts. She takes too long to decide sometimes, and other times she backs down too readily after deciding, especially when challenged by Pete."

"She takes too long to decide sometimes, and other times she backs down too readily after deciding."

Jean was frankly comforted to learn about the Enneagram Six. She was relieved to be able to name her operating style and understand that she wasn't alone. This also made it easier for her to admit the depth of her anxieties. She readily agreed she had been defeating herself and was delighted to recognize so clearly how she had been doing it. Learning to sharpen her strategic thinking, as Pete had recommended, would clearly be to her advantage, but Jean had kept finding reasons to postpone the task. As she explored her reluctance, she saw she had been afraid to test herself. Like other Sixes, she had an unfounded certainty that her actions would bring negative consequences.

Coaching Analysis

Coaching Jean

As she prepared for the feedback session with Jean, Mary decided to abandon her usual practice of first emphasizing a client's strengths. She knew that, as a Six, Jean would not trust the good news until she heard some bad news. Jean probably had worst-case fantasies about how others had described her. Mary took care, however, to offset Jean's negative expectations with positive details that Jean may have overlooked. She confirmed Jean's worry that Pete thought she should be more strategic, but also offered examples from Tom and Joe of how Jean had already demonstrated some aspects of strategic thinking. She told Jean other people were annoyed when she procrastinated—but added that some of Jean's slower decisions had been especially effective in easing departmental frictions.

Now that Jean trusted the feedback, she was pleased to hear that people appreciated her loyalty and felt energized by her. Mary elaborated: "You're intense, focused, and goal-oriented with high standards; yet appropriately friendly and thoughtful. You can maintain discipline; you're clear about what people need to improve, but they know you're in their corner."

Mary expected that Jean, like most Sixes, would seek more detailed information in order to feel secure. So she brought a comprehensive description of the Enneagram to the feedback session, and answered all Jean's questions about Sixes. After reviewing others' feedback, Mary helped Jean see how her problems had their taproot in the habits and motives of being a Six. Examples were how Jean limited her strategic thinking by only focusing on what could go wrong, the way she blurted out ideas to quell her anxiety about acting, and how she became defensive and accusatory because of her self-doubt.

Reframing "Strategic" Thinking

She realized that her planning was not thorough because she focused on problems and often failed to see the bigger picture.

To satisfy her job requirements, Jean wanted to learn a formal strategic planning process. Mary encouraged her to do so, reminding her: "Until now, you've targeted only what could go wrong, particularly when looking into the future." Understanding her Enneagram style helped Jean reframe her negativity. She realized that her planning was not thorough because she focused on problems and often failed to see the bigger picture.

As a Six, Jean tended to respect authoritative sources while simultaneously doubting authority. Mary took descriptions of Sixes from nationally known Enneagram authors, but restated them in a way that invited Jean to strengthen her own authority:

> "Your self-doubt is particularly likely to emerge when someone in authority questions your intelligence or conceptual ability, as Pete has. Discovering what people think of your strategic skills can be an advantage when the discovery places opportunities for action in your own hands instead of leaving you powerless."

From this opening Jean decided to take a hard look at her analytical and conceptual potential—in order to place opportunities to act in her own hands. She and Mary created a questionnaire based on validated rating scales[1] and sent it to more than 30 people important to her success. The results showed that Jean was a solid citizen in their eyes, stronger in analysis than in conceptual thinking. These written comments rang true to Jean:

- "She naturally distills a situation down to core elements that can be acted upon."

- "Jean is good on her feet, in tune with what's going on all the time. You can sense the gears turning."

- "She's very intelligent and doesn't confine her approach to 'here and now' but always looks for the implications of decisions to the entire organization."

- "Jean is street-wise and usually anticipates potential roadblocks by developing what-if scenarios."

---

[1] See *Competence at Work*, Spencer and Spencer: analytical thinking = breaking a situation down systematically, seeing multiple causes, making complex plans/analyses; conceptual thinking = identifying underlying patterns, seeing the larger picture, creating new concepts.

- "She effectively orchestrates concepts into action strategies."

Jean was pleased with the results and particularly agreed with one comment: "She could use a more sophisticated process, but she provides good advice based on her experience and investigation."

She was now able to take action into her own hands because she knew exactly where her strengths and development needs lay. Specific information calms a Six's worry habit. She worked on identifying the larger picture, and sought feedback from Mary and others about ways she was beginning to demonstrate this capability.

It became clear that Jean's only real problem in being strategic was her tendency to focus on what could go wrong and to voice those fears too quickly. All her secondary problems related back to this central tendency. Mary and Jean created the following actions together:

Specific information calms a Six's worry habit. Jean worked on identifying the larger picture, and sought feedback about ways she was beginning to demonstrate this capability.

- In planning, list the negative prospects in the left-hand column, then a balancing alternative in the right-hand column. (This solves two Six problems. It creates the obvious balance, but it also moves the negative from an emotion, or hunch, or projection—all Six tendencies—into the real world, on paper, where it is objective. Sixes don't fear real problems nearly as much as suspected ones.)

- When trying to get others to face a real or potential problem, remember that they may not see it as you do. Understand them and their contribution; then you can integrate their worldview and yours.

While always an excellent contingency planner, Jean could now create a plan based on a more balanced vision. Much more important, she was able to observe and interrupt her Enneagram patterns of doubt and anxiety. Occasionally she'd ask Mary, "Is this a Six thing?" Alert to Sixes' tendency to seek authority outside themselves, Mary would hand Jean's power back to her by asking, "What do you think is going on?"

Bungee Jumping

Relaying the feedback that she seemed a puzzle, Mary encouraged Jean to observe several Enneagram patterns that were affecting her decision-making ability. Jean understood her bungee jumper quality—a tendency to take risks with reckless abandon—as a way to counter her anxiety about making a decision she'd regret. Pete, Tom, and Joe had all described Jean as second-guessing herself. Mary gave an example: "They're concerned that it took almost a year to fill a key position, when they felt you had at least two capable candidates early in the process." After exploring with Mary her inner dialogue when trying to decide, Jean created the following reminders:

- Ask myself what my own criteria are. How do I determine what the right decision will be? From whom do I seek counsel? Consensus?

- Notice when I find myself internally debating and/or second-guessing a decision. What am I telling myself? Whose voice is telling me I'm going to fail?

Reaching Inside

Jean said she wanted to be considered as backup to Pete but didn't feel confident. "It seems to others that you seek an answer outside of yourself," Mary told her. "Your peers say you worry too much about what others think of you, and that you become unnecessarily upset when you feel people don't value what you've done." Jean could then bounce from this emotional stance to assume hidden agendas and place blame on others. With Mary's help she worked out two ways to become less defensive and accusatory:

- Respond to criticism without defensiveness. Criticism may be helpful, may be true (at least part of it). Don't fight, run, or cry inside. Ask for specifics and focus on what I need to learn.

- Accusing others is a way of giving away my power. When I find someone else at fault, see if what I dislike in the other person may be a disowned part of me. "Try on" their behavior or attitude with self-talk (e.g., "I'm angry with the part of me that's like Pete, the part of me that questions my own competency").

Bit by bit, Jean was able to observe her pattern of doubting herself and others. She learned to interrupt that pattern and to find her own inner power. When starting to react to someone else's opinion she was able to "reach inside and let it go." She learned to take a deep breath, focus inward, and trust her answer to, "What do I think is true?"

Bit by bit, Jean was able to observe her pattern of doubting herself and others. She learned to take a deep breath, focus inward, and trust her answer to, "What do I think is true?"

We wrote in Chapter Two about the use of story and metaphor. As Jean began to make significant shifts, Mary gave her a gift to celebrate: a 3-D art book. Jean looked puzzled. Mary explained, "I want to honor your well-tuned antennae, knowing that's your gift, and that you're no longer limited by focusing only on the negative. Take a look at the last page." Jean opened the book to the marked page: "I've never done this before. How does it work?" "You have to hold the page close to your eyes," Mary responded, "release your customary focus, and move the page slowly away until you see the hidden picture." There was a moment of silence while Jean experimented with this new way of seeing. "Ah!" she exclaimed. "It's a crystal ball!"

Coaching Style Six

Cal Norris called Mary because he was burned out in his teaching job and excited about the possibility of becoming a professional coach. He'd found her web site and was intrigued by the Enneagram. "No question I'm a Six," he announced, and proceeded to give her examples of how his self-doubt had been triggered by administrative changes and by perceived criticisms from the unpredictable school principal.

To fear the worst often cures the worst.

Shakespeare
Troilus & Cressida

An open, endearing, and impetuous man in his late thirties, Cal was interested in the possibility of being financially independent, but he had some worries. He wanted to know all the details about going into business for himself. What was coaching really all about? What would be required to market himself? Who were his potential clients? How would he know? In particular, Cal wanted to know what could go wrong. Was he dreaming to think he could exceed his modest but secure income?

When you coach Sixes, you will build initial trust by giving lots of details and by holding nothing back, so they don't assume or look for a hidden agenda. Mary was attuned to this in her first conversation with Cal, so she maintained a balance between encouraging his excitement and outlining the specific barriers he'd have to overcome to become successful in his own business. He was enthusiastic and eager to learn during their next two coaching sessions. Mary reinforced this in an e-mail following their second meeting: "I'm continually renewed by your quick absorption of insights and your unusually high self-awareness."

When you coach Sixes, you will build initial trust by giving lots of details and by holding nothing back, so they don't assume or look for a hidden agenda.

Cal came to their third coaching session with a troubled look on his face. He said, "I noticed at your web site that you've created development plans for Sixes. What should I be working on?" Mary realized that the work they'd done wasn't satisfying Cal's doubt because she'd been building on his positive skills and potential. She asked, "What's behind your question?" His answer told her that he'd been waiting for the other shoe to drop: "My perception from reading about the Enneagram is that people don't see for themselves where they're stuck. Surely you see some problems with me that you haven't talked about yet."

You'll notice lots of clues in early interactions with clients that lead you to good guesses about their Enneagram style. This doesn't mean that you approach them directly with your observations about their Enneagram patterns. It probably won't help a Six, for example, to be told, "You're driven by fear." But the process of your interaction with clients is rich fodder for learning. Mary used this opportunity to show Cal how his doubt of others was a Six pattern that showed up when he assumed she was hiding something dreadful from him.

Coaching is a partnership in which clients begin to find solutions to their own dilemmas. This is especially vital when you work with Sixes. If you become an authority you can unwittingly reinforce their ambivalence in relationship with you. Instead of telling Cal where he might be stuck, Mary gave him a list of strategies for increasing self-awareness in Sixes. Together they added to the list and Cal chose the areas he wanted to work on: (1) Be aware of my habit of suspecting compliments and modify my "ESP" by focusing on others' positive thoughts instead of hidden agendas. (2) Analyze my underlying assumptions about those in power and ask, "How am I giving my power away? (3) Don't assume anything about who's in charge; develop a partnership by asking others to clearly state their expectations and together create guidelines for how we're going to interact. (4) Take my fears seriously, but also ride them out before reacting, do reality checks, and use my imagination to picture positive future outcomes.

Coaching is a partnership in which clients begin to find solutions to their own dilemmas. This is especially vital when you work with Sixes. If you become an authority you can unwittingly reinforce their ambivalence in relationship with you.

As they learn their Enneagram style's typical patterns, Sixes will begin to see themselves quite readily. Your efforts as a coach will show them how their suspicions of others and self-doubt can be transformed to a level of trust in themselves and others that leads to effective action.

Opposes Self

Pay attention to these four habits of in-the-box Sixes:

Opposes self

Gives power away and frightens self

Sorts for negatives

Substitutes worry for action

Sixes can be the most contradictory of the nine styles because they have phobic (overtly fearful) and counterphobic (doing what they fear) manifestations. Some Sixes will seem clearly phobic or counterphobic while most display a mixture of the two, as did Jean. When phobic, Sixes are afraid to act; when counterphobic they act in order to overcome their fear, but may do so without thinking through the consequences.

As a coach, you will usually work with Sixes on their fears and reactions to fear. Even counterphobic behavior is based on fear. When they're operating more in a counterphobic mode, you may have to work your way through their overtly challenging and risky behavior to see the fear and self-doubt. One of Mary's clients, Ray, was tough and adventurous. "I come from a working class family," he said, "and I'm pretty much a loner. Both of my parents were strict so I was rebellious and roamed the streets. I had friends on the honor roll and friends on dope. I was raised to give no quarter—if you showed that things bothered you, it was considered a fault. I went off on my own at age 17, and took up construction work. From the beginning, they'd send me to the top of buildings because they knew I'd try anything. I kept telling my boss we needed to do more demolition work because that's where the money was. But we fought all the time about it. I got so pissed off at him one day that I quit without a dime to my name. After almost a year of scrabbling, doing free-lance demolition, I started my own construction company on a shoestring. I've nearly been killed a couple of times, setting explosives in buildings that were about to collapse, because I didn't check out the building's structure thoroughly enough. But, hey, you learn as you go."

So how do we know Ray is a Six? Listen to his language and notice his behavior. All Sixes challenge the way things work. When counterphobic, they tend to criticize and even attack those in authority. Ray defined his rebelliousness as a reaction to his parents' authority. As a young adult he was constantly at odds with his construction boss, and again acted impulsively to counter his boss's power over him. Sixes can act impulsively to avoid feeling their fear, and may take unnecessary risks. Ray did this when he quit his job on the spur of the moment and risked his life setting explosives, both without proper planning. You can almost hear his internal mantra: "I'm not afraid! I'm not afraid!" You can also recognize this as counterphobic behavior because of its extremity. At the other end of the spectrum, a phobic six may plan things to death.

Sixes have phobic (overtly fearful) and counterphobic (doing what they fear) manifestations.

The shift from phobic to counterphobic will often be confusing except to coaches familiar with Enneagram dynamics. Jean's peers, for example, recognized when she acted impulsively. Cal's wife, also, was aware of his counterphobic tendencies. When he told her he was thinking of changing careers, she took a deep breath and said, "I want you to be happy, but please don't act precipitously."

Beneath this apparent contradiction in Sixes lies a deeper set of conflicts. They habitually second-guess themselves, examining their thoughts and plans in the light of remembered warnings from Mom, memos from the boss last year, and the imagined opinions of others. They also assume others will second-guess and criticize them. This mental habit makes potential enemies of everyone. The net result is that Sixes become their own worst enemy.

Sometimes, when in-the-box Sixes project their own negative assumptions onto others, they play the victim, and consider themselves innocent while locating the evil "out there." Even when they are at fault, they may twist the facts around until it seems like the other party is the aggressor. This can turn into us-against-them mentality—we are good, they are bad—just as it did when Jean formed such a strong bond with Joe.

Polarization means being divided against ourselves in some area. Sixes, in particular, are self-opposing.

Their self-doubts may also cause Sixes to distrust achievement and they may be most anxious at times when they have a clear success. They may feel like their success is too good to be true and wait for the other shoe to drop, as Cal responded to Mary's supportive feedback and positive reframing. In the Enneagram, we call this *polarization*, and it means being divided against ourselves in some area. Sixes, in particular, are self-opposing.

Their characteristic ambivalence is a clue to self-opposition in Sixes. They can simultaneously hold positive and negative feelings toward people and actions. Jean was so influenced by other's opinions before coaching because her own opinions were not stable. During her year's procrastination over hiring a key executive, she was criticized for giving both the pros and the cons of every decision and then not deciding: "Shall I hire this guy? Well, our workload is awfully heavy and I'm worried about burnout if I don't hire him. But I really don't have time to train him during the rush season." While she vacillated, her teammates didn't know whether she was going to take action or not and if she was, which way she would decide.

Under pressure of circumstance, Sixes can finally take action, and in so doing they alleviate their anxiety. As leaders, though, their habits of reacting to fear by acting precipitously, freezing, and/or second guessing are confusing to others and make them seem like "a package of contradictions."

Help them discover what triggers their patterned responses. This level of observation will offer clues about how to interrupt the pattern.

The first step for you as a coach is to raise your Six clients' awareness of how pervasive their self-opposition can be. Then they can observe themselves to see how frequently and in what form this inner dynamic manifests. Help them discover what triggers the behavior and their patterned responses. Usually this level of observation will also offer clues to both of you about how to interrupt the pattern.

Gives Power Away and Frightens Self

Jean needed to learn to see how she gave her power away. The operative question is how. How did she picture her co-workers? How did she see herself talking to Pete? How did her self-doubt serve her in some important ways? What was in it for her? Were there other ways than inaction to get what she wanted?

Style Six is the mostly explicitly fearful of all nine. This fear creates a posture of hypervigilance born of the conviction that the world is a dark and dangerous place. Sixes tend to focus their attention on what is threatening, missing, or deceptive. As soon as they see something that meets one of these criteria, they go through a process of frightening themselves. One of Jean's favorite expressions before coaching was, "I guarantee this is going to fail." A guarantee in this context meant that she was only looking for what could go wrong. A world in which everything can go wrong, as she guaranteed it would, is dangerous. By looking only at the danger she reminded herself of that menace and frightened herself.

Because they see the world as menacing, Sixes may notice real dangers and take precautions. In a world of broken machines, one learns to be a mechanic. In-the-box Sixes don't confine themselves to solving existing problems. They can also try to solve future problems. They frighten themselves with *possible* dangers by repeatedly asking, "what if?" It's not necessary to demonstrate probability or even to gather evidence. They just keep asking, "What if?" "What if the car breaks down?" "What if my boss betrays, dislikes, overworks, under-appreciates, ignores, or fires me?" It's not possible to take every precaution against all those possibilities. But because any one of them might happen, Sixes adopt eternal vigilance.

Because they see the world as menacing, Sixes may notice real dangers and take precautions. In a world of broken machines, one learns to be a mechanic.

Jean had told Mary, "My teammates don't see my creativity because often when I have an idea I assume everybody has already had it, then somebody else will bring up the same idea and people will love it and I'll kick myself for holding back." That's a helpful statement to a coach. Why did Jean assume everybody else was smarter? The assumption was not based on current evidence, so what was it based on? The answer is on the first page of this chapter: "They wouldn't trust me." When her parents didn't trust her, it confirmed her intuition that she couldn't trust herself. Her Six assumption that whatever she did was going to bring negative results (especially from authority) is at the heart of how she gave her power away. As long as Jean assumed she couldn't be trusted and everybody was smarter than she was, she gave away her power.

Sixes will sometimes imagine others as either larger or older than they are. When they frighten themselves with this process of shrinking themselves and enlarging their inner vision of others, they often do this out of loyalty to parental opinions. This application of loyalty is an example of a good quality pushed so far it becomes a liability. It is at the heart of being a Six. Sixes have usually received a double message from parental figures that they've now incorporated into their own self-talk. These voices hold them to high ideals but reinforce low self-worth: "We expect great things of you even though you're incompetent."

Mary's client, Elaine, had insisted through months of coaching that her mother was a wonderful woman against whom she'd had no need to rebel. Elaine almost idolized her mother for being so caring and supportive. Yet she felt there must be some basis in her background for her poor self-image and emotional stresses. A breakthrough occurred when she told Mary about a recent phone conversation with her mother, and Mary played her words back to her. Elaine sat stunned as her eyes welled up with tears. When she was able to speak she said, "My mother has always treated me like a child. She still does. I never realized before how much I want to prove to her that I'm a grown-up." Now aware of this pattern, Elaine remembered that her mother often said, "You'll never get married," at the same time frequently arranging for Elaine to meet the sons of friends. No wonder Elaine was confused: "Does she think I'm marriage material, or not?"

Sixes most frequently give their power away to those they consider a higher authority. One Six office manager received a glowing evaluation at the end of the year. Her boss said, "I can't find a single thing to complain about." She answered, "Do you know how hard I had to work to make sure you couldn't find one?" Sixes take authority seriously, paying attention to everything authorities say. At the same time, they don't trust authority. They expect, and try to protect themselves against, criticism by those above them in the organizational hierarchy. When Mary asked Jean what she wanted from coaching, Jean first replied with what her boss said: "Pete told me I need to be more creative, more strategic and analytical, less focused on the down-side." With equal energy, she constantly complained about Pete's shortcomings—being stingy with praise, for example.

Sixes most frequently give their power away to those they consider a higher authority.

Because of this contradictory response to authority, some in-the-box Sixes tend to draw negative attention. Three successive bosses called a sales manager on the carpet for turning in expense reports late. Each time he nodded and smiled, agreed to comply, but after a couple of months would again begin to forget, even when reminded that the accounting department could not complete year-end reports without them. When the third boss fired him, he felt victimized. By his non-compliance, he gave his power away. Another Six might have done what he was asked, but still criticize the boss, as Jean did.

Sixes will probably know, or want to know, what the authority in any field thinks before taking action. They tend to prefer the authority's opinions to their own. Mary used her knowledge of this pattern early in her relationship with Jean by drawing upon authoritative Enneagram sources. It is important to note, however, that Mary embedded a solution in her summary of Sixes that led to Jean's self-initiated survey of people's opinions: "Discovering what people think of your strategic skills can be an advantage when the discovery places opportunities for action in your own hands, instead of leaving you powerless." This link to her own action broke through Jean's habitual pattern as she began to empower herself. Without this reframing and break in the pattern, Sixes can be like hostages who are brainwashed to be dependent on their captors, while unconsciously suffering tremendous psychological conflict.

Even with conflicting feelings about authority, Sixes often make bureaucracies work. Particularly when phobic, they find security in structure. They tend to comply with existing rules, customs, and organizational climates. As managers they appreciate obedience and value time-honored virtues of punctuality, diligence, and carefulness. They expect to obey and be obeyed. They may praise employees for bringing up negatives but will condemn any sign of disloyalty. Six managers usually make this utterly clear. Jean trusted and was trusted by the people who reported to her. Mary praised Jean for instituting a process of mutual feedback: Jean's pattern was to uncover the negatives, but in the context of her self-development this pattern became a source of concrete information to help her change.

Jean indirectly gave her power away and frightened herself in another way. She described herself as being too open and wearing her emotions on her sleeve. Sometimes when Sixes do that, it is an attempt to disarm an environment that is perceived to be hostile or at least dangerous. The belief is, "If I am completely open, then perhaps you will be, too, and then I can get all the emotional and operating information I need." It can also backfire when the Six shares information that others feel should be private.

How do you help your Six clients break this pattern? Start with their focus. When Jean finds herself being more open than she thinks she ought to be, the first question for her to ask is, "What danger am I trying to avert? Is there another way to avert this danger?" Help Sixes become aware of their narrow focus on danger by keeping track of what they worried about yesterday, last week, last year. What is their batting average in predicting disaster? How much precaution can they afford if the statistical probability is one percent?

Help Sixes become aware of their narrow focus on danger by keeping track of what they worried about. Then ask them to examine their self-talk.

Then ask them to examine their self-talk. Whose voice is warning them of danger? Clarence once rode to an airport with a Six. As it got dark she warned him that some cars might come out of the side roads because the drivers love to drive full speed in the dark with their lights off. Now that is a dangerous world!

One way Sixes can deal with danger is to move from their imagination into reality. Sixes fear internal creations of danger more than external reality, the future more than the present. They live in constant tension, protecting themselves against what they imagine will happen. The phrase "fear of fear" is almost right, and in the case of anxiety or panic attacks (common in Sixes) it is perfectly correct. They are really afraid of what they imagine, of what might happen. Putting their fears down on paper takes them out of their imagination and moves them into the "real" or at least shared world. Clarence asked his client, Barry, to list all the reasons why he feared something wouldn't work. Barry came up with quite a list—seven or eight negative elements—then looked up and said, "I think we can make this work!" Once he had the negatives pinned down, Barry realized his resources and how he could overcome the perceived barriers. There is another reason why this is an effective exercise. We know that Sixes often second-guess and challenge their own conclusions. So Barry saw the negatives and attacked them himself, even though it meant doing the project!

Jean was worried about Pete's disapproval. She could have made a list of what he might disapprove of, when he disapproved last, and what percentage of the time he disapproved. By clarifying the real fears, you can help bring the Six's perceived fears into the light of everyday and interrupt a pattern by reframing the purpose of habitual behavior.

By clarifying the real fears, you can help Sixes bring their perceived fears into the light of everyday.

Sorts for Negatives

Mary began coaching Jean by telling her the negative feedback about her. Until Mary satisfied Jean's preoccupation with the negatives, she couldn't pay attention to the positives. With Cal, on the other hand, Mary relied so much on positive reframing that he suspected she was holding something back. To get inside the heart of a Six, go watch a horror film. Listen to the music and feel your fear as the heroine goes into a house that we all know contains an unspeakable monster. You really can't breathe until you know the face of the monster. Once you discover the monster, you select your weapons—or flee. When Sixes face the monster, they develop courage, and many Sixes are wonderfully courageous. You would be, too, if you fought monsters every day.

Sixes worry. The Scout motto "Be Prepared" fits them well. They are often brilliantly analytical, even if looking for what's wrong flaws their analysis. They anticipate every problem and will be reluctant to make a decision until all the negatives are explored.

A concrete negative problem focuses their free-floating anxiety and energizes them: "Here's the problem. Let's go." Polarizing against the problem helps them know what to do. Clarence's Enneagram Six friend broke his hip and a number of people commented on how well he handled the crisis. "Well," he said, "you have to remember, I've been preparing for this all my life!" When the worst finally happens, as they know it will, Sixes are fully prepared, calm, and resourceful. The known enemy, the trouble at hand, isn't nearly as frightening as the unknown.

They are often brilliantly analytical, even if looking for what's wrong flaws their analysis. They can profitably look particularly for information that contradicts their assumptions.

Clients of this Enneagram style will routinely challenge optimistic expectations or projections. If presented with hard data they will probe for data of the softer kind—hidden meanings, intentions, what others think—as well as information that may be missing: "Why did the accountant think we could get 7 percent interest? Why did the marketing department say we could expect a 1.5 percent pull on a direct mail piece?" The good news is that their projects tend to have few unexpected difficulties. Jean was described as "street-wise." Sixes can be brilliant at trouble-shooting because they habitually anticipate what can go wrong, so Jean could learn to trust her ability to solve problems. She was strong when the task was negative: finding out what needed to be protected so things would work. She needed to learn to be more confident and talented at coming up with daring, practical, positive suggestions.

Sixes are often accused of reading into information what isn't there. They may even be inclined to read into others the worst possible intentions. Take this seriously as their coach. It stems from the Six conviction that one must be on guard. Many Sixes report listening for what is not said. They sort for omitted information and hostile intent. What they don't realize is that by paying so much attention to what is not said, they miss what is actually said. You can help them take a small but important step: make sure they really did hear and understand the information given to them. They can profitably look particularly for information that contradicts their assumptions. Mary did this when she got Jean to gather concrete data about her strategic thinking capability. This was also an element in Jean's decision to "ask for specifics" when criticized. All Enneagram styles maintain their worldview by holding onto generalizations. When you coach your clients to move from general labels to specific and descriptive information, they become better communicators *and* they break free of their general assumptions about themselves.

All Enneagram styles maintain their worldview by holding onto generalizations. Coach your clients to move from general labels to specific and descriptive information.

You'll find that many of your Six clients love detail. Mastery of detail enables them to breathe easier and prepare for the unexpected, as a defense against the dangers of a frightening world. They want the detail to guarantee that everyone has done their work and explored all the negative possibilities. This is also a gift that Sixes give to the team in organizations. They are loyal to the company and will feel they are not doing their duty unless they do a thorough job. For the always-conscientious Six, people who only look at the big picture can leave too much room for slippage.

Their naturally fearful stance in life prompts Sixes to seek allies, and they can be the ultimate team players. We have heard a number of Sixes describe themselves as "the glue that holds the group together." Jean's boss said, "Jean appreciates the roles of everyone." Because suspicion is second nature to Sixes, loyalty is demanded, exchanged, and rewarded. It is not assumed. They will listen for information leaks about a loyal employee's deviance from their expectations. Sixes require full sharing of information—the data and the employee's interpretation of it. They want full commitment and cooperation to assure themselves that at least for today, all is well. Tomorrow will bring another question.

> *Their naturally fearful stance in life prompts Sixes to seek allies, and they can be the ultimate team players. We have heard a number of Sixes describe themselves as "the glue that holds the group together."*

Jean's subordinates were pleased that she helped them balance career and home life and they were fiercely loyal to her. They also described her as having high standards for them in meeting department goals. Jean's reputation for good interdepartmental communication was well deserved. On the down side, this level of cooperation fed her habits of worrying and sorting for negatives to assure herself that she knew exactly what was going on everywhere. On the up side, Sixes do have a strong sense of how things ought to work, and how the community should function. They're natural facilitators, whether in a meeting or structuring a project. While their excessive concern about what others think can make them too easy to influence, this concern can also be an asset. They know how to make a group blossom. They care, and they will work unbelievably hard for the sake of the group.

Substitutes Worry for Action

Jean's anxiety about competence was a central knot in her Enneagram style. Did she really want to be a CEO? Many Sixes function beautifully in middle to upper management. They frequently do not aspire to the top job. They expect that their work will attract only negative attention. "It's the tall grass that gets mowed" is their motto. Mary coached one CEO who had been recently hired to run a manufacturing company. It was the most visible position he'd ever held and he acknowledged that he'd been terrified about attending the first social function in his new role: a board of trustees dinner to celebrate his being hired. "I was sweating so hard," he admitted, "I felt like rendered meat."

Deciding does not come easily to in-the-box Sixes, and the knowledge that everyone talks about the boss can ignite latent paranoia. They often love to be part of the community, so top executives of this style may feel isolated. Preference, not talent, is the issue here. Sixes should take a top job only if they truly want it, not because someone else thinks they should. Many Sixes have strong intuitive ability, so Mary could have suggested to Jean that she become quiet and ask her body what it thinks.

Because Sixes tend to expect all attention (especially from authority) to be negative, they can substitute worry for action. Why hadn't Jean made the requested improvement in her strategic thinking skills? This is a good place to further your clients' understanding of the difference between a phobic and a counterphobic Six. If they are certain they are going to receive bad news or fail, do they procrastinate? Or do they jump right in and "get it over with"? Show them how they have pictured themselves inwardly small and feel frightened in a hostile world, perhaps one even organized against them. If they freeze and don't face the issue, they are being phobic. That's what Jean sometimes did. In other situations she moved from phobic to counterphobic and "bungee jumped." She couldn't stand the tension, so she acted precipitously.

Thinking replaces doing when Sixes worry. They may accept a position rationally but not be able to act on it. This occurred with Jean before she worked with Mary, when she took almost a year to fill a key position reporting to her. She was new, the organization had a new direction, and she was far too concerned that her selection might not meet with everyone's approval. You can coach Sixes by using their own questioning habit against the worry habit. Had Mary been there during the hiring process she could have asked Jean, "What's the worst that can happen? How likely is that? If the worst does happen, what are your internal resources?" Focusing on their internal resources helps Sixes bring their power back within themselves instead of continuing to frighten themselves by giving their power away.

You can coach Sixes by using their own questioning habit against the worry habit. "What's the worst that can happen? How likely is that? If the worst does happen, what are your internal resources?"

You might also use the metaphor of health/sickness to show Sixes how to face their dangerous world. There are two ways to stay healthy. One is to live or try to live in a sterile environment. In-the-box Sixes take this approach. In extreme forms, they can become agoraphobic and stay inside, just like someone in a sterile emotional bubble. The other way to stay healthy is to develop a strong immune system. This is nature's way and the way of Sixes who are able to break free of their focus of attention on danger.

Humor can help, too. Push your Six clients to see how exaggerated their fears are: "If you hire the wrong person, are rejected, fail in this project, lose your job, then what? Then what? Then what? Will you survive? Are you sure?"

Jean's lack of confidence showed up when she assumed that if she had an idea, everyone else had already thought of it. In-the-box Sixes often don't speak up because they fear their ideas may separate them from the group. They avoid deviating from the group norms and even the group's opinions. Sixes, especially phobic Sixes, usually keep rules, honor traditions, and obey authority. So when Jean decided everyone else must already have the idea, she was over-using her natural ability to build, contribute, and mesh with the group. Remember that Sixes live largely in their heads. They step out of the box when they become concrete and practical. If coaching Jean, you could ask, "Which one of the group will object to the idea? Why? What's the worst that can happen if someone objects?" When Jean gets specific, she will attack her own idea, think of all the objections, probably answer them, and come up with a stronger presentation.

Remember that Sixes live largely in their heads. They step out of the box when they become concrete and practical.

Sixes may never completely rid themselves of this tendency to worry, but you can help them use their Enneagram energy to help themselves. For example, Jean could second-guess her habit of second-guessing: "Is this really the right way to decide?"

The Six's Vision: Shift from suspicion of others, doubting self to trusting self and others

The vision for the transformed Six is self-empowerment. Ultimately Sixes will learn to trust themselves and those around them, to rely on their own power to act and create.

These clients can reach a point where they hear their inner truth instead of torturing themselves and looking outward for affirmation and direction, where they act with courage instead of giving their power away, where they see the full picture instead of sorting only for the negatives, where they recognize their own contribution to situations instead of worrying and projecting blame outward.

Grin and Bear It

After 24 successful years in customer relations, 50-year-old Jack Millman faced a crisis: His career with a large trucking company had been sidelined. Ben Canova had promoted Jack to vice president of customer relations, but a year later, Ben called Mary with second thoughts. "Jack's a very capable guy, and I saw his potential, so I put him in charge. Now it's clear my superiors don't have the time of day for him. I'm beginning to question my own judgment to put him in such a responsible position. Technically he knows his job and he's bright as hell, but he's not deep in his analysis of existing problems."

Jack had significantly improved customer service since Ben gave him full responsibility, but Ben told Mary he thought Jack wasn't tackling the big issues: "He's optimistic to a fault. At my team meetings everybody else outlines potential problems and how they're going to solve them. Jack paints a bright picture, which I pass on to my boss; then I find Jack didn't do his homework. He pisses me off every day, for a whole bunch of reasons. I can't sleep at night knowing there are so many issues out there, but he seems unaware of them. His objectives are abstract and he doesn't seem to see that he has to have specific plans to achieve them. Even under questioning he can't give much detail, when something in my gut tells me things just aren't right."

Mary began to realize Jack was an Enneagram Seven. She had worked with Ben previously and saw the potential for conflict. She knew that Ben, as a Six, was preoccupied with how things could go wrong, and she expected that Jack might be expansively optimistic. "He has no regard for spending money," Ben continued. "He has phone mail on his car phone—give me a break! And while I like to give a guy a little headroom, he abuses it when it comes to spending money on his employees. Some of that is appropriate, but he goes overboard."

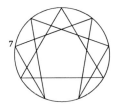

Ben was surprised and somewhat hurt that Jack seemed to ignore his feedback. "Typically I'm on the same wave length with people who report to me," he explained, "but Jack and I are miles apart. I spent several hours talking to him about my concerns two days ago, and his reaction was to 'yes' me to death. The next day he told me he wasn't sure what I said. The guy's in la-la land!"

At their first encounter Jack met Mary with a wide smile and introduced her to everyone on his team. He told her about that day's rally for service calls, made sure she had coffee, then went off on a tangent about how to make great salsa! When Mary raised the issues Ben had brought up, Jack said he was confused: "Ben's promoted me twice in the last two years. But the last time we met he told me we have a 'communication problem.' Then he said I'm 'not a team player,' and after that I went into a fog—I couldn't hear anything else he was saying. I have no idea where he's coming from because my whole organization is team driven. I know all my people by name, spend time with them, even take them out to lunch. Ben never does that. I'm more of a cheerleader than he is."

When Mary mentioned Ben's concern over lavishing fancy food and expensive hotels on his team, Jack said, "He told me I entertain more than any of his other managers, but my people represent the company every day and I need to keep them pumped up."

Mary told Jack he seemed upbeat, in spite of having had a conversation with Ben less than a week before that seemed to threaten his career. Jack nonchalantly replied, "Well, I could open a closet full of skeletons, but I don't dwell on them. I try to learn from my mistakes and move on." He was somewhat concerned about his career, however: "I haven't lost many promotions, but senior managers in this organization don't reach out to me, and I'm not sure why. The only recognition I've gotten has come from customers and from the people who report to me."

Jack's peers had a more balanced view of him than Ben had predicted, and strongly supported Jack's view of himself as a good leader. "He has a Star Wars vision of customer service," said one person, "though today we don't yet have the people or technology to support it. But he keeps the goal in mind and little by little works toward it." "He's very focused on the future and communicates his vision with passion and emotion," said another. "He's inspirational and earns a tremendous amount of respect from his people."

He talks about how great his team is instead of outlining the results they're getting. So others don't take him seriously.

However, his peers also reported that Jack got in his own way by his constant positive reframing: "I think his measures are world class—clear and objective, but he talks about how great his team is instead of outlining the results they're getting. So others don't take him seriously."

Jack earned raves from everyone who worked for him. "He even has union employees motivated," said one of his team leaders. "He promotes an open atmosphere with lots of sharing of information and it's a very feeling climate—we really like each other!" Another commented on Jack's approach to change: "He communicates that you don't want to lose what's valuable about what you've been doing, just do it in a different way. You walk away feeling good about a change you don't even like!" Concerning delegation and professional development one person said: "He wants his managers to grow. He knows his people and pushes involvement to the lowest levels." And most telling: "He makes new requests every day even though we're maxed out with work, but we can be at wit's end, call him anytime, vent, and he always turns it around to something positive!"

Jack's lack of interest in details showed up in feedback from those who worked for him. One employee reported, "He's very supportive, but leaves us to figure out the particulars. I really thrive on this approach because it makes me demand more of myself." Another, though, acknowledged frustration with Jack's lack of structure: "He wants us to manage with the goal in mind but without specifics."

Allowing for these relatively minor flaws, the threat to Jack's career came almost entirely from his overemphasis on the bright side with peers and senior management. In spite of his colleagues' positive observations, senior managers didn't trust him because he monopolized conversations and his boundless cheerfulness was too "one note." At times he could seem condescending in his jokes about others. "He thought it was funny to tell me I couldn't see the forest for the trees," one senior executive reported. "I didn't laugh." They also found Jack hard to read: "He always has a smile on his face, and I don't know if it goes deep down because his expression never changes." The perception that Jack's smile wasn't real and that he skated over the surface was reinforced by his responses to attempted feedback—he did not want to hear any bad news. At times he'd react to criticism the way he did with Ben, by going into a fog, and at other times he was defensive. One executive noted, "Jack's too quick to come up with all the reasons why something happened instead of absorbing the information and then coming back and saying, 'Here's what I'm going to do.' Instead he just talks on and on."

The threat to Jack's career came almost entirely from his overemphasis on the bright side. Senior managers didn't trust him because he monopolized conversations and his boundless cheerfulness was too "one note."

Coaching Analysis

Coaching Jack

Mary congratulated Jack on his passion for the business and his ability to make creative changes in the organization. She appreciated how he could coax out innovative thinking from a team that had been stifled under more traditional management. She also acknowledged the gifts of his style: "Everyone appreciates your energy, enthusiasm, optimism, and sense of humor. You are fun to be around, rarely negative, and you communicate well. You visibly exude joy, and can evoke enthusiasm in others."

Mary then pointed out another side of Jack's style. She told him he had a reputation as a lightweight who glossed over problems. She predicted that he could not succeed in that company unless he (1) demonstrated comfort and familiarity with the details of management and (2) showed more than a happy face to his boss and peers. How Mary coached Jack is covered in detail below.

How to Do the Rhumba

Mary began: "One of your team members said it very well, 'Jack is not a minutia person. He doesn't need to understand the details because he gets the essence of it, and that's all he cares to hear.'" She continued, "You have improved your team by making people accountable and by encouraging them to solve problems more creatively. Like your boss, though, these people know there's more to the picture than just the up side. And many of them need more specific details than you give them. You want them to do the rhumba because you know it's a fun and energizing way to get across the ballroom floor, but they need dancing lessons. When they bring you a problem they want to talk through the issues, consider possibilities and solutions with you, and to receive at least some direction."

He retained his gift of focusing on the positive while breaking his habit of denying any down side of a situation. He began to value details and problems as an important way of inspiring others to see his vision.

Jack set out to balance his one-sided positive focus. Before, he had treated employees'questions as their concern: "I don't want them always coming to me with problems." He learned to discuss problems in a way that encouraged them to see potential solutions. He then reinforced their good ideas. This approach helped him retain his gift of focusing on the positive while breaking his habit of denying any down side of a situation. He began to value details and problems as an important way of inspiring others to see his vision.

The Shadow Knows

Mary helped Jack accept that his personal charm also made him appear superficial. He was not respected because his approach lacked balance or moderation: "Senior management has questioned whether you are serious enough to lead as the business expands. They also made blunt reference to your 'shithouse' politics—meaning that you can exacerbate problems by 'gossiping about them' instead of solving them."

Following this discussion, Jack started talking more about business issues in meetings and less about the players and personal topics. He also began encouraging colleagues to talk in depth about problems instead of trying to cheer them up. He acknowledged that his tendency to entertain peers with stories had stemmed in part from his impatience with the "agonizing details" of their conversations. Mary pointed out that his annoyance with co-workers who "can't see the forest for the trees" was similar to his reactions to employees who came to him with problems: "You have astute business observations and you want to see your organization move into the future, but your impatience can frustrate your own goals."

Jack started talking more about business issues in meetings and less about the players and personal topics. He also began encouraging colleagues to talk in depth about problems instead of trying to cheer them up.

Mary coached Jack to accept certain negative traits in himself. "Your ideal self-image currently doesn't allow you to accept feeling down," she suggested, "and then you become impatient with others who aren't cheerful." She encouraged Jack to notice how he also became annoyed with others because he wished to escape tedious details. "The detailed work that's required for true collaboration may make you feel trapped and prompt you to want to move on, but it's precisely what you need to do."

Coaching came too late to save Jack's job. He had made progress in learning how to solicit and accept feedback and had greatly improved his ability to listen to others instead of always telling stories. He had achieved more balance when he presented business problems. Ben and he had worked with Mary to blend their different leadership styles: Ben had learned to be more optimistic and to focus more on possibilities; Jack had learned to work with more details and plan more for potential problems. But senior management still saw Jack as a lightweight. Ben had to let him go, but did help him find a comparable job in another company.

Some time later, Jack faxed Mary this cartoon:

A man is standing by his bed in polka-dot pajamas and bunny slippers, stretching and saying, "Ah! Another GREAT day!" Meanwhile there's a bolt of lightning crashing through one window and an explosion visible through the other, a one-ton weight is crashing through the ceiling directly over him, his dog is lying dead on the floor, a circle is being sawed through the floor beneath his feet, the news reporter on TV is showing a Wanted poster with his picture, and from the phone—which is lying off the hook on the bedside stand—his boss is shouting, "You're fired, you grinning jerk!" Underneath, Jack had printed, "A SEVEN!!!"

Coaching Style Seven

An inordinate passion for pleasure is the secret of remaining young.

Oscar Wilde

Characteristically, Sevens are charming, upbeat, and humorous, tell lots of stories, and focus on the positive. They can also show a lack of attention to details that makes an in-the-box Seven scattered and unreliable. Coaching these clients can be energizing because they're playful and inventive. They love to talk. You'll develop rapport quickly if you ask lots of questions. They may also convince you they're ready to change when they respond to suggestions quickly, but their early enthusiasm could lead you to have unrealistic expectations.

Peggy, a Seven, hired Mary to coach her because she felt she'd been a dilettante in her work. She wanted to establish a career she could envision as deeply satisfying over the long haul. She had changed jobs and life goals often and easily and felt blown about by every wind.

Mary and Peggy established some tentative goals together. A few weeks after they started coaching, Mary reinforced some concrete steps Peggy had taken toward her career goals. Following that session Peggy wrote, "From deep within me came the full weight of the realization of what I had accomplished and this brought me to tears. When I first started down this path, all I wanted was to find and release that happy little kid inside. Little did I know what that journey would entail—having the desire and courage, as Joseph Campbell said, to go into the forest where no one else had ventured. I KNEW that was the journey I had to take yet was hesitant to take. I am amazed at the tenacity I have demonstrated. I, a lightweight Seven, have simply refused to stop hacking my way through the forest of my emotional and psychological landscape. Thank you for helping me with this breakthrough."

We're tempted to write – light-heartedly, of course: "And everyone lived happily ever after." In the session above, Peggy felt she made a significant breakthrough. As with all of us, though, the process of transformation waxed and waned. Every week she would find a new and fascinating approach to envisioning a more fulfilling career, and every week Mary encouraged Peggy to take action instead of losing herself in the thrill of generating ideas. It's not always easy to help Sevens corral their buoyant energy and move from imagining possibilities to creating a durable framework for change.

Coaching Sevens is one of the few times you want to help clients become less optimistic.

Coaching Sevens is one of the few times you want to help clients become less optimistic. They need to have a more sober picture of their tasks, and to observe how they tend to run away from anything too detailed or problematic.

Your Seven clients may be somewhat scattered and unreliable in the beginning, but with your coaching they will become more realistically enthusiastic while remaining visionary.

Fears Confinement

Sevens are polarized between creating pleasant options and feeling confined. You'll often hear these clients describe feeling trapped, and they may even use prison metaphors. One Seven told Mary, "A friend of mine who went to prison handled it very well, but I don't know if I could stand being cooped up like that. There are times when I feel that way about this company. I'm making so much money here, I feel completely trapped, realizing I can't leave no matter how bad it gets. Then I think, 'I can't wait to get out of here and be free.'" Another said, "The biggest problem in my job is that everything's so programmed. Sometimes every hour is scheduled. It's a problem because I love to make connections but usually feel I have to say, 'Gotta run now, goodbye!'"

Pay attention to these four habits of in-the-box Ones:

Fears confinement

Escapes into pleasant options

Acts childlike or childish

Substitutes charm for substance

Sometimes the confinement lies within Sevens. They are more easily addicted than other styles and feel trapped by whatever they're addicted to. You'll improve your coaching skills as you recognize how addiction plays out for them. One of Clarence's clients said, "I get a kick out of a game on our home computer, and I'll play it before I go to bed, much more than I should. I'm not a gambler because I have strong moral feelings about it, though I did go to Reno with a friend to test a theory. I set a limit on what I would spend, but found myself wanting to do it more. This bothers me because I want to think of myself as self-disciplined, but when I really make up my mind to do something—such as losing weight—that can be addictive, too. When I read a book for pleasure my wife tells the kids, 'Say goodbye to Dad, guys.' When I get close to the end, I'll stay up till 3:00 AM to finish it, no matter what I have ahead of me the next day." Another Seven admitted to Mary, "I smoke pot, and it gets worse when I'm under stress and feel there's no escape. It's not that I think smoking pot is bad, certainly no worse than having a couple of drinks. It's the compulsion that bothers me. I was smoking and eating breakfast at the same time this morning and heard myself saying, 'You're going to enjoy this if it kills you.'" A coach might ask Sevens to notice when they experience a surge of appetite—for food, sex, caffeine, or entertainment. The desire may signal that they're running away from something.

When Sevens start a project it feels like an adventure, but when the demands of the project get heavy, they feel confined by the boredom or difficulty. They may find a way to circumvent the real work. When they do, find out where they feel trapped. Sometimes you can coach them to do the most unpleasant tasks of a project first, so it doesn't hang over them like a threat. They can experience a sense of relief at having broken the back of a task that was oppressing them. One Seven's motto: "Worst first." Help these clients focus on what to finish instead of what to begin and you will more effectively bring about a second-order change. Self-improvement programs bring a rush of early energy, but perseverance brings about results.

Sevens may come to coaching because of external pressure. They can feel trapped by the demands of someone else—boss, spouse, doctor, or lawyer—and will be eager for escape rather than change. They will verbally agree to change, but will often change some superficial behaviors and then look for wiggle room to avoid internal effort. If they lack internal motivation they may only want to avoid unpleasant consequences

You can help Sevens by giving them a model of change with some structure. The model should assure them in some detail that the process does have an end.

Their fear of confinement may underlie a conviction that unless they can escape their crisis, they're going to be stuck in this struggle forever. You can help Sevens by giving them a model of change with some structure. The model should assure them in some detail that the process does have an end. We often use the familiar business model that moves from denial through resistance and exploration to commitment. They can relax a bit when they see where they are in a finite process and can realize they are not really trapped.

Sevens love to move at high speed and will feel burdened by the slower pace of a group. They fall more easily into the Lone Ranger syndrome than most. If they belong to a group, their role is often cheerleader or spokesperson. Their usual complaint is that the group is too slow or boring. Jack admitted to Mary, "I get impatient with people who ramble on. I got called on it the other day by a colleague who pointed out my hand gesture indicating 'move it along.'" One way to slow Sevens down is to move them from their heads into their hearts. Mary suggested to Jack that when he found himself thinking, "I'm bored," he visualize placing his hand on the other person's heart and let himself experience what that person might be feeling. After trying it he told her, "Though it took great effort, I felt incredible empathy for the person I'd been bored with, followed by a wonderful sense of joy." His was true joy, not the high he experienced when he was running on automatic. He felt the difference.

Confronting Sevens on their issues is delicate. They may easily shift the responsibility for change over to you. Then you are their confinement, you become the one who wants them to change. You'll be effective if you give descriptive and specific feedback in a caring tone so they can see consequences they've never noticed.

Confronting Sevens on their issues is delicate. They may easily shift the responsibility for change over to you. Then you are their confinement.

Escapes Into Pleasant Options

In-the-box Sevens find it difficult to face tedium or unpleasant matters. A coach will want to be alert to a number of their escapes.

The first escape is purely mental. With their low tolerance for pain, they may too quickly reframe painful experience into a positive learning one. They will miss the lessons of failure because they rationalize them away. They will explain that they didn't try harder because the project didn't have much chance for success. "It was the wrong time," "We couldn't have foreseen what actually happened," "We learned a great deal and will do much better next," are typical dodges. This rationalizing defense is frequently invisible to Sevens, and they regard it as a type of creativity.

They defend themselves against unpleasant information, or all information from people they consider unpleasant, by making light of it. They don't argue much; they're more apt to shake their heads or laugh it off after the messenger leaves. If they are in a management position their employees learn not to bring them bad news. Jack complained if his people brought problems without solutions. They saw him dance away when they need discussion to figure out how to break through a problem. Mary took advantage of the Seven's ability to reframe things from negative to positive to help Jack see bad news as a key to solve problems.

Seven managers further avoid nitty-gritty problems by giving employees the big picture and then leaving people alone to figure out how to carry on. One Seven told Clarence she was strong at delegating. She asked her employees to handle the details, telling them, "This is far too important for me to do it. I need someone really competent." This pleasant maneuver dispensed her from mastering the details and left her a bit vague about how much time and money to allocate to a task. Delegation can become mere "dumping," as the Seven moves on to something more fascinating. As one of Jack's team members said, "He wants us to manage with the goal in mind but without specifics."

Sevens typically don't want to hear bad news themselves, and omit it when they report to those in authority Jack displayed this trait and his boss described him as "optimistic to a fault." Sevens are often verbally facile; they love to speculate and create scenarios that glow with promise. Unfortunately, they may have done little homework and based their optimism on little or no concrete evidence or even any specific plans. We describe this as a blue-sky virus. One Seven announced to Mary, "With a few basic principles, you can run just about anything." A Seven's ungrounded optimism can frustrate a coach. You'll help most if you keep pushing for "how." You may have to ask many times and be rather blunt.

A Seven's ungrounded optimism can frustrate a coach. You'll help most if you keep pushing for "how." You may have to ask many times and be rather blunt.

In-the-box Sevens can also try to escape through simple denial. When they ignore the bleak side of things, they see only the possibilities and miss the problems. Unless they are forced to see problems, they assume that everything is working well when that may not be true. This is what worried Ben when he discovered Jack "hadn't done his homework." Jack was surprised to learn that Ben was disappointed in him. He hadn't wanted to see Ben's increasing concerns. Another of Mary's clients reported, "I told a friend I had the perfect life. My wife divorced me within eight months."

Sevens can escape unpleasant tasks by switching their attention and energy to something more pleasant. Mary's client Allen came wanting help with his marriage to a spouse he described as verbally abusive. But within one short week, he shifted his focus in the coaching sessions from the serious problem in his marriage to the exciting growth in his new business. His new focus was his attempt to escape his real issue.

With their love for novelty and variety, Sevens seek out new and innovative approaches. They like the edge rather than the familiar middle of conventions or ideas or customs. They will try new and daring projects, but then may have trouble doing the grunt work to implement last week's new idea with today's labor. This unwillingness to commit to a difficult or unpleasant task has its roots in a lack of confidence to accomplish what they picture to themselves as impossible or unbearably boring. They remain flexible so that when the expected failure comes they can move on to something more promising.

If Sevens are not able to escape into novelty, they may escape into excess activity. Too many tasks, too little time. In-the-box Sevens have a peculiar relationship to time. One way they distort time is to have a vague picture located in the future in which all their ideas come together eventually. This optimistic vision can blind them to contradictions easily seen by others. This time-expansion gives them a false bounty within which all things can be accomplished. For example, they might simultaneously proclaim a policy of tight cost-control while laying out grandiose plans for growth. This same time expansion explains why Sevens double-schedule and over-promise. When they promise or schedule, they tell themselves they will have plenty of time, but when the deadlines and appointments hit, they can't always deliver.

Many Sevens will see their workload as infinite because of their time expansion. They may fill their expanded time with tasks to do, then feel overwhelmed and look for a way out. At that point they often cut corners, break promises, and substitute their notion of creativity for doing what they promised.

Sometimes Sevens escape into hyperactivity. Everything seems better at high speed. Movement feels like accomplishment. You can break this escape from real engagement with questions such as, "How will you address (your real issue) right now?" "What are you feeling at this moment?" You do Sevens a favor when you pleasantly but persistently face them with real issues.

Humor can substitute for serious effort in Sevens. For example, two consultants worked with a large firm to deliver diversity training. After their first event one reported, "I can't continue doing this because they're just juggling abstract concepts. They're not involving the key people or attempting to change the system, so I doubt if any real change is possible." The other, a Seven, said, "It was great! They loved me! I kept everybody laughing."

Sometimes Sevens escape into hyperactivity. You can break this pattern with questions such as, "How will you address (your real issue) right now?"

Humor or entertainment can serve as a pleasant escape route for some Sevens. They can laugh at how seriously others see problems, or make fun of those who predict disaster. They may be funniest about their deepest issues. Jokes about their boss or spouse, for example, may reveal serious problems or hostility issues.

Sevens need to understand humor's power to hurt and its use as a defense. Jack had alienated his colleagues by monopolizing conversation, and his witty, acerbic asides in meetings had seemed like barely disguised attacks. When fear erodes their inner authority, they may adopt an attitude of superiority, employing humor to put down anyone who threatens them. When coaching Sevens, watch how they may bury issues in cartoons, e-mails, and office jokes. One Seven, when called on his mean humor, replied straightforwardly, "Never use a tomahawk when a needle will do." If Sevens try to entertain or even mock you as a coach, probe for their fear.

Notice when they replace feeling with thinking, usually about the future. Help them see how this may be an escape from the present, and from feelings. The journey into deeper feelings may challenge a Seven. One told Mary: "I have a theory on people becoming introspective, that we all have four layers. The first layer is the outer shell. At the second layer is something you don't necessarily like about yourself. Below that are deep, deep fears, a place where you have to

When coaching Sevens, watch how they may bury issues in cartoons, e-mails, and office jokes.

recognize the 'ugly' and ask yourself, 'What's really back there?' The pain of examining this layer is excruciating, just horrible, but when I can get through it to the fourth layer, that's where the light is."

Seven clients with a religious bent will be assured by the words of Thomas Keating, a well-known teacher of Centering Prayer, in his book, *Intimacy with God.*

> …a person in the dark night normally has an intuition that these trials are going someplace, such as the growth of a nonjudgmental attitude…greater detachment from things….The spiritual journey from the aspect of the dark night of the soul is a course in growing up and becoming liberated from childhood fixations at emotional levels that have become disruptive of our adult life and that interfere with our relationships.

Not all Sevens are willing to agree to a journey that is associated with discomfort. When Mary's client, Jenny, wanted to learn how to observe her dysfunctional patterns, she told Mary she didn't want to stop and meditate. Mary offered self-observation as a way to look inward without judgment. She stressed the objective, neutral aspect. She knew that Jenny, or any client, can gradually face the deeper feelings that are inevitably aroused by the phases of self-discovery. She assured Jenny that as she developed, she would learn to see how the general patterns of the Enneagram act out specifically for her and that she would become less attached to these patterns. One Seven, for example, reported picking up flowers for a large dinner party and, noticing her desire to buy fifty bouquets, stopped for a moment to ask, "How many is enough?" She bought thirty bouquets instead. She then laughed and said, "I guess even thirty is a lot." But how many bouquets she bought is not the point. She was learning to observe her patterns and she took a few steps out of her box.

Acts Childlike or Childish

Of all the ways Sevens exercise their ability to reframe unpleasant into pleasant alternatives, none works better than their ability to turn work into play. The most famous example in American literature is Tom Sawyer's reframe of whitewashing the fence from a tedious task into a neighborhood privilege. Tom was a Seven and when Sevens share their vision, they can inspire a group and set a tone of high adventure. Sevens in a position of authority can motivate people with this ability to make work attractive. One of Jacks' employees said with admiration, "He even has union employees motivated!"

Sevens can set a tone of high adventure. Be careful. They can also lure you into their magical world.

This is the childlike gift of Sevens. Be careful. They can also lure you as a coach into their magical world. Peter Pan is their model and Sevens may try to convince you that you can fly, too. Remind them that reality has its own magic. When in the box, this childlike ability to turn work into play degenerates into a willful reluctance to finish what they start. If the task is enjoyable, they will do just fine, but as it becomes tedious they fade, lose focus, and switch attention to something more interesting.

When Sevens teach, their instinct is to turn to stories. They much prefer narrative to explanation, because narrative entertains and persuades as it instructs. They can compress information into metaphor, example, and slogan. But they are often much better at imparting information than facilitating a process. It takes effort to pay close attention to all participants. The immaturity of some Sevens makes them reluctant to spend such effort to bring forth the resources of others, preferring the limelight themselves. You can coach them to ask open-ended questions, encourage discussion, and field questions back so others discover their own resources.

The immaturity of some Sevens prefer the limelight themselves. Coach them to ask open-ended questions, encourage discussion, and field questions back so others discover their own resources.

Substitutes Charm for Substance

Given an ability to tell stories and jokes, a penchant for rationalizing, and a preference for escape over conflict, it is not surprising that Sevens try to get their way through charm. It's probably going too far to call them con artists. It is fair to say that they rely heavily on an ability to persuade.

The Seven's positive reframing of difficulties comes into play here as a way of avoiding conflict. On the spur of the moment, which is often when Sevens are at their best, they will try to change the way people look at a situation: "You see it as carelessness, but sometimes when people are enthusiastic, they get carried away and miss details. We don't want to put a wet blanket on enthusiasm, do we?" We honor reframing as a technique to influence change—to see habits in a different light. Sevens do it compulsively. When they reframe as a means of getting off the hook, it is a defense against conflict or perceived danger. They charm to disarm.

They will use charm to avoid effort. A Seven explained how he got through college without much work: "If I had too much information, I just dumped it on my test paper without much thought. But if I only had a few facts that I had to nurse through three or four pages, I really developed style!" He was bright, so he did some good work, but when he ran out of substance, he turned to charm.

If Sevens rely on charm, they are seen as lightweights. They don't seem to have analytical ability because they glide over the surface, just looking for highlights. One of Ben's first comments about Jack was that that he "wasn't deep in his analysis of existing problems." Jack's peers had a slightly different take on the same charm. They said, "He always has a smile on his face and I don't know if it goes deep down because his expression never changes."

Sevens lead with a smile. It is said that pessimists come closer to the accurate evaluation of reality, but that optimists accomplish more. Sevens take advantage of this with gusto. They make optimistic decisions and inspire the group with enthusiasm because they "know" this project will be fantastic. The group gets excited, works hard, and the Seven turns out to be right. Sometimes. For Jack this charm worked with his team and led to success. But he killed his career because his relentless good cheer charmed senior management not at all.

Lead Sevens to admit their unacknowledged fears, show them their escape routes, and help them explore why they work so hard to be charming.

When you're coaching a Seven, you will deal with someone who is charming, funny, energetic, and slippery. Don't be deceived. Constant change is the same as any other rigid pattern. It is a burden to others, a threat to their own happiness, and a source of pain. What can you do? You begin, as usual, asking them to do non-judgmental self-observation so they have nothing to fear. As they become aware, they can let go of their defenses. Because Sevens don't mind interruptions—they love spontaneity—feel free to break in any conversation with observations that they are executing one of the four patterns we've described. Lead them to admit their unacknowledged fears, show them their escape routes, and help them explore why they work so hard to be charming.

The Seven's Vision: Shift from being scattered, unreliable to being realistically enthusiastic, visionary

Mary once facilitated a review meeting for a group of hospice social workers who had a discouraging job. They and the families of the patients had to be satisfied with small rewards. Sevens need that lesson more than most. They can achieve significant breakthroughs, as Peggy did after only a few coaching sessions, yet still be faced with the day-to-day patterns and habits of their Enneagram style. They learn to value small real triumphs instead of veering off to a grandiose vision of transformation.

For example, after several months of coaching, Peggy recapped her progress: "I don't have the same resistances I had in the past where I would totally distract myself from staying with something. Now I'm doing things that are at least tangentially related, instead of stopping to say, 'Oh, look at the beautiful sky!' and never getting back to what I was doing. It comes down to instituting those habits into my day-to-day routine. Bit by bit, I'm better able to do that."

The Affectionate Tank

Chapter

10

Chris Johnson directed a small but profitable company she created to sell state-of-the-art software to hospitals. When she met Mary, Chris summarized her problem: "I have enormous energy that rarely lags, so I get exasperated with people who are too cautious or who whine a lot. Some people who work for me have a Goody Two-Shoes mentality, and I want to push on that. I'm tired of doing everything myself. I don't have enough faith in others to let them take over, so I'd like you to work with my team to help them become stronger."

Mary challenged her. "What about you? They need to see you're willing to go first. I hope you don't find that too threatening." Chris took the challenge. In a booming voice while making piercing eye contact she responded, "There's very little fear in me. But don't expect to make me into something I'm not. I had enough of that as a kid!"

When Mary agreed to her terms, Chris said more: "I set an explicit goal to treat my kids differently from how I was treated, which was being pounded with negative feedback and trying to make me something I was not. My mother was like the mother in *Ordinary People,* constantly disappointed in me—I was too heavy, too loud, and too aggressive to suit her." As Mary questioned further, Chris acknowledged that her husband's more laid-back style had acted as a buffer when her own parenting style got too tough. "We have a perfect marriage," she cracked. "A man who can't say no and a woman who won't take no for an answer." Mary asked about their social life. "I plan all our vacations, our evenings out, and my husband sometimes acquiesces, then complains about it because it's not what he really wanted to do. But he won't flip over and initiate anything. When we're on vacation it's a hoot, because his idea of fun is water, sun, and a book. Mine is a boat, scuba gear, a set of golf clubs, and nine dinners out—I'm a perpetual motion machine."

"And you see some similar patterns at work," Mary reflected. "Yeah," Chris replied. "I'm good at grabbing people and moving them toward a vision, but

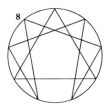

I sometimes jump ahead too fast and leave others behind who wanted to be involved. Then they give me a hard time. When there's a hot agenda item and people waste time it drives me nuts. I'm pretty tenacious and sometimes I can be obsessed with control. Then when I get exasperated with people, I think 'F--- it! I'm the CEO. Why can't I throw my weight around?'" Mary was puzzling over a response to that statement when Chris laughed, and said, "That reminds me of a great story I heard about the community organizer, Saul Alinsky. He was with a group of people eating breakfast where one woman had asked twice for some syrup for her pancakes. Alinsky stood on his chair and shouted, 'Bring me the goddamned syrup!' I like that."

"So, how is that style working with your team?" Mary probed. "I know some of them are intimidated," Chris admitted. "I've certainly heard that often enough. And when I really forget myself I can be verbally abusive, even mean. Also, while I have a good sense of humor, I'm not sure when I'm going over the edge with it. Sometimes it bites people. So I'm not getting the most out of them that I could." Mary asked. "What do you want for yourself?" She was touched by Chris' answer: "I'd like to go deeper into myself and find that I'm not a monster."

Chris set up an appointment for Mary with Hal, the board chair. "The board is happy with Chris. When she starts talking people listen," Hal mused. "There's little bluff to her—she doesn't shoot any bull. She never seems to hesitate about what to do. She is outspoken, lets everybody know what she wants, and she usually gets it. It would take two or three people to replace her." Hal also focused on the more personal side, because he and Chris and their families had become friends: "She's quite lovable when you get to know her. She truly has a tender heart and her family and friends are important to her. She has a great respect for life, including animals. She's very moral, will even sacrifice popularity for principle. It's simple with her: you don't compromise your values."

Chris is not particularly big, but she can fill a room when others act contrary to her expectations.

Chris' administrative assistant, Anne, was one of her trusted supporters. Anne buffered Chris at work in the same way Chris' husband buffered her at home: "Chris starts out well in most situations because she's smart and knowledgeable, but she's burned some bridges behind her that I've had to rebuild. She's not particularly big, but she can fill a room when others act contrary to her expectations. If she thinks people have been incompetent she'll let them have it with both barrels, and she doesn't care who they are. She's made people look like dopes who needed to be handled with kid gloves. I've overheard her a couple of times on the speakerphone in an attack mode." Anne obviously felt supported by her boss, though, and wished

Chris had a more balanced life: "She has huge intensity but she works too hard. Her stamina and dedication go to unhealthy bounds. She expects from others what she expects from herself, but she has unreasonable expectations."

Mary interviewed two of Chris' staff who represented opposing reactions to her style. Charley was self-confident and able to stand up to Chris respectfully, so he related well to her: "I expect her to tell me like it is, but others aren't so open. She may not have the best of manners. She certainly isn't subtle; she's kind of brash and abrupt. But deep down I don't believe we'd have achieved what we have without her offensive posture. It's a known business strategy that some people get to wear the black hat." When Mary asked Charley if Chris treated him the same as she did the others, he said, "She trusts me and I rarely feel over-controlled. She's forceful, and we've parried a bit, but that doesn't bother me because she is concerned with doing what's right and I would expect her to speak up. She won't back off, so if you think you're right you've got to hold your ground with her. I consider this a strength, but she intimidates people who have trouble standing up to her demanding approach. A couple of my colleagues find her controlling. If she disagrees with something, she says so immediately. Overall, she comes off as gruff and overbearing."

When asked what he would recommend for Chris, Charley said, "She needs to learn to listen, and not control situations so tightly. She needs to bend more when dealing with different people on the team. She could show more tact and diplomacy, back off a bit, and occasionally bite her tongue—for example, not embarrass someone in a large meeting."

Jerry spoke from the other end of the spectrum: "In my dealings with Chris," he said, "as long as she's getting her way and others subordinate their independence, everything is fine, but if someone offers a different perspective she confronts them. Things I see as taking initiative she views as disrespect." Mary asked Jerry if Chris had done a good job as CEO. "She has accomplished a lot for the company," he acknowledged. "My only question is whether she could have accomplished the same results with a different approach. She sees the world as adversarial. For example, she tends to assume someone has screwed up if they don't answer her phone calls right away. Chris can really blow people away. She conveys that you're incompetent or a lightweight. She's opinionated and overbearing. You can see this in her approach to solving problems. She questions you unmercifully until she finds a weakness and then exploits it. As much as I like her, when she does that I dig in my heels as if I were one of her kids!"

She's opinionated and overbearing. She questions you unmercifully until she finds a weakness and then exploits it.

Picking up on Jerry's admission that he did like Chris, Mary asked him about Chris' positive traits. "There are a lot of things about her that I find inspiring," Jerry confirmed. "She has a tremendous capacity to love and care for the underdog. She has a kind of naïve honesty: what you see is what you get. When she's at her best she exudes a quality of fearlessness, calm, gentleness, and positive outlook. She believes she can do anything, and she will do anything for you. But she does what she thinks you need. She absolutely doesn't know how to get inside other people's framework. She doesn't understand that people adapt by incorporating new ideas into their own way of thinking. She just wants them to 'do it!'"

Coaching Analysis

Coaching Chris

When Chris picked Mary up at the airport for their first meeting—and for scheduled interviews with others—one of the first things out of her mouth was a challenge: "I don't want you giving me any bullshit."

Mary reframed the meaning of power: "A leader's real power lies in acknowledging vulnerability as well as showing strength."

The night before her feedback session with Chris, Mary cut out a set of paper teeth and sewed them onto the mouth of a small teddy bear. Remembering the admonition for "no bullshit," Mary dropped all attempts to be nice when summing up others' feedback. "You've got a big bite," she said bluntly, looking directly at Chris, "and you've left some people nursing their wounds." "A couple of people have seen your tender side," she added, and handed Chris the teddy bear with teeth. Chris loved it.

To match Chris' worldview, Mary acknowledged the importance of leading with strength, and also drew on the Eight's value for justice: "Ethical leaders don't push their own agenda without regard for others' beliefs and values." Mary reframed the meaning of power: "A leader's real power lies in acknowledging vulnerability as well as showing strength." The overt message acknowledged and legitimized Chris' worldview, and warned of possible abuse: "Powerful leadership is interactive. It rests on your relationship with followers, more than on your overt power." Mary highlighted two key points:

1. "Strong leaders bring out childhood patterns in many employees. As head of the company, you are a parent symbol to them. So they will react to you somewhat the way they did to their parents. Your aggressive style and their unconscious patterns explain both why you are so powerful and why you get resistance."

2. "It's an abuse of power to use it only for your own ends. To be ethical as a leader you need to teach others how to lead. You will be really strong when you make your followers strong. To do this, encourage them to think critically and creatively. You can only accomplish this by developing them to be independent and to question your views."

The paradox was not lost on Chris. In order for her subordinates to be strong, she had to be open enough to solicit and learn from their criticisms of her style and her point of view. Together she and Mary used *tough love* (Chris' term) as a framework for coaching. They drew skills from a study on forceful and enabling leadership. A leader who is too forceful is insensitive and callous. A leader who accommodates too easily is nice to people at the expense of the work. One who is both forceful and enabling makes tough calls when necessary—even when it affects people adversely—but is also compassionate and responds to people's needs and feelings.

Practicing these tough love skills began to break down Chris' either/or mentality and she learned to see more nuances.

Practicing these tough love skills began to break down Chris' either/or mentality and she learned to see more nuances. Before, she had seen weakness as the only alternative to strength. Now she saw the mutual strength in cooperation. She still reverted to her old win/lose tactics, though, when she negotiated with vendors. Mary and Chris rehearsed with Fisher and Ury's *Getting to Yes* audiotapes to help Chris focus on principles ("What is your objective in pushing for this option?") instead of positions ("No, we've got to do it this way"). They laughed aloud at the program's subtitle: "How to Negotiate Agreement Without Giving In."

Coaching Style Eight

With all Enneagram styles, you can earn trust quickly when you acknowledge and validate their worldview. One way to do this is to use language familiar to your clients. We've suggested, for example, that you match Fives early in the coaching process by using intellectual words. With Twos you need to start with relational language. Eights can be brusque, tough, somewhat loud, what-you-see-is-what-you-get people. They also have tender hearts, sometimes carefully hidden. You want to show Eights the same consideration that you would with any client. But if you get too flowery or long-winded or act intimidated, they may see you as weak. Then you aren't as likely to develop the deep rapport that leads to transformational coaching.

There is always room for a man of force, and he makes room for many.

Emerson

Buddy Halstrom called Mary and said, "I need someone to teach my people how to stand up to me." Mary guessed he might be an Eight. Buddy's trusted

If you get too flowery or long-winded or act intimidated, Eights may see you as weak. This could impede the deep rapport that leads to transformational coaching.

aide had told him people on his team found him too aggressive, controlling, and intimidating. Consequently, when he confronted them, they tended to beat around the bush. Buddy knew he could intimidate people. In fact, he sometimes reveled in that. But he didn't realize how much his own behavior invited the response he most despised. He wanted them to "tell it like it is!" Yet he pushed and challenged everyone, inviting them to "waffle," as he called it. Then he would see them as "wimps" and reassure himself that his view of the world was accurate: "I have to be strong. There's nobody else."

Chris Johnson loved getting the teddy bear with teeth. Buddy had a similar reaction after Mary talked to his team and reported back: "People shrivel up like raisins in your presence." He grinned at that. He looked a lot more uncomfortable when he shook her hand as she was leaving, looked her directly in the eye, and said, "Thank you for caring." He saw that she knew him and liked him just the way he was. Paradoxically, feeling known and appreciated as we are allows us to envision changing. When we don't have to defend ourselves, anything becomes possible.

Eights who seek coaching will most likely be locked into a power-seeking, war mentality. As you bring out their best, they will become more compassionate and just.

Preoccupied with Power

Not everyone relishes being in charge, but Eights usually do. They are natural leaders. They prefer to be on top, in control, and making things happen the way they want them to happen. They gravitate toward action, power, and aggression. Their style might be called Euclidian: "The shortest distance between two points is a straight line." In-the-box Eights don't finesse, they don't schmooze, they don't ask. In business, they typically claim power and use it directly, without worrying whether people like it or not. They don't pussyfoot around, and *wimp* is their term of ultimate scorn. The Eight's power is visible, like a holstered gun in a western movie. They are not fond of taking prisoners. Their posture is frequently "in your face," and their speech direct, blunt, clear, and loud.

Eights can contaminate their love of power with a suspicion that others are not handling power well. They are sensitive to all forms of power: information, relationships, expertise, money, talent, and energy. If anyone on their team (read: under their command) abuses any form of power, they take it as a personal betrayal and deal with the issue quickly and forthrightly. Typically, they only share information if it won't weaken their power base. They demand more information than most styles. Because they experience themselves as larger than life, they

Pay attention to these four habits of in-the-box Eights:

Is preoccupied with power

Uses toggle-switch thinking

Confronts as search for truth

Fails to distinguish revenge from justice

assume they can deal with all information. Unlike Sevens, who want good news, or Sixes, who expect bad news, Eights want all the news, unvarnished. They monitor all the news carefully, like a general assessing a battle plan.

They can require personal information from their employees. Others' self-disclosure is important because Eights tend to view business and all of life as a kind of war. They want to know where everybody stands. Others must state their positions, opinions, and needs clearly and succinctly or in-the-box Eights won't get it, because they often don't listen very well or easily empathize with others. When they get personal disclosure from someone, Eights can relax and admit that person into their inner circle. Once admitted, this person is then entitled to the Eight's protective side. But they don't want any back talk or evaluation of themselves. That's why it was key that Mary reframed feedback and evaluation as ethical demands. This reframe was crucial to Chris' new view of her world.

Eights often find it hard to delegate. They usually don't want to share power and prefer a hierarchical structure in which they do the deciding. Notice that Chris made all the decisions and did all the planning for vacations with her husband. Eights usually prefer to make or approve all decisions in the company. They may allow initiative, but usually want to stay in control and be kept informed, preferably in detail.

Eights tend to polarize between power and vulnerability because they assume that the presence of one vitiates the other. They may feel extremely vulnerable inside, almost unprotected. Their tough persona is a virtual suit of armor to protect that soft inner self. The few people they allow to see their vulnerable side—some spouses, for example—often describe Eights as "pussycats." The wife of one of Mary's Eight clients died unexpectedly. He was devastated. A few months later he was still grieving but began to see other women. Mary asked him what quality in his wife he had loved the most that he could seek in another woman. He replied simply, "She babied me."

Eights may feel extremely vulnerable inside, almost unprotected. Their tough persona is a virtual suit of armor to protect that soft inner self.

In part, the tendency of Eights to see others as weak is a projection of their own childlike vulnerability. However, Eights who can't or won't access or acknowledge their own vulnerability can be ruthless, steamrolling over everyone in their path.

They can wield power so vigorously that they don't realize their own strength. In-the-box Eights may remain unaware of their inner workings and not understand how anger motivates their behavior. They tend to apologize for their use of power only after it's clear they've hurt someone they didn't intend to hurt. For example, they might criticize someone brutally without being aware of any inner rancor, but the recipient experiences them as fierce and hostile. If these people who feel attacked reveal their pain in these circumstances, Eights may be surprised and apologize because they didn't mean to draw blood.

Johnny Cash's popular country song, "A Boy Named Sue," illustrates why Eights often make life difficult for those they love and nurture: A father says to his son that he named him Sue in order to make life harder for him so he would survive in a tough world. Consistent with their belief that life is a jungle, many of your Eight clients will be physically armored with heavy musculature. When provoked, they may *muscle up*, grow larger like a cat that wants to frighten its perceived opponent. Remember Anne's comment about Chris: "She's not particularly big, but she can fill a room when someone acts contrary to her expectations." When coaching Eights, get information about any exercise regimen they have (weight lifting is likely) and move them into more fluid, holistic approaches—like yoga, tai chi, or dance—that are geared toward getting past the armor.

Get information about any exercise regimen they have and move them into more fluid, holistic approaches.

Not only may your typical Eight clients not be good listeners, but they might systematically mismatch. If you nod your head yes, they might remain still or shake their head no. This pattern may be evident in their interactions with you. Clarence sent an e-mail to an Eight friend who'd missed a meeting that was fun and covered a lot of ground in a short period of time, but not in a very orderly way. "The meeting was lively," Clarence wrote, "but a bit unnerving for some. People were talking all over the place and the chair kept tapping her pen on the table to get people's attention." Notice the opposite reaction in the Eight's response: "That shows a lack of respect for the person in charge. If I were chair for this group the Roberts' Rules of Order would be brought into play real quick!" He completely missed the amused tone of Clarence's message and jumped to action: how he'd bring things under control if he ran things his way.

Eights can make good use of active listening if it counters their habit of learning about the other's weak points: "Listen so carefully that you can argue the other's position."

Eights can make good use of active listening, but if you recommend this without explaining how listening can change their focus, they might use the technique simply to feed their power needs; to learn more about the other's weak points. With clients who are ready to go to their edge, you can be direct with fieldwork that counters this pattern. For example, "When arguing with someone, try to match their body posture and feel your impact on them." Or, if they say how hard it is to hold back when someone challenges them, you might push on the boundaries of their box: "You're not that fragile, you can handle disagreement." When they seem unready to tackle their habitual behavior directly, a good tactic is

156

to start with their worldview but subtly introduce a shift: "Listen so carefully that you can argue the other's position."

Many Eights, especially males, have naturally loud voices. You will invite a different response if you suggest they install a volume control. Point out that even though they may not have been aware of it, many others are intimidated by volume. You could suggest they gauge their volume and notice carefully the differences in feedback they get to different volumes.

Mary helped Chris distinguish between authority and control by dissolving Chris' polarized assumption that if you're not strong, you're weak. You can also help your Eight clients widen their field of vision by breaking down the meaning of the word *control*. Then you can dream up fieldwork that creates a continuum between no control and too much control. A thesaurus comes in handy for this kind of task. Here's a range of words from no control to too much control that will make the process amusing for both of you: *crumble, capitulate, ignore, mollycoddle, influence, motivate, inspire, empower, galvanize, magnetize, pressure, dominate, subjugate, incapacitate, terrorize, murder.*

> *You can help your Eight clients widen their field of vision by breaking down the meaning of the word control. Then you can create a continuum between no control and too much control.*

Mary's Eight client, Brad, was angry at the company president for putting him last on the agenda for a coming board meeting. After exploring Brad's self-described range of reaction between wimpdom and rage, she encouraged him to consciously choose his approach when he discussed the agenda's sequence with the president. After that meeting he wrote, "When I met with him my impulse ranged from groveling gratefully to be on the agenda at all (are you kidding?) to kneecapping him. I found more constructive middle ground by asking why he put me at the end. He wasn't even thinking of the order on the agenda. The discussion highlighted our need to agree on the strategic direction we present to the board."

Uses Toggle-Switch Thinking

In-the-box Eights seem to harbor a secret wish that everyone be issued athletic team jerseys at birth so they can tell who's on their side, and relax. This will be true in your coaching relationship as well. It usually happens in one of two ways. Either they test you to see if you're a wimp or not (as both Chris and Buddy tested Mary), or you show your underbelly and ask implicitly for their protection. When they are your protector, they are knights in armor, usually shining, but always on your side. Eights demand and give total allegiance, and in business they can create fierce team loyalty. They also reward loyalty with money, benefits, security, and recognition. One of Mary's Eight clients gave his personal assistant a company bonus in the form of stock in a business he knew was going to grow rapidly. He didn't ask his assistant how she'd like to invest her bonus. This was a tremendously generous and affectionate act on his part, and a bit tank-like.

In-the-box Eights' thought can lack nuance. We call this *toggle-switch* thinking, in contrast to the black and white thinking of Ones. Instead of a right/wrong polarity it's a simple on/off. Eights tend toward quick, impulsive solutions: "Let's go with it!" No middle ground. As with Clarence's friend who immediately e-mailed back a way to bring people under control in a meeting, they may be so driven to take charge that they miss the subtleties. All Enneagram worldviews are sustained by an either/or posture. Out of the Eight's war mentality, it's "are you with me or against me?" This creates a bull in the china shop approach as they barge around trying not to notice they feel vulnerable inside. It's safer to see themselves as strong and others as weak. From this frame of reference they convince themselves they're compassionate when they offer their protection. Jerry described Chris this way: "She will do anything for you. But she does what she thinks you need. She absolutely doesn't know how to get inside other people's framework."

They tend toward quick, impulsive solutions. Suggest that they listen a long time before they speak (counting to ten is a long time for an Eight).

Mary had an Eight client, Jake, whose wife told him she wanted to celebrate her sixtieth birthday with him, her son, and her daughter-in-law. Her son's thirtieth birthday was two days after hers and a milestone for him also. She planned a quiet double celebration for the day between her birthday and her son's, asking her son to cook lasagna—her favorite of his culinary masterpieces. She would bake the cake. Near dinnertime on the day before the planned family party, Jake said he had a surprise for her. He was pleased as punch. He'd invited all their friends, her son, and daughter-in-law to celebrate her birthday that night—a big party for a big occasion. Because there would be more people coming he'd asked her son to cook a big spicy pot of Jambalaya (Jake's favorite by the way). He was angered by his wife's obvious discomfort when he popped the surprise. She said he had not really listened to her wish for a small double celebration. She also reminded him that she was recovering from an ulcer and would have a long night after eating such a spicy dish. He kept a dour face as she talked. He was thinking, "What a drag, she doesn't know how to have fun." When she tried to explain that becoming sixty was not something she felt like having a big party about, he told her she needed to face reality. He didn't want to hear about her feeling vulnerable.

In-the-box Eights can often be sure they know what to do and steamroll everyone to accomplish it. In business their micromanaging is about power; not an attempt to correct things, as it might be for a One, or a withholding of information, as it might be for a Five. They want it done now, their way. They want a sense of victory. One reason that conflicts involving Eights often degenerate into an out-and-out power struggle is because they can see things almost in cartoon fashion. In many newspapers, the most savage criticism of public figures lurks in the cartoons and comics. With nuance absent, conflicts degenerate into a struggle between good guys and bad guys.

Jake was not about to accept his wife's disappointment. That would mean he'd lost and, besides, he had to prepare for a party! So Eights can try to solve conflicts by charging ahead and winning. If they resort to diplomacy it's usually for a change of pace—simply another battlefield strategy.

Eights tend to see others as caricatures and use derogatory labels that justify attack. Getting specific will help break the trance these generalizations induce.

Eights tend to see others as caricatures so they describe them with derogatory labels, like soldiers use for enemies or bigots use for those racially or politically different. Seeing people as caricatures justifies attack without considering personal feelings. Soldiers might have trouble killing a person, but "gooks" or "krauts" are different. Eights can't inwardly justify scalding a person, but a "wimp" needs it.

Chris saw people in her organization as caricatures when she called them Goody Two Shoes. Like the rest of us, Eights often despise in others what they are afraid they might have in themselves or long to have in themselves. Chris didn't understand how she carried a "Goody Two Shoes" desire to be sweet and gentle within herself.

Generalizations often support an Enneagram style, so getting specific will help break the trance generalizations induce. Mary pushed Chris to become specific. "In what way are they Goody Two Shoes? What do they do exactly that leads you to that conclusion? How is each of them different from the others?"

Like some in-the-box Eights, Chris also displayed the Eight's relish of profanity. "F--- it!" Chris said. "I'm the CEO. Why can't I throw my weight around?" Their profanity can stem from the same process that underlies their caricaturing. Simple unadorned street talk streamlines out nuance. Real people are complex, including Eights. Without complex language, Eights can lose this complexity and individual uniqueness.

To deal with this language habit, Mary invented some playful fieldwork with an Eight client. She asked him to look up all the synonyms for *f---*, make a note of them, and begin to substitute them in his conversation. This exercise had the desired effect. It introduced more complexity and heightened his awareness of how the constant use of the word over-simplified his thoughts and maintained his drive to overpower others by scaring them. When he interrupted this pattern he stopped using so much profanity and began to be more specific about his feelings.

As you coach Eights, you may find they're certain they are right in a conflict. When in the box, they often do not even know the information that supports an opposing view. Point out that this is dangerous. What others think and know is crucial to wise decisions or even to victory. As a coach, you can help them listen. It was only after Jake backed off from his first reaction to his wife that he could really listen to her needs and apologize. The ability to apologize, even if they need a little nudging, is a sign of health in Eights. They don't mean to hurt people.

Often, angry Eights cannot see or hear when they're in combat, which is how Jake saw the challenge from his wife about the change in party plans. Suggest to your Eight clients that they listen a long time before they speak (counting to ten is a long time for an Eight). You can also help these clients become more aware that people are naturally afraid of them, and that if Eights don't listen, people will assume they're going to wipe them out.

Grant them that they can do it their way. Then ask, "How much will it cost?" Sometimes Eights don't consider the cost. Start with money, but don't stop there. Move on to other costs like morale, loyalty, moral health, or the quality and stability of an important relationship. Jake didn't run his birthday plans by his coach. Had he done so, Mary could have helped him get a bit more in his wife's shoes, and anticipate how the change he made—which to him was a great idea—might have an unanticipated effect on her.

Confronts as Search for Truth

Eights handle conflict directly. "My way or the highway." Whereas Ones point to the rules and Sixes to tradition and authority, Eights self-validate: "It's right because I have the power to make it happen." Clarence was present when a Catholic Sister, at a national broadcaster's meeting, was challenged as to why she rejected a certain submission for public airing. She answered curtly, "Because I own the station." End of discussion.

They're not about to give any power up unless they know they can trust you, that you're on their side, and that you're strong enough to hold your own with them.

Eights confront people in order to test them, to see if they believe what they say and if they are for real. Fighting is a search for moral truth. They put pressure on people for the same reason military units have hazing. In a battle situation, you have to know whom you can count on. Putting pressure on people is just part of the Eight's battleground view of life.

Charley related well to Chris because he was able to stand up to her respectfully: "She won't back off, so if you think you're right you've got to hold your ground with her." Jerry, on the other hand, became defensive and dug in his heels with Chris. Their relationship was definitely boss/subordinate. We recommend to people who deal with Eights to hold their boundaries, but do so with respect. Eights will stake out their territory, and in the face of no opposition will take it all. Many people assume there's no way to counter their power. Not so. Eights unconsciously feel burdened by their responsibility and want others to help shoulder it. But they're not about to give any power up unless they know they can trust you, that you're on their side, and that you're strong enough to hold your own with them. This is why Mary felt confident to tell Chris she'd left some people nursing their wounds, and to tell Buddy people shriveled up like raisins in his presence. The implicit message was, "I know you want it straight, I'm not afraid of you, I'm strong, too, and I'll tell you the truth." But she didn't attack either of them. She spoke and acted with humor and compassion. If you attack in-the-box Eights, they can't resist escalating until they prove they're stronger than you. They have to do this to protect their worldview that it's not safe to be weak.

Eights can reflect our culture's masculine stereotype, just as Twos can mimic a female stereotype. A *New York Times* article[1] described a support group of women who'd been told their no-nonsense ways intimidated people. They named their group "Bully Broads." As much as any Eight can be intimidating, female Eights have a particularly hard time being accepted, in business or in their personal lives. Chris was told as a child, "You're too heavy, too loud, too aggressive." Society has low tolerance for women who display stereotypically masculine behaviors. The Bully Broad's leader coaches them to "become ladies first." Our approach is different. We believe the real task is to help Eights, male or female, break free from their worldview that life is a jungle where they must carve out their kingdom. A coach can help them free their inherent compassion.

The real task is to help Eights break free of their worldview that life is a jungle. A coach can help them free their inherent compassion.

Eights hunger for action. They don't mind difficulty. It's ease that bores them. Chris' administrative assistant, Anne, said of her: "She has huge intensity but she works too hard. Her stamina and dedication go to unhealthy bounds." More is better. Chris compared her husband to herself on vacation: "His idea of fun is water, sun, and a book. Mine is a boat, scuba gear, a set of golf clubs, and nine dinners out. I'm a perpetual motion machine."

An Eight writer on economics sent off a scathing letter to *Forbes* magazine about their handling of a story. In telling Clarence how angry he was about the subject,

[1] Business Day, August 10, 2001

the 70-year-old warrior grinningly remarked, "You know, adrenaline is better than Geritol."

Eights test themselves as well as others. This can show up in subtle ways, as with an Eight Mary coached for whom food (and life) could never be too spicy. In some restaurants specializing in spicy food, the waiter offers a heat range of one to six. This Eight always asked for the hottest level and then for more sauce on the side. He was never happier than when his face turned red and sweaty: "Now *that's* hot!"

When the energy subsides in the absence of conflict, Eights feel less effective and can lose interest. If a problem emerges, they come to life and attack it with full vigor again. The latent dynamic is that in the absence of real problems, small office politics or insignificant details can draw their full firepower. It's a danger for in-the-box Eights when things go too well, and they will stir the pot just for the sake of challenge. Before working with Mary, Chris and her husband had taken their 16-year-old daughter on vacation with them. They'd had a great time, but when Chris checked in with the rental car company she discovered there'd been a snafu in the rate she would be charged. She raged against the sales rep, that person's boss, and the next in command until her husband and daughter were embarrassed. That's what they ended up remembering about their otherwise happy and laid-back vacation.

Eights can base a whole business strategy *against* someone or something. Because of their propensity to see life as a battlefield, they may see enemies where they could see friends. In our example, Chris negotiated ruthlessly with the company's vendors. However, many contemporary businesses do the opposite. They make friends, allies, and co-workers out of their vendors, giving them privileged information so the vendors will tailor their own strategies to serve them better. A good coach can help Eights learn that the world is as full of friends as it is of enemies.

Despite their jungle mentality, Eights love the outdoors. They often profit emotionally from time in nature. Sometimes it helps to suggest they learn from nature: the cooperation of many species, the abundance of gardens in complete harmony with their environments. Also point out how few things, numerically, eat one another; how flowers, insects, climate, soil, moisture, and sun merge to make a single plant or animal. Eights often publicly espouse the saying (and an inner attitude of) "survival of the fittest." Observe that in nature *fittest* always assumes a context.

Fails to Distinguish Revenge From Justice

Out-of-the-box Eights have an agenda of justice. In-the-box Eights think they pursue justice while they really seek vengeance. They assume people are not using power correctly. Chris revealed this when she said she felt treated unjustly as a child ("being pounded with negative feedback and trying to make me something I was not"). They feel a need to correct a cosmic imbalance. Every injustice is seen as one more example of how things need to be changed. They feel the strength to change this injustice and they go to battle. One of Mary's clients, Ed, had once been a mercenary; a tough job for a tough guy, full of danger. But in his world he was serving justice: "These were bad guys who didn't deserve to be in power." In psychological terms, in-the-box Eights compensate for the injustice they felt as children by taking justice into their own hands.

Even the least self-aware Eights are typically protective of children, but in general they need to develop their tender side. This can show up early on as tenderness in relationship with a lover or with a friend. As their level of trust grows, their compassion grows as well. "My years as a mercenary ended," said Ed, "when I was walking down a street with a woman, and a kid reached out and pushed her. He was with a bunch of other kids and they were just goofing off. It was basically harmless, but without thinking I struck out and whop! hit him hard in the face. The woman with me didn't realize what had happened because we kept on walking, but I know I left that kid with some broken bones. I don't think I killed him, but that was the end of that life for me. I realized that something in me was becoming damaged. I asked myself, 'Along the road I'm going, what can become of me? Who would I be?' Certainly no one I could live with."

Even the least self-aware Eights are typically protective of children, but in general they need to develop their tender side.

Eights battle most fiercely when fighting for the underdog, the underprivileged, and the weak. Even Jerry, who found Chris "opinionated and overbearing," grudgingly admitted her "tremendous capacity to love and care for the underdog… She believes she can do anything, and she will do anything for you." Not able to acknowledge weakness in themselves, Eights are sensitive to it in others and marshal full force to help the weak. This is a form of projection in which they do not take care of themselves (overwork is common), but they will often take exquisite care of the people entrusted by life to them. Many Eights are excellent community servants, either under company auspices or their own.

163

This keen sense of injustice often pits them against authority. Sometimes this happens within a company, but other times it could be the law, the IRS, the medical establishment, or simple incompetent government bureaucracy. Jesse Ventura, the wrestler-turned-politician, is a vivid Eight who became governor of Minnesota running on a platform of simplicity and hostility against government bureaucracy.

Along with this sense of injustice there is a quality of innocence. Many Eights do not see themselves as fierce, but as gentle giants. Their deep love of nature expresses this. As managers, though, they may consider themselves innocent and the others guilty before they consider the evidence.

Justice includes a search for human equality. You can help Eights share power with their teams or in their marriages.

Justice includes a search for human equality. You can help your Eight clients share power with their teams or in their marriages. They can learn that sharing power multiplies it. That may not feel right to them at first, but it gets wonderful results. If they don't share power, they have themselves to blame when they find only wimps surrounding them. Help them discover, as Buddy did, that their own tough behavior invites waffling from others. As they stop looking for weakness and begin to relate more equally, they will notice others' strengths. A healthy Eight understands the advantages of a strong team, not just one stellar player.

Eights often cause fights and conflict just for the sake of intensity. It is this hunger for intensity that the Enneagram puts at the center of the Eight compulsion, labeling it *lust*. Help Eights become clear about what they are defending or seeking. They will often begin with some form of seeking power, so remind them that power is always for the sake of something else. That something else is value. They usually will say something concrete like "more money" or "fair play around here." When they do, move them up one level of abstraction: justice, or revenge, or intimacy. Then see if their current strategies fit that abstract noun to the best of their ability. By putting Eights in touch with values, they can let go of petty quarrels, power plays, and personality clashes. The key question to ask is, "How else can you achieve this value?" In-the-box Eights can be narrow and blind. Asking for other routes, other assumptions, and other allies breaks their Enneagram focus and toggle-switch thinking.

Help your Eight clients own their personal needs. This requires a high level of trust. They have censors that delete information contradicting their belief that it is not safe to show your soft side. Sometimes metaphors can get past those censors. After reading Seamus Heaney's poem, *Double-take,* Ed acknowledged how his own unmet needs drove him to be tough ("Human beings suffer, / they torture one another, / they get hurt and get hard"). Ed had experienced profound depths of feeling sitting on the deck of his sailboat watching the sun go down over the ocean. Heaney's last lines gave him hope, "for a great sea-change / on the far side of revenge…"

> Call the miracle self-healing:
> The utter self-revealing
> double-take of feeling.

The Eight's Vision: Shift from war mentality, seeking power to being compassionate and just

When they have broken through some of their habitual patterns, Eights can shoulder huge responsibility without having to control everything. Reaching beneath the surface, they allow their soft hearts to show, manifesting the innocent openness they never had a chance to express as children. Now able to empathize with, listen to, and respect others, their protective, compassionate strength can inspire people to make a real difference in their life, their work, and in the world.

Chris arranged a two-day workshop with Mary where she and all her team members talked about their Enneagram styles, how they knew themselves in that worldview, and how it affected their interaction in achieving company objectives. Chris discovered that she didn't need her protective gear. Far from being seen as a monster, she found that she was among friends who were touched by her "utter self-revealing." When she asked Jerry if he still felt intimidated by her, he said without embarrassment, "I love who you have become, Chris."

Vanilla Sundae

The Dalai Lama told a reporter he had workout equipment in his office to keep himself from being tense, then added with a laugh: "But I don't like to sweat." This metaphor for Enneagram Nines hit home for Mary's client, Dale Robb, who said with a deep sigh, "I force myself to work out to keep my weight under control, but I keep a moderate pace so I don't break into a sweat." Though somewhat serious, Dale had a quiet smile. She nodded frequently in response to Mary's comments, and almost disappeared as she leaned back into the overstuffed armchair she kept in her office for informal conversations.

In a mellow voice Dale described her childhood: "I was praised for being well-behaved, so there was no need for a lot of rules. My parents left me pretty much to my own devices. They never came to school events. As a teenager I took up golf so I could play with my father, but he was so engrossed in his own game he never noticed how I was playing." When asked how she felt about that as a child she pondered a moment, then answered: "I realized that's how things were and figured there was no use getting upset about it."

A laissez-faire manager, Dale had taken on increasing responsibility as her organization grew from a small, start-up company to become a leader in its industry. Most of her decisions had been made by consensus. She was now being considered for promotion to vice president, but that was in question because she lacked decisiveness and the ability to engage in healthy confrontation with peers. Her boss recommended that she work with a coach and she agreed.

Her peers described Dale as kind, considerate, and genuinely concerned with the common good, but they, too, questioned her capability to be vice president. "Dale always seems up to date with what's going on in our company, and could probably sit in the vice president's chair," remarked her colleague, Al. "However, she needs to show more visible leadership. 'Passion' is not a word you'd associate with Dale. For the most part, she doesn't inspire excitement." Another colleague said, "Dale's

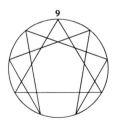

better informed about the new technology than anyone else in headquarters. She works with her team by consensus, and I've seen her handle very well a tough situation—a dispute between two people who report to her. But I'm not sure she'd be decisive enough in her boss's job." "I often wonder why she doesn't take a stronger position. She's a nice person, maybe a little too nice," concluded a third observer. "Her voice is so quiet she's sometimes hard to hear. I've heard her say her piece if she feels strongly, but she needs a better ability to sell herself."

"She's easy to be around," commented Dale's boss, Sam, "and a valuable asset in many ways, but she has a kind of 'vanilla' quality. She needs to be more directive at times. Another problem is her glass half-empty response when projects have to change direction. Her first response is 'I can't do it' or 'I don't have time.' She is usually mature in knowing what she can't do, but sometimes I think she's just tired. To my mind she internalizes stresses and then becomes disengaged or remote."

The people who worked for Dale showed respect for her as "a human kind of person." She had hired people who could tolerate uncertainty, but the constant changes going on in the organization required close teamwork with other functions, and their roles were unclear. "Ambiguity is our middle name," said one person who worked for her. "She's trying to do so many things she doesn't have time to set parameters." Others on her team made the following comments: "She thinks things are clear to us when they're not." "My guess is that she hasn't thought the details through." "Often she's the only one with the answer, which makes it hard for us to act on our own."

People were confused by Dale's rare but puzzling bouts of anger, which ranged from a disapproving frown to abrupt explosions: "She's been very helpful in regard to my weaknesses, making suggestions and giving positive feedback, but she initially intimidated me. She can look distracted and people think she's disapproving or angry." "If she blows up, she immediately apologizes, and never stays in a foul mood for long." "She doesn't seem to realize her impact. One employee resigned because of the way Dale spoke to him. This person couldn't attend a meeting because of something going on with his mother and Dale made the crack, 'You have to ask your mother?'"

The contradictory behavior of being overtly nice to people most of the time, yet becoming stubborn or occasionally angry and critical, was especially true in Dale's interactions with peers. "She's a global thinker who can connect the dots, and generally she engenders confidence," said one, "so she gets buy-in from us at a high conceptual level. But once she's made sure her vision aligns with the top brass, she goes off on her own course, sometimes to the point of withdrawal, so we don't know how the details are working out, or how it will affect our areas. Then when one of us opposes her at the point of implementation, she moves into a convincing mode that can sometimes degenerate into a temper tantrum instead of her usual ambassador mode. She's an enigma to me." Another commented, "I experience Dale as having a soft quality of really listening, really wanting to learn. But she's very private and I don't have a reference point for her personally. She's hard to get to know. She doesn't engage in constructive confrontation. Instead, she gets stubborn. I've lost patience with her anger. Sometimes it seems to be a game she plays because she gets angry out of the blue, in marked contrast to her usual laid-back style."

"She doesn't engage in constructive confrontation. Instead, she gets stubborn."

Coaching Analysis

Coaching Dale

In their coaching work Mary addressed both Dale's vanilla quality and her anger, which were related. Dale learned that stammering when trying to set a boundary was a signal she was tamping down her feelings. If she failed to attend to these feelings and wishes she would later feel anger, which often appeared without warning. Mary focused on how Dale could express her anger in the moment and be more assertive. Below are some highlights.

The Dormant Volcano

One of Dale's peers commented, "Sometimes it seems to be a game she plays because she gets angry out of the blue." This was not a game Dale played. She told Mary, "When someone suggests something, I'm persuaded, even conciliatory. Afterwards, I feel ambivalent about what I've agreed to, but I don't want to look wishy-washy, so I keep trying to make it work. Then my frustration builds, and before I know it I've blurted out an angry statement. I think to myself, 'Where did that come from?'" In response to the feedback that some of her questions seemed to veil criticism, Dale said: "The power of discipline and structure—and fear—when I was growing up was with my father. There was no way to overtly question any of his ideas. Then I had a teacher in fourth grade who was a tyrant. One day she called me out of a classroom, took me to a dark hall, and said, 'You told some children on the playground that I'm a blabbermouth.' I didn't say that, but she wanted me to admit it and I wouldn't do it, so she kept me in that dark hall all afternoon. I still can't stand to be bossed or to have my wishes ignored."

Dale needed to break this pattern of stubborn silence and give herself permission to feel anger before it erupted unexpectedly. She and Mary explored her physical

Dale and Mary explored Dale's physical reactions and mental states for signs of anger such as anxiety, fatigue, confusion, or ambivalence.

reactions and mental states for signs of anger such as anxiety, fatigue, confusion, or ambivalence. For fieldwork, Dale agreed to sit down at least once a day and fill in the statement, "If something today could have triggered anger, it would be _____." After only a week of this practice, Dale saw how often she tamped down her feelings to get along with people. In the ensuing weeks she became able to talk about her reactions before they reached epic proportions. For example, she described her annoyance with a subordinate who was consistently late to meetings. She rehearsed how to combine knowing what she wanted with a direct request: "Bob, it's a problem for me that you come late to these meetings. I work hard to prepare for them and want you to take my ideas seriously."

Say What You Want and Want What You Get

Dale described her optimistic and receptive style: "Generally, I approach people in a trusting way. I've found a way to work with almost all of the varied people in my life. I've been told I'm a safe harbor. I don't like to be demanding because I feel people do the best they can do." Mary asked Dale what she saw as her weak points. "It's very hard for me to decide what I want," Dale admitted. "I find myself responding to other people's demands a lot of the time. Sometimes I forget to take care of myself. Only yesterday someone asked me to take over their project when I already have almost no space of my own, and I stuttered and stammered before I finally said I couldn't."

Dale learned to figure out what she wanted by asking herself what she did not want, then translating those into statements of what she did want.

Mary asked Dale to take a deep breath whenever she was at the point of agreeing to something, and ask herself, "What do I want?" She encouraged Dale by pointing out that even though she might not give herself an immediate answer, the practice of asking would eventually open up choices for her. Dale also learned to figure out what she wanted by asking herself what she did not want, then translating those into statements of what she did want. She began to make conscious choices about whether to agree with a task, say no, or find someone else to do it. Once she could be clear about her wishes, she also learned to reframe her reactions to organizational changes as a search for alternatives:

- *Clarify* the other's point of view by using open-ended probes.

- *Confirm* by playing back my understanding of the other's values, needs, assumptions, and objectives.

- *Give credit* by focusing first on what I agree with or value about their point of view.

- *Be creative.* Instead of stating my concern as a barrier, construct some outcomes that will alleviate my concern.

Rehearsing these skills contributed to Dale's being more direct with people, which energized her considerably. Within two months, others commented that she was much more dynamic and influential, a positive counterpoint to her earlier vanilla reputation.

Coaching Style Nine

Style Nine is the most peaceful, harmonious, powerful, and sometimes maddening style on the Enneagram. It would be easy to stereotype Dale and others like her as peacemakers and miss the point that the relationship of this Enneagram style to anger is very complex. An exaggerated modesty covers an internal conflict: Nines are polarized between self-effacement and the ensuing anger. That's why their most common coping behavior is passive aggression.

Beware the fury of a patient man.

John Dryden

People often underestimate Nines because of their low-key approach, but a remarkable number of them have been world leaders. You might even say it's a Presidential style in the U.S., including Clinton, Reagan, Ford, Eisenhower, and Lincoln. Some Nines are humble to the point of self-effacement, not owning their power. Someone who worked for Dale said: "She doesn't seem to realize her impact." Dale lacked awareness of both her anger and her power, leading to the resignation of someone to whom she made the passive-aggressive joke, "You have to ask your mother?"

If you offer structure you will find Nines easy to coach, too easy if they are unaware. An in-the-box Nine will go along with whatever you suggest and then often not do it. "I'm so sorry, I forgot," is a common refrain. This is because they will lose themselves in your agenda—even seeking structure from you—then their passive aggressive behavior kicks in. Once you have trust and commitment from your Nine clients, this self-forgetting pattern offers important and useful data that you can use to reflect back how they keep themselves in their own box. Be alert, in particular, when they ask, "What do you think?" Nines need to state their own preferences.

If you offer structure you will find Nines easy to coach, too easy if they are unaware. An in-the-box Nine will go along with whatever you suggest and then often not do it.

Mary's client, Frank, seemed clear in his goal when they first talked: he wanted to be better at addressing upper management, "so that my ideas will be heard." He was very quick to use the Enneagram to pick up others' styles, especially the more aggressive ones, but his reports of conversations always blamed others. They never had time for him, they didn't take his ideas seriously, and they weren't clear enough in their expectations. As he began to see his own part in this pattern—ways in which he held back ideas, sought structure, and criticized others for "keeping him in a box"—he felt overwhelmed and helpless. He wanted easy answers and was not ready to be coached to shift his patterns. But in typical Nine style, Frank didn't tell Mary directly. Instead he kept forgetting to call at the appointed time and forgetting to send a check for the agreed-upon fee. When Mary challenged him to stay with the process he said it would take "too much energy." He had heard his wake-up alarm and hit the drowse button. Two years later, when his job was in jeopardy, he wrote, "I'm ready to work."

We have had several Nine clients who signed up for coaching because someone else suggested they do it. We learned the hard way to get a commitment based on the client's own wants and goals.

We have had several Nine clients who signed up for coaching because someone else—a friend, a spouse, a boss—suggested they do it. We learned the hard way to get a commitment based on the client's own wants and goals. This is not easy and usually cannot be handled directly when beginning to coach a Nine. If you ask, "What do you want?" there will be either a very long silence or an honest, "I don't know." Instead of a "to do" list, we often recommend a "want to do" list for Nines. You can build on a Nine's comfort with consensus by collaborating to help them find their focus.

Nines often know what they don't want, so you can help them work their way to a goal by starting there. For example, Jo reported in her first session with Clarence all the things she did not like about her current work environment. She moved in a positive direction when he asked about each of those dislikes, "So what would that look like if it weren't a problem?" Another way you can encourage Nines to take initiative is to offer some alternatives and let them choose among them. For example: "Would you rather change the way you ask for things, or talk directly to your boss about the problems you see, or write a proposal for improving the work environment?"

Nines can be immobile and indecisive. Your coaching will help them become focused and initiating, while retaining their gift of inclusiveness.

Practices Mediation Naturally

Pay attention to these four habits of in-the-box Ones:

Practices mediation naturally

Presents only a pleasant self

Falls asleep to deepest needs

Tends to minimize difficulties

Serene and centered, out-of-the-box Nines bring cooperation to any situation. They are highly capable of dealing with others' problems and building consensus. They have a natural tendency to honor diversity, and can get along with almost anyone, as Dale did. Their considerable gifts as mediators stem from their ability to see all sides of a question. Because Nines think globally, they can interiorize everyone's side of a conflict and have an intuitive grasp of what it feels like to hold each position, as well as all the strategies and value systems at play. When Mary first learned about the Enneagram, she laughed at the realization that her career as an executive coach had flourished precisely because of her ability to resolve differences among others. She had developed tried and true strategies and handouts—on collaboration, negotiation, and conflict resolution—and was known for her skills in team building, especially when teams had not been getting along.

There is a flip side to this gift. While adept at mediating conflict among others, it is particularly difficult for Nines to take a strong stand for themselves. They can see all points of view. They just have trouble weighing the relative merits. The global thinking that enables them to see all sides now blocks them from choosing any. A particular kind of distractibility goes with this difficulty in taking a stand. Nines habitually allow themselves to be drawn away from their own agenda by a wide variety of distractions: other tasks, momentary impulses, worries, re-arranging furniture or priorities—anything but what they start out to do.

In the same day that Mary became aware of the driving force for her conflict resolution skills, she also noticed for the first time her habit of drifting off from what was important to her. Realizing that she was onto something big, she decided to make a pot of coffee and spend the morning reading more about the Enneagram. She spent the next hour drifting into side projects—the laundry, a call to her mother, searching through yesterday's mail. When she decided to go back to her bedroom and get dressed she saw the Enneagram book lying on her bed and remembered her agenda for the morning.

You will also hear this distractibility in Nines' wandering conversations with you. You may ask a question and have to listen carefully because they will go all over the map. Sometimes they will notice this and may even mutter, "Where was I going with that? Oh, yeah…" A trainer Mary coached would stop during a training session and say, "Where am I?" Not likely to engender confidence in an audience! In-the-box Nines can frustrate people who live or work with them by their vagueness and indecision. They may agree to something and then not do it. They are not faking agreement. They merge so completely with another's wishes that they believe they really agree, just as Dale said: "When someone suggests something, I'm persuaded, even conciliatory." Later they will feel ambivalent, as Dale did, but because of their distaste for confrontation will not bring it up. Instead, they find ways to avoid doing what they have agreed to, or they will do it, then their frustration builds until they begin to dig in their heels.

You will hear distractibility in Nines' wandering conversations with you. You may ask a question and have to listen carefully because they will go all over the map.

Nines often avoid choices by going for consensus. That way everyone gets heard. Tom Condon's *Enneagram Movie and Video Guide* notes that American movies usually stereotype Indian Chiefs as Nines. The American Indian tradition of having every person speak—and not taking action intolerable to anyone—is the hallmark of a Nine culture. Nines typically offer consensus as a type of diffuse and general support. The genius of the consensus approach lies in its inclusiveness. Nines can make everyone feel important (except themselves) as they consider all opinions carefully. If they reach consensus, as they often can with their mediating skills, then everyone is on the same page and everyone works together. They usually manage to snuff out factions by reaching decisions this way. But they still hold onto all these varied points of view, which in Dale's case led her employees and peers to have trouble getting all the necessary details from her. One said, "My guess is that she hasn't thought the details through." In fact, she had thought them all through. She could not choose among them.

We pointed out in the introduction to this section that Nines can learn to choose by first uncovering what they don't want and turning that into an action step. You might say, "You could change the way you ask for things, or talk directly to your boss about the problems you see, or write a proposal for improving the work environment. Which of these is least interesting to you?" You can be more oblique: "If you could choose among these, what might you do?" Or have them practice making arbitrary decisions, starting with something non-threatening.

Have them practice making arbitrary decisions, starting with something non-threatening.

Mary's client Herb began to observe his typical response when friends asked where he wanted to go for dinner. He was surprised to notice how often he said, "Whatever you want is fine with me." He made a list of all the restaurants in town and when a friend called, he'd close his eyes and put his finger down somewhere on the list. "Chinese," he'd say. "I'm in the mood for Chinese food." Nines need to exercise their power to make decisions. It's a good idea to suggest they tell others how they're changing, because unexpected decisiveness may be a shock. "You were always so easy-going," complained one of Herb's friends who didn't know he was working with a coach. "What's gotten into you?" As with any Enneagram style, have your Nine clients set up a system of support to reinforce their new behavior.

Presents Only a Pleasant Self

In her novel *The Green Knight,* Iris Murdoch writes about a woman greatly admired:

> What he saw might have been her pity for him, her sympathy. Or perhaps just her kindness, the way in which, ever after as he watched her, she instinctively made all things better, speaking no evil, disarming hostility, turning ill away, making peace: her gentleness, which made her seem, sometimes, to some people, weak, insipid, dull. "She's not exactly a strong drink!" someone said.

Nines are not exactly a strong drink when it comes to taking a position. In-the-box Nines loathe conflict above all and avoid it masterfully. To state a strong opinion invites disagreement. Becoming involved in a disagreement can be their biggest nightmare. "She doesn't engage in constructive confrontation," said one of Dale's teammates. Dale acknowledged this: "Only yesterday someone asked me to take over their project when I already have almost no space of my own, and I stuttered and stammered before I finally said I couldn't."

Even an evolving Nine may have to overcome inertia in order to disagree. The result can be a more abrupt statement than is necessary because Nines have to push through their tendency to quietly mull things over and not say anything. Mary's client, Tom, told her about a dinner party with church members where a man named Homer said, "I don't think kids are ready to grasp religion until they're in their early teens." Tom retorted: "I have to challenge that! That's too cerebral. I believe that if we live our spiritual lives in the way we love and interact with our children, they will develop faith at an early age based on what we model." Concerned about the ensuing brief silence, Tom then tried to smooth the waters: "But you were probably talking about understanding the philosophy of religion, and I agree with you totally that children need to mature before they can take that in."

Tom's urge to be conciliatory still lingered: "I think he was hurt that I accused him of being cerebral." He wanted to make an apology. Mary asked him how Homer had interacted with him after that conversation. "Well, actually, he asked my opinion about something else. And right before we left, he said he was really glad to have met me." Mary and Tom talked about how, when we act counter to our boxed-in patterns, our ego kicks in and tries to keep us from stretching. Tom's fieldwork for that week was to stay with the discomfort of not being nice. No apologies necessary.

Mary and Tom talked about how, when we act counter to our boxed-in patterns, our ego kicks in and tries to keep us from stretching. Tom's fieldwork was to stay with the discomfort of not being nice. No apologies necessary.

Farther along in coaching, Tom was asked by a very persuasive colleague, Beth, to participate in a conference. Tom liked Beth, felt flattered to be asked, and was all set to agree. But he now knew to buy time to become clear about what he wanted. As he centered on himself he became aware of ambivalence, often a good sign for Nines that they are merging with someone else's agenda. He thanked Beth for asking but said no, explaining what he wanted—to use that time to complete a project important to him.

How a Nine manages conflict—or anything else—will depend a great deal on the context. Nines absorb their environment. They merge and mold with the energy and the values of their surroundings. Their distaste for rocking the boat is evident in their personal lives and extends to their relationship with their company or community. If you have an aggressive, fast-moving company, Nines may merge with that style of operating. If a fast pace isn't required you'll hear the kind of comment made by Dale's boss: "She's easy to be around and a valuable asset in many ways, but she has a kind of 'vanilla' quality." Her consensual approach had worked for her in that company, up to a point.

In-the-box Nines have trouble finishing. In the beginning of a project or assignment, many possibilities and points of view are available. But one choice excludes others. Nines often make a public decision that seems to exclude many other options, but these options still live. When a Nine says, "Yes" a silent, "No" may still be inside waiting for a chance to be heard. Closure requires decisive action and that can feel like judgment day.

Nines may also have trouble asking for something. Clarence's client Ruth wanted to talk to her husband about the lack of spontaneity in their lovemaking, but said she kept finding excuses to put it off: "He just got home from work. This isn't a good time. Maybe after dinner." After dinner she told herself, "He's obviously tired; maybe tomorrow." Ruth had answered the question, "What do I want?" She wanted more intimacy in her marriage. But taking action that might incite an argument was very difficult. "I couldn't feel more reluctant," she told Clarence, "if I were walking the last mile to my own execution."

Nines benefit from developing assertiveness skills. It's a relief for them to discover they can ask for what they want without trampling on others' rights and needs.

Nines go with the flow. This approach works better when they have some temporal room to wiggle, but as deadlines approach, they feel stress. Responsibilities have to be assessed, options have to be winnowed, and they may have to do some prodding. They will fear they're being too pushy. Nines benefit from developing assertiveness skills. They can learn to distinguish between passive, aggressive, and assertive behavior. It's a relief for them to discover they can ask for what they want without trampling on others' rights and needs. They no longer inwardly frame deciding as an issue of keeping the peace or starting a war. They can find or create other options. Nines will also benefit from observing how unnecessarily toxic they consider conflict, and learn to reframe it as neutral. You can suggest that they study conflict resolution texts, because the good ones all start with a counter-argument to their unconscious belief that conflict is bad. Conflict is normal and healthy, and can actually bring people closer together by ferreting out unspoken values, beliefs, and assumptions.

Nines often process information kinesthetically, so in face-to-face contact it is important to be aware of their body language. If their gestures are incongruent with their words (which they often are), they signal inner confusion. Many times you will see them extending their hands and arms as though they are feeling for what they are trying to say. In phone calls, you can listen for signs of confusion or ambivalence in how they express themselves. They may also repeat themselves a lot—evidence that they don't expect to be heard. In either case, calling attention to what you see or hear has a secondary side benefit. They experience being present to someone else, an affirmation on a deep level for Nines that they are not, in fact, invisible. In the beginning you may find them surprised to be noticed. This habit of humble self-forgetting will shift over time as you help them to know themselves. You might say, for example, "You have repeated that idea, with slightly different words, five or six times. I wonder what part of you doesn't expect to be heard."

Notice these clients using the expression, "I found myself living with my mother," or "I find myself (fill in the blank)." This is a sign of their invisibility, even to themselves. In-the-box Nines don't take the initiative. Things just happen. Mary's client, Patsy, opened a coaching call by saying she had been reading Joseph Heller's *Something Happened* and suddenly threw the book across the room. "I don't know why I did that," Patsy admitted. Familiar with the book, Mary suggested that the main character, Bob Slocum, is a Nine to whom things "just happen." Patsy was helped to see how she had identified with Slocum, and hadn't wanted to look into that mirror of her own inertia.

Falls Asleep To Deepest Needs

Out-of-the-box Nines have a natural charming modesty that attracts and empowers those who interact with them. In business they often excel at giving recognition, supporting career paths and goals, and facilitating the personal and professional development of those who work for them. They are natural mentors because they get out of the way so well. They usually will not compete with or be threatened by the initiative of even aggressive young workers.

When in the box, Nines merge with others' preferences and forget theirs, preferring peace and tranquility. Often referred to as *self-forgetting,* they can work mightily in service of someone else's goals.

Nines often flourish in predictable situations. Routine structures feel like support so they don't have to decide anything. All decisions have been made earlier or by

Calling attention to what you see or hear with Nines has a secondary side benefit. They experience being present to someone else, an affirmation on a deep level that they are not, in fact, invisible.

someone else. They get a great deal done on automatic pilot and can split their attention off from what really matters to them. This comfort with structure leaves some Nines quite inflexible. Dale's boss, Sam, described her difficulty with change as a glass half-empty approach. Listen for such comments that others have made to your clients. Many of these will illustrate their Enneagram style.

Nines may go unconscious to their own preferences through repetitive behavior. Keep asking them, "Why are you doing this?"

Sam said of Dale, "Sometimes I think she's just tired." Nines often resist change by manifesting low energy. The absence of enthusiasm can be a clue to their inner resistance. Dale's low energy alone would have enabled many coaches to suspect she's a Nine.

Paradoxically, Nines may suppress their own desires in order to make their fullest contribution to a project or cause. They may consider that to offer their best work, they have to let go of their own wishes. They prefer peace, tranquility, and order to disagreement with how things are going. Highly structured work provides that peaceful order. They may go unconscious to their own preferences through repetitive behavior. Keep asking them, "Why are you doing this?"

In business, Nines can govern by pleasantly administering clear detailed rules and regulations. They typically don't find rules offensive and can offer rules without stirring up resentment. The rules are there for the sake of love and order, to keep peace, to avoid conflict, to minimize confusion (where personal preferences might have to enter), and to create a harmonious environment. Who can fault them for that? But in their quest for harmony they hide their own agenda, especially from themselves. Nines are sensitive to the needs of others—too sensitive at times. They can merge with others' agendas without even realizing it. Nines will excel at surfacing the plans, hopes, and agendas of others, yet may find themselves at a loss to state their own clearly and distinctly. Dale's colleague, Al, as much as he cared for her, admitted, "'Passion' is not a word you'd associate with Dale. For the most part she doesn't inspire excitement." Other, more aggressive styles will find they can't get a bead on a Nine. It's like attacking Jell-O with an axe.

With their non-judgmental, accepting demeanor, people with this Enneagram style often make wonderful coaches and counselors. Carl Rogers, the famed creator of client-centered therapy, was a Nine. The technique of reflective listening is the center of Rogerian therapy.

A psychiatrist once evaluated a young delinquent for a school Clarence worked with and listed all the youth's crimes and times served. But he felt compelled to add: "Despite his many infractions, Billy is unlike most delinquents. He's very likeable and has no hard edges." Nines are often well loved because of their willingness to go along with the demands of their environment. Billy was a Nine. He had gone along with some tougher kids because they offered him a path to follow. Nines can get along almost anywhere. But, as with the young delinquent, they sit on a lot of anger and have trouble handling the anger of others. When Nines listen to everyone, mediate disputes, and put everyone else first, they assume they will be universally loved. Maybe not.

Nines can create precisely the conflicts they try to avoid by their passive aggression. Their own anger is turned in on themselves, so they frequently consider others' expressions of anger improper. Some Nines explode periodically and then quickly get over it and make amends. This was characteristic of Dale: "If she blows up, she immediately apologizes, and never stays in a foul mood for long." Other Nines never get overtly angry but become covertly retaliatory. Take it seriously if one of your Nine clients ruminates excessively on others' misdeeds. If they do not do something up front, they are quite apt to sabotage or ambush the "villain." This was signaled in Frank's conversations that always blamed others in his organization. They never had time for him, they didn't take his ideas seriously, and they weren't clear enough in their expectations. Frank expressed his anger at these perceived slights in oblique and passive ways.

Some Nines explode periodically and then quickly get over it and make amends. Other Nines never get overtly angry but become covertly retaliatory.

If Nines are really in the box, they don't share what they have the most of: knowledge of the complete situation—information, points of view, and suggestions. It's hard to catch them at withholding information, because nobody knows everything they know. The Nines themselves probably don't realize why they're holding back. Keeping others in the dark is a fine passive aggressive strategy in a hostile situation. It also signals fear that if they do not hold back, they may not be able to stay in control of the situation.

Nines can also punish in subtle, passive ways. First, they may refuse to give direction. When they give vague or no directions in a business setting, they hang team members out to dry and create resentment. One of Dale's staff members said, "Ambiguity is our middle name." Being without direction from a Nine supposedly in charge—a manager or a parent, for example—can leave others feeling alone and without resources or guidance to act appropriately. Nines can also let others make all the decisions, then criticize what happens, leaving the other person wondering, "Where were you when we decided on this?" Nines' spouses typically complain that they plan vacations without a word of disagreement, then feel let down when their Nine partner is unhappy with the choice once they get there.

Nines can also be subtly punitive by asking questions that carry an implied criticism they don't even recognize. The people they interact with feel the criticism, but have difficulty engaging in conversation about it, because it is subtle and the Nine can look hurt and say, "I was only asking a question." Or in Dale's case, "I was only joking." A friend described shopping for a small rug with her mother, a very accommodating, humble Nine. Trying to translate her mother's preferences from things not said, or said obliquely, she held up a rug and said, "Mom, this is just what you were looking for!" Her mother asked, "Do you think it has enough grip so it won't slide?" Along with the frown on her mother's face, the message was clear: "I don't like this one."

Your Nine clients may not be aware that they ask questions as a way to avoid stating a dislike directly, which might invite argument. But you will hear them repeating conversations with others that manifest this tendency, and they will ask questions of you that imply a preference. This is both a clue to their Enneagram style in early coaching, and a cue for on-the-spot coaching. You might offer, "You mentioned a course that's been recommended to you, and asked me if I think you should sign up. Even if you don't feel strongly about it, turn that question into a statement of preference." You can also get them to come forth with a decision with the question, "When you ask yourself if you want to take it, what answer do you get?"

Nines may honestly not know how to get on with their lives. When they find out they do not know what they want, it can be a shock to their whole system and they will need your support. On the other hand, you will at times have to make them uncomfortable in order to help them stretch. There is no easy answer about how to hold this balance. When Mary challenged Frank to see his own part in not being heard by upper management (holding back ideas, seeking structure, blaming others), he backed away for two years because of the energy it would take him to ignite that level of initiative. In the beginning, holding up the mirror and collaborating with Nines is the most effective strategy. As their hidden light begins to shine and they gain more confidence in their heretofore hidden strength, they will re-energize themselves by building on their successes.

As their hidden light begins to shine and they gain more confidence in their heretofore hidden strength, they will re-energize themselves by building on their successes.

Tends to Minimize Difficulties

As demonstrated by Frank's reluctance to change his mode of operating, Nines often have a quiet fatalism about what will go wrong or what they can't accomplish. Clarence asked 28-year-old Claude why he got such low grades in school with his 140 IQ. Claude said he remembered the day in the third grade he gave up. He was promised a spot on the fast track in math if he did his homework. He did the homework, he did not get in the fast track, and so he gave up.

A prevailing attitude can be, "It's easy for you to talk, you've got a life." This fatalism stems from a lack of energy to do anything about what might happen if they don't take action. This fatalism also tends to show up in their inability to be proactive. The technical name for this attitude in the scholastic Enneagram tradition is *sloth*. Sloth does not refer to laziness, as laziness is usually understood. It means an unwillingness to take the action needed for spiritual growth. Nines may express this unwillingness by saying they "don't have the energy." When they show lots of energy, activity, and effectiveness in their social world, it is often based on others' criteria. Help your Nine clients notice when high energy is another way of staying asleep to what is important to them: a reluctance to do the one thing they need to do to save their soul, their marriage, their job, their reputation—whatever is in jeopardy.

They can even minimize a life-threatening situation. Clarence coached a Nine who was substantially overweight. When the matter of his weight was brought up, he casually stated that he thought he would wait until he had a heart attack! An extremely bright man, he had shrunk the menace of a heart attack to a bridge he would cross if and when he came to it. The move from "no big deal" to something that has to be dealt with is a matter of waking up.

One way Nines put themselves to sleep is by minimizing. When they define a large concern as a small one, they admit the problem but deny the size of it, and still may not address it. Minimizing is a mode of what Enneagram theory describes as putting oneself to sleep: *narcoticization*. Minimizing fits right in with eating, drinking, working, and sleeping too much. All of these are oblique ways of dozing through problems Nines can't find the inner will to address. You'll hear your Nine clients make comments such as, "Oh, it's O.K., it doesn't matter that much." Dale's parents had ignored her, even when she took up golf to be with her father. Remember her comment when Mary asked how she had felt as a child: "I realized that's how things were and figured there was no use getting upset about it." Here is perhaps the ultimate example of minimizing:[1]

> Alone on Foal Island and waiting, Nathan Staples turned on his bed... A familiar lack was stitching up his arms and then climbing further to jab at his brain. All psychosomatic, he knew, all self-inflicted, but all inescapable just the same. He exhaled with care, sidestepping the start of a sigh. Audible despair depressed him, most especially his own.

[1] A.L. Kennedy, *Everything You Need*

But things could, most assuredly, be worse.

The Persian Eye Cups, for example… They'd prise back my eyelids and bed the cups right down… I would try to claw. But then I'm quite sure that they'd have their way with me, irrigate each cup with the correct corrosive dose and watch it bite…

Which would be worse—of course it would.

As Nathan Staples did, your Nine clients may compare themselves to someone who's in worse circumstances. By comparison, they're in fine shape: I felt sorry for myself because I had no shoes until I met someone who had no feet. Alcoholic Nines will compare themselves favorably to drug addicts: "At least I don't do drugs." The comparison shrinks the size of the problem. The overweight executive Clarence coached was deeply concerned about his son's weight, "because he is so young to be fat." The unwritten subtext was that being overweight goes with getting older. Nothing to be concerned about when it occurs later in life.

"I was hurt when my boss joked with me about how slow I am," said one client, "but that's O.K., he jokes with everybody." "My wife was angry with me to the point where I numbed out," said another, "but I couldn't argue because her points were well taken." In truth, no one else can discount us unless we accept their opinion without challenge. Nines fear being discounted, but feeling discounted becomes an inner steady state. Out of their drive to keep the peace, they unwittingly invite being overlooked. Because they withhold opinions or challenges, others come to expect that Nines will go along with them and tend not to take a Nine's tentative suggestions seriously. Notice that after Tom challenged Homer over dinner, Homer asked Tom's opinion about something else.

The greatest gift you can give Nines is the awareness of their own value to the world. Help them see how they minimize their own importance when they minimize difficulties. This can bring about a huge shift that excites and energizes them. You might suggest that they keep a journal, noticing when they feel overlooked or overlook themselves.

Nines often freeze when asked, "What do you do?" or "Tell me about yourself." Even successful Nines are somewhat ill at ease talking about themselves, especially to someone new. It helps to probe for how they don't want to be when talking about themselves. A Nine said: "I hate it when someone brags. I don't want to be that way." This is an either/or position. The client felt that either she would have to discount herself or she would be an aggressive braggart.

The greatest gift you can give Nines is the awareness of their own value to the world. Help them see how they minimize their own importance when they minimize difficulties.

Coach your clients to create a continuum with more options. You might, for example, reframe "bragging" as "self-referencing." Then ask them to collaborate with you to create a scale of self-referencing, using their own terminology. The Nine mentioned above created a scale that ranged from *Too Humble* to *Self-Referencing* to *Self-Promoting* to *Total Obnoxious Showboat.* As fieldwork she observed others who seemed comfortable talking about themselves and ranked them on her scale. From those who seemed self-referencing or even appropriately self-promoting, she created a model for self-presentation that stretched her without the fear of being overbearing.

Coach Nines to create a continuum with more options so they have a model for self-presentation that stretches them without the fear of being overbearing.

The Nine's Vision: Shift from being immobile and indecisive to being focused and initiating; they remain inclusive while remembering their own agenda

Dale said in one of her last coaching calls with Mary, "I feel as if I have new blood coursing through my veins!" This was not due to a transfusion. Dale's heart had been pumping life into her all along, but at such a slow rate that her own initiative wasn't getting enough exercise. This is somewhat like Yogis who decrease their heart rate to the point where they can be buried alive for long periods of time.

Nines who wake up to themselves no longer avoid being visible in the world. When they break through their habitual patterns, they have no trouble taking decisive and appropriate action. They unleash all the energy that has been tamped down. While maintaining their inclusive, collaborative style, they also take appropriate credit, sell themselves and their ideas with vigor, and stay focused on what they want without being distracted by others' agendas.

Connecting the Dots

An Overview

You're about to complete your introductory meeting with a potential client and it's time to "close the sale." Right? No. Getting someone to pay you for your work is not your primary goal in a good coaching session. You will be more authentic and useful to your clients if you fully engage with them. Whether you seek commitment at the beginning or want them to renew their coaching contract, your goal is to build a compelling relationship.

People will hire you because they experience you as competent and caring, and—most important—because you take a step in the very first session to open up their inner universe. They will continue with you because you mirror their patterns and suggest fieldwork that changes the way they understand the problems that brought them to you. You were introduced to the language of change in Chapter Two and have seen ways to bring about second-order change in the nine case studies and analyses of each Enneagram style.

As you become competent in this powerful approach, you will find that most of your clients quickly gain insights, make dramatic shifts in their worldview, and accomplish significant change within a period of months. On rare occasions, you may coach someone whose needs evolve and who gains substantially from continuing with you for a year or two. Even when the desired breakthroughs occur in a shorter period of time than is possible in traditional coaching, your clients will be grateful for your significant help, and a transformed client provides a number of referrals.

In this and the next chapter we will specify how to help clients break free of their self-imposed limitations and significantly affect their behavior: how to partner with your clients, how to listen to and be part of their world, how to use everything that comes up (even resistance), and how to be relentlessly optimistic.

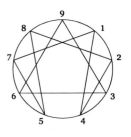

We'll review the detailed techniques of our coaching approach in Chapter Thirteen. In this chapter, we concentrate on how to give potential clients the opportunity to convince themselves they want to hire you. In an introductory meeting you want to get the facts, highlight their needs, imply some solutions, and expect a positive response from them:

In an introductory meeting you want to get the facts, highlight their needs, imply some solutions, and expect a positive response.

- Answer their questions about your coaching experience and style, but put most of your emphasis on their experience of you as a coach.

- Be fully present, ask questions, and listen closely. Draw out their description of a problem until it is specific. Heighten their awareness of the problem, then lead them to a shift in perspective, an "aha" moment.

- Mirror back a shift of any degree ("That was a long pause and a sigh... something got to you there?"), then refer back to it as the call comes to a close ("I've noticed a couple of times that something has hit home for you—a realization that you sometimes haven't stood up for yourself, some new thoughts on what has triggered your anger").

- Use open-ended questions that assume they will work with you ("How do you see yourself benefiting from continued coaching?").

- If they haven't convinced themselves within the allotted time, but they're close, extend the call a bit. People naturally fear change and may wait to bring up a key issue until they think there won't be time to deal with it!

Mary's client, Bill, got to the crux of an issue with only five minutes left on the initial call—anger toward the people he worked with. Mary deepened his experience of his anger by asking, "Give me an example of the most recent time you felt angry. What was that anger like for you?" She broadened his awareness of his anger by asking, "What other situations have triggered your anger? How has it shown up differently with different people?" Mary then showed Bill how to work with his feelings in a healthy way instead of stifling them or blowing up. When she asked, "How shall we move forward from here?" (a positive expectation) Bill paid for three months in advance.

Sowing the Seeds

Think of your initial meeting with a client as an invitation to grow. You do this by laying the groundwork, unearthing fertile soil, and sowing the seeds of change.

Get the Facts

Ask questions that will give you answers about their situation. Go deep enough to identify opportunities for growth. For example, Clarence probed for more facts from a potential client, Derek: "You mentioned in your e-mail that your goal is to be the kind of person who appears on Oprah Winfrey. Describe that kind of person. How are you different?" Derek replied, "Well, I think of somebody who's a great motivational speaker, like Stephen Covey. I have great thoughts, too, but there's a block that keeps me from bringing my intelligence forward."

Ask questions that will give you answers about their situation. Go deep enough to identify opportunities for growth.

What Derek stated as "a block" points out an *unmet* desire. Sometimes clients describe their coaching need as a *problem,* as Lesley did when she told Mary, "I need to get more business in the next two months or I'm going to go bankrupt." Mary thought, "Ouch. That's not much time to help her do what's necessary." But Mary trusted that if she listened well she would be able to help. To get more facts, Mary asked, "What do you see as your challenges?" Lesley responded, "In other markets I've been successful in turning cold calls into leads. But this market is based on whom you know, so I've had trouble even getting in the door to make my pitch." Lesley's perception of the problem was a good start, but Mary kept asking questions until she saw Lesley's Enneagram pattern more clearly.

Clients may know their Enneagram style. If so, you can ask, "How have those patterns shown up for you?" and learn how their style plays out. Keep in mind the low side of their style as the source of possible problems, and what resources their high side offers. You can also use the Enneagram to guide your work if they don't know their style, or even if they aren't interested in the Enneagram.

Clients may know their Enneagram style. If so you can learn how their style plays out. You can also use the Enneagram to guide your work if they don't know their style.

Derek, for example, didn't know the Enneagram. But he said he hoped to be on the Oprah show and described someone he envied (he didn't say he was envious; Clarence sensed it from his words and the tone of his voice), so Clarence suspected Derek was a more introverted or withdrawing style, probably a Four (envy is central to the Four style), but possibly a Nine or a Five. Clarence dug a little deeper: "Tell me more about that." Derek said, "I have so many ideas, but I seem to be a little out of phase with the world, and I get tired of trying." This was another clue that he might be a Four—they often feel they're from another planet. Clarence used this as a working hypothesis and continued unearthing the facts: "Have you held your ideas back assuming people weren't ready for them, or have you offered your ideas and found no one's interested, or has it been something else?"

Lesley, who was having trouble getting in the door to market her business, knew of the Enneagram but said that she was "confounded by her test results." She thought she was either a Five or an Eight. She added, "My vision was that I could get enough business by force of intention." Mary listened to Lesley's language. "Force of intention" sounded Eight-like. But "confounded" is a word more likely to be used by a Five. Mary listened further to Lesley's tone of voice, pauses, and pace of speech. Lesley continued, "In the longer run I want to have the option not to work, to get more into my spiritual practice." Notice two things: Eights— who fear being vulnerable—would not readily discuss their spirituality during an initial call, though it's possible if they're very self-aware. Besides, Lesley's statement completely separated spiritual practice from work, which points to a Five's tendency to compartmentalize. Her words were thoughtful. She paused at some length to think through answers to Mary's questions. At this point it seemed clearer to Mary that Lesley might be a Five. Mary didn't pour this in concrete. She simply operated from it as a possibility.

All the questions that we suggest to open a coaching relationship are open-ended.

Notice that both Clarence and Mary asked open-ended questions to encourage elaboration. If you operate from a sales mentality, you will gear all questions to get one answer—the answer you want. In contrast, all the questions that we suggest to open a coaching relationship are open-ended.

In Lesley's case, the question, "Do you have a mission statement?" would be closed. "Tell me about your mission statement" would be more open, though it could still get a short answer, especially if Lesley didn't have a mission statement or didn't yet see the value of having one (we've heard clients say, "I never bothered to write it down," or "I put mine in the drawer a year ago and forgot about it"). Mary said, instead, "Tell me what you think your business contributes in your industry." Lesley answered this open-ended statement in detail with facts Mary needed to understand Lesley's situation.

Highlight Needs

Slant your fact-gathering a little to make sure you – and they – are aware of the extent of their needs that could be resolved.

Once you have identified a problem area, you want to heighten clients' perception of their need. We're not suggesting that you make them feel worse, only that you slant your fact-gathering a little to make sure you — and they — are aware of the extent of their needs that could be resolved. Their awareness creates more options for both of you. Also, you'll begin to see glimmers of solutions that working with you could offer. But it's not yet time to share your insights. Keep asking questions that deepen and broaden the field.

Derek, who wanted to be more like Covey, said, "I have so many great ideas, but they're not embraced and then I get tired and drop them, switch to something else before I reach success." Clarence's deepening questions included, "When people haven't embraced your ideas, what have you thought the rejection is based on?" And, "Describe your experience of having been tired." Clarence also asked a broadening question, "How has feeling tired affected the rest of your life?" And even broader, "In what other ways have you felt blocked?"

With Lesley, whose business was in danger of going bankrupt, Mary asked this deepening question: "Tell me more about the trouble you've had getting in the door to talk to clients." Mary's broadening question was, "How else has your business been jeopardized?" Then, a very broad question: "What else has been going on in your life and work that you would like to talk about?"

We'll elaborate on how to focus on solutions in Chapter Thirteen, but the short version is this: Speak of problems in the past, solutions in the present and future. Notice the past tense in, "Describe your experience of having been tired," "Tell me more about the trouble you've had getting in the door to talk to clients," "What was that anger like for you?"

Imply Solutions

Once you have the facts and have heightened the needs that coaching can satisfy, begin to imply solutions. For example, in answer to Mary's questions about Bill's goals for change, he offered, "I would like to go in and *make my case* in a non-emotional way. When people think, 'You're a raving maniac,' they don't *give me credibility*."

As Mary dug for more facts, deepened and broadened Bill's perception of need, he added the following: "I can be very expressive and may be over the top in my enthusiasm. My optimistic side has enabled me *to bring people along with my ideas,* but sometimes I'm *overly harsh in my criticism*. I'm particularly likely to get angry *with people I don't respect*."

The phrases in italics above contained the seeds of Bill's wish to change. Mary reflected in a way that implied a solution for him: "So, when you are enthusiastic without being angry or critical—even with people you don't respect—you will be more credible, better able to make your case, and bring people along with your ideas." Notice the present and future-oriented language in the implied solution.

Once you have the facts and have heightened the needs that coaching can satisfy, reflect back in a way that implies a solution. Speak of problems in the past, solutions in the present and future.

Reinforce Signs of Breakthrough

Think of your initial conversation as a process, not a linear, sequential set of steps. You may go back and forth between getting the facts, highlighting needs, and implying solutions. It's especially important to reinforce signs of breakthrough as they happen.

In person-to-person coaching, you'll see signs of a shift: their body might relax, they may sit up and look at you more directly, or smile, or look confused. On the phone, you can hear verbal and nonverbal signs. In both cases the client may tell you clearly, "That's a good question," meaning, "I've never asked myself that question," or, "I've never thought of it that way." A small shift. Respond in a way to reflect the possibilities that working with you offers: "So that's a new insight for you."

It's especially important to reinforce signs of breakthrough as they happen. Respond in a way to reflect the possibilities that working with you offers.

The most frequent signal of an "aha" moment over the phone is a perceptible pause in response to a question, often accompanied by a sigh. Sometimes their voice gets noticeably quieter or slower. Or maybe the client laughs. Appropriate laughter is often a sign of insight that you can reinforce. Inappropriate laughter is also a good cue. Perhaps the person laughs bitterly while talking about feeling discouraged. That opens an opportunity to do some brief coaching then and there. If you're not sure what's going on, ask.

In response to Mary's questions about his anger, Bill relived a recent meeting. As he got into the details, Mary could hear him breathing harder into the phone. After mirroring back the thoughts and feelings he described, she joked, "Now let's stop and talk about your heavy breathing." He laughed, asking, "Was it that obvious?" He then shared his sudden realization of how frightened he was of his own anger. Both his laughter and his insight were signs of a breakthrough, and an opportunity to do some on-the-spot coaching.

Of all the ground they'd covered, working with his anger and fear seemed most likely to bear some fruit and help him experience Mary's coaching style. She laughed with him and said, "Sometimes in talking with someone like me, you'll discover things about yourself that might otherwise remain hidden." Mary asked him to keep breathing raggedly, to find the place in his body where he most experienced the fear, and to name it. "It's in my stomach," he said, "like a balloon that's expanding gradually, about to explode." "Make it expand a little," she suggested, "then watch it begin to deflate. Tell me when you feel that shift."

Presuppose Positive Outcomes

In the example above, notice Mary's language: "Sometimes in talking with someone like me, you'll discover things about yourself that might otherwise remain hidden." She reinforced his discovery and at the same time spoke in a way that implied he would continue with coaching. We refer to this as a presupposition. This is highly influential language. When harnessed, presuppositions create a self-fulfilling expectation of change. For example, Mary suggested that Bill make the balloon in his stomach "expand a little, then watch it begin to deflate." She added, "Tell me when you experience that shift." When, not if. Of course he did experience a physical shift as she suggested he would.

Presuppositions are statements or questions that create a self-fulfilling expectation of change. This is highly influential language.

While an immediate outcome of an interaction this powerful may be the decision to hire you, your positive expectations set the client on a course of change, without or without you. You have given a valuable gift.

It will be easier to refrain from "asking for the sale" if you see yourself and your potential clients as co-creating outcomes with mutual advantage. Offer honest appreciation for what they have added to your day, such as, "Thank you for being willing to try that exercise. I feel touched by your reactions." Or, "Wow, I'm impressed with your readiness to dive in." Then review what they've gained from your time together. Mary summarized to Bill, "You've had some insights about the fear behind your anger, and a chance to experience a shift in your feelings from working with me today." Most often, clients will agree with this kind of specific observation, as Bill did: "I had no idea we could get this far in a single session."

Then you can suggest (not ask) that the client continue. Do this with a presuppositional question, one that embeds a positive expectation, however subtle: "How shall we move forward?" or, "What else would help you decide to work with me?"

Respond Creatively to Concerns

If clients aren't ready to decide at this point, they will raise concerns. We mentioned earlier that factors outside of their experience of you as a coach may influence their decision to continue or not.

Some Enneagram styles have trouble making decisions on the spot. In-the-box Nines are notorious for this. They don't know what they want. Fives typically want time to think it over. Sixes may set their self-opposition in motion and be unable to trust they're making the right decision. Use your knowledge of the Enneagram to help them through this.

You can also use a simple creativity technique when clients raise concerns:

- **Clarify the facts, even broaden and deepen their concern** (this takes faith on your part, since their concern is now about hiring you). At the end of their first call, a potential client named Shelly told Clarence, "I've gotten a lot out of this session and I'd like to work with you, but my children are home for the summer and I know I won't have time. Besides, I like to relax with them, take the summer off. I'd rather start with you in the Fall."

- **One of the generic boxes that people carry around with them is either/or thinking.** In an interior monologue, shift into both/and thinking. Clarence thought, "Shelly is assuming that either she has time for coaching or time with her children. Actually, it's possible to both have her children at home *and* find time for coaching."

- **As you confirm the client's thoughts and feelings, roll concerns into a statement of possibility.** Think of "X" as the problem and "Y" as the possibility. Ask, "How can you do both X and Y?" Clarence asked Shelly, "How can you sustain the momentum you gained in this session while still relaxing with your kids?"

When clients raise concerns, clarify the facts, identify either/or thinking, and roll their concerns into a statement of possibility.

The example above illustrates a common barrier: other demands on a client's time. Financial concerns are another reason people balk at making a commitment to coaching. If they bring up cost as an issue, chances are that one of two scenarios is in operation:

- **They knew coming in that they had financial constraints but hoped the session would be of such value, they'd find the money somehow—** perhaps rethinking their budget. If this is the case, then raising money as a barrier could be an excuse to avoid saying your process didn't match their expectations. You can check this out by asking an open-ended question: "Tell me two things you wanted in this session that have not yet happened." No matter how good you are it simply isn't possible to always meet everyone's needs. If they are disappointed but don't say so, they aren't ready to tell the truth and may not be coachable at this point. Be willing to let go.

- **They really want to work with you.** You can presume a positive outcome by saying, "You've said you feel really good about some significant insights and you'd like to continue with me to build your business, but you're feeling a financial pinch. So let's think about that together. How can we move forward in a way that makes coaching a value to your business?" Notice that we don't recommend saying, "What will be the losses to you if you don't invest in coaching?" Keep your emphasis on possibilities. If your instinct tells you they're just too broke, suggest free services you know about such as SCORE[1] for business development, other people with whom they might barter coaching, or other resources in their own community. This is honorable, and will be appreciated. You never know how this good deed will circle back to you. We have also on occasion tailored our services to offer options that fit a variety of budgets.

The question, "How can we move forward in a way that makes coaching a value to your business?" presumes a positive outcome.

At any rate, all you can do is be the best coach you know how to be, offer your honest opinion about what a client can accomplish with you, and then be willing to let go if it's not the right time or the right match.

Out of the Box Coaching

Not only clients get stuck in boxes. So do coaches. Each Enneagram style has a corresponding coaching style that will be intuitive and comfortable—and will have certain areas that require breaking out of your own box. Remember the Nine-Dot Problem where you're asked to connect nine dots with only four straight lines?

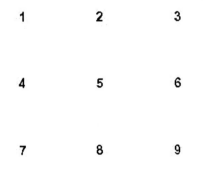

We've used numbers instead of dots so this riddle can serve as a metaphor for you as a coach: how to go beyond the limitations of Enneagram habits—yours as well as clients'. Many people who see this puzzle for the first time can't figure out how to connect all nine points with four straight lines because they assume they must stay within the visually implied box. There is no box in the diagram, as you can see, but our generic worldview is one of boxes. The only way to solve this problem is to go outside the box, in this case by creating four lines that extend past the numbers:

[1] Service Corps of Retired Executives

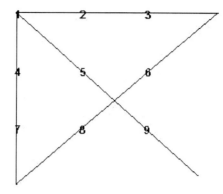

Your clients can step out of their habitual patterns; so can you, whether in the initial call or during the coaching process. The Enneagram tells you, with more detail and precision than you may find comfortable, what kind of box you may be in. Every Enneagram style is the over-use of a gift. What is your gift and how do you over-use it? Use other styles as models—how people motivate, challenge, unite, support, protect, and advise others. You will unearth a whole treasure chest of differing approaches. Each approach will at least partially teach you how you can coach outside of your own box. Compare your approach to the eight others, become more self-aware, and notice how the Enneagram points to your growing edge.

Our generic worldview is one of boxes. Your clients can step out of their habitual patterns; so can you.

Ones

Ones are great at holding clients to demanding standards. If you watch Ones coach, the experience may remind you of your best and strictest teacher. They criticize with surgical precision. Watch how helpful exact feedback can be, especially when balanced with the healthy One's infectious idealism, which can bring out the best in their clients. They model how to hold a vision of what's possible. On the other hand, these coaches are apt to take some of the pressure off the need for individual change and shift it to how to function within the system. This is fine for first-order change, but if you're a One you may need to hold your focus to your clients' transformational needs. If you have a set of standards that you want your clients to meet, you'll find yourself trying to convince clients what they ought to do. Because you are highly motivated to do what's right, you may wrongly assume that the same motive will energize your clients. This can be a turn-off, especially in the introductory call, when they can't yet hear the caring behind the criticism. Threes, for example, do not respond to the slogan, "Virtue is its own reward."

If you're a One, you may find yourself trying to convince clients what they ought to do.

They will want to see some kind of tangible reward, perhaps only recognition from you or others for their efforts. If you stay within your box, you're apt to think of clients like these as less than noble.

Twos

When you watch Twos, you'll notice first the emotional support they offer. They are attuned to the other's every mood, spoken and unspoken, and they know what to say to support a struggling client. Notice, too, how accepting and understanding they are. Clients are sure that the coach is on their side. Listen to Twos' advice on networking, diplomacy, and motivation. These are what they do best. If you are a style Two, you think coaching is a great idea. You've been helping people all your life and now they're paying you for it! And you know just what a client needs. You have this little irritation—not large, you understand—when they won't do what is good for them. You're such a wonderful listener you may feel sure they owe obedience to your suggestions for the time you spent in rapt attention. You may have to be a little clever, even devious, but they will realize you have their best interests at heart. Maybe. The temptation for the Two is to manipulate people into doing what you think they need. You may especially be tempted to do this to get them to hire you. And if you're really in your box, you will make them dependent on you and your marvelous suggestions. Watch for your conviction in the initial session that what they really need is *you*.

The temptation for the Two is to manipulate people into doing what you think they need.

Threes

Even if your relationship with clients is going well, you may still need to sharpen your skills in how to set goals and objectives, measure progress, and help your clients get the results they need. If so, go see a style Three in action. And we mean action. Threes know their clients want measurable results and that's the Three's specialty. Threes can help their clients act effectively. These coaches will also anticipate what behavior will get you in trouble or get you applause. Few coaches are more in tune with the corporate culture than Threes, but they can also be models for making rapid progress with personal goals. If you can't find a live Three to model from, read some books on time management. They are usually advice on how to be good Threes, written by Threes for Three aspirants. If you are a Three, you probably assume the standard motivation of fame and fortune at the top of the heap. You believe that if you play your role well you'll succeed. This doesn't work for many of your clients, even when they say they want to do a good job. You may not leave nearly enough room for the subjective and interior dimensions of life (go to Fours for this inspiration). You will have to work hard

Pay attention to the process if you're a Three, rather than focusing, laser-like, on the goals.

to get inside the world of your clients, especially in the initial session, when your every molecule is screaming, "Get the sale! Get the sale!" Pay attention to the process rather than focusing, laser-like, on the goals. You may also need to work on your tendency to define your own success by clients' approval. Really good drivers dim their headlights so others can see by theirs. Let your clients shine.

Fours

Now watch some Four coaches. Healthy Fours trust their take on things without losing sight of the client's novel circumstances. Notice their empathy. It gives clients faith that they're in good hands while they experiment with innovative approaches to their problems. Nobody appreciates subjectivity like Fours. They are masters of the unique: this jacket is *you,* this job only *you* can do; forget the system, do what feels right inside. They have intuitive insight into the individual, as opposed to understanding the system the way a One or a Three might. "Objectively, Beethoven was the greatest. But subjectively Tchaikovsky is perfect for you because you're a Four and so is he." That kind of appreciation of the individual is the gift of the Four. Notice how these coaches are careful never to make their clients an example of a trend. Four coaches will teach you how to follow the book as far as you need to, then put it down gracefully and address the client's unique self and situation. If you're a Four, you may try too hard in the first call to come up with daring and original solutions to impress clients as the most creative of coaches. Later in the process, you may find their mundane concerns a bit boring. You may not pay enough attention to the real criteria clients have to face. Others' expectations may be terribly important to them and you might have trouble seeing why other people's standards are such a big deal. After all, one should work according to one's own lights. You have to establish trust before clients can appreciate your unusual approach.

Fours may try too hard to come up with daring and original solutions to impress clients.

Fives

Look in on Fives, the master planners. Watch how they allow plenty of time to think things through. Clients who are coached by a Five know that everything they say will be noticed and reflected on. Pay attention to how well Fives prepare. They will have notes and comments from last time, possible references, and resources. They will have relevant useful information and the session planned out quite thoroughly in their heads. Then see how objective and balanced is their advice. For cool wisdom, you can't beat a Five. If you are a Five, you might be surprised when clients don't use information you give them. You know, in your head of heads, that information is the key to solutions. If that's the way you think about it,

If you're a Five you might have trouble helping someone work through a block that is primarily emotional.

you might have some trouble understanding that the process of helping someone work through a block can be primarily emotional. Even in the initial call, their emotional state is important information. Counter your tendency to sell them on your expertise. Good coaches form an emotional alliance that is an understanding of deep mutual trust. You can learn much from all the other styles, but especially from the healthy Two's emotional intelligence. You may also need to be feistier, more connected with others, at which Sixes can excel.

Sixes

If you don't like trouble (or troubling emotional interaction), spend some time with talented Sixes. Look closely, and you'll see they look closely too—at what could possibly go wrong. They look at every process, every decision, and every person or idea to see what might be dangerous or stupid or expensive. If you want to learn how to avoid problems by thinking of them ahead of time, watch them do it with amazing thoroughness. They help clients discover all the things they have to watch out for to make sure their ideas work. They will also doubt or challenge much of what the client says, so the client can become more honest and self-aware during the process. This is a gift in on-going coaching. If you're a Six, though, you may have trouble trusting your client's information. You are naturally suspicious, so it may be difficult for you to see things from their point of view. No matter what information they give you, you can use it as a starting point for coaching. Whatever they say is grist for the mill. Your natural sorting for what can go wrong may make you too critical of what they're doing, a particular hazard when you haven't yet signed them up. When asking questions, try not to sound like you're giving the third degree. In a corporate environment, you may have a tendency to blame the authorities for whatever is wrong and not give clients enough credit for having the power to change the situation. You may also doubt yourself, holding to some ideal of coaching expertise, believing that you won't otherwise have credibility. Learn to trust your own common sense. Trust your "Sixth" sense as well: your antennae have been finely tuned; use them!

You're naturally suspicious if you're a Six, so you may have trouble trusting your client's information.

Sevens

It may be fun to learn from Sevens because their gift is turning hard work into play. They offer all sorts of interesting suggestions, and frequently use humor. While clients have a good time with a Seven's anecdotes and aphorisms, they learn and change. Appropriate one technique that Sevens use especially well: positive reframing. They will show you how to stand a situation on its head—how to start a salvage company out of a car wreck. You can change a lot of situations by simply changing the way you look at and think about them. In an initial call, this can be an advantage because potential clients will be excited about the possibilities. If the coach is not self-aware, however, reframing can be a way to influence clients to buy into the coach's dream instead of their own. As a Seven, your way of doing this will be different from Twos—you'll see yourself at times leading with charm, carrying them along with your enthusiasm instead of using the client's resources. Because you're such a good storyteller you may forget to listen (see what Fives have to offer) or to pay attention to potential problems (learn this from Sixes). Notice your temptation to make clients happy, not better. In fact, you may not be willing to confront them about destructive approaches they take (Eights are your models here). Your natural aversion to pain, especially conflict, may prompt you to overly accentuate the positive. You work extremely well with first-order change, but might camouflage the need for second-order change.

If a Seven, your aversion to pain, especially conflict, may prompt you to overly accentuate the positive.

Eights

Eights are responsible and hold their clients accountable. Notice how they don't let anyone get away with flimsy excuses. Nobody confronts like an Eight. Rationalizations, half-efforts, careless follow though—none of those get by an Eight. Many of us have trouble calling people on their games. It's the gift of Eights. Learn from them. You can also learn from them the importance of passion. They fire up everyone with their own gusto. When an Eight coaches you, you will want to win, however you define *winning*. If you're an Eight, pay attention to your potential down side: you may forget to listen and instead try to bolt down clients' commitment based on what you think they ought to do. Eights can be surprised at how much listening is involved in persuasion. Remember to listen—especially in your initial call—even though you think you have a pretty clear idea of what must be done; even if it irritates you when someone pussy-foots around the problem, wallows in self-pity, or cowers in fear. You will have an urge to tell them to stop whining, get to work, and let the chips fall where they may. If you have to hold their hands for a while, you may have a tendency to scorn them for it. It may be difficult for you to enter into a strong relationship with someone you consider weak.

An Eight may try to bolt down clients' commitment based on your idea of what must be done.

Nines

Let's say you're a bit rigid. You're an uptight Six, a scolding One, or a toggle-switch thinker like some Eights. If you want to learn how to be flexible, watch Nines at work. Notice how they support their clients at every turn. Notice how able they are to assimilate the client's views into their own conclusions. Notice how carefully they listen. Watch how they implement the notion of partnership on an emotional level. You'll have to be alert, because they are smooth. They have no hard edges; they don't alienate. If you yourself are a Nine, you may be too nice. You will be fine identifying with clients and their struggles, but when it comes to insisting they go beyond their comfort zone, you may assume that all you have to do is unconditionally support them. You may have trouble bringing the initial call to a close. You may also find it difficult to call people on the games they're playing. You're able to merge so fully with their agenda that you don't see the agenda that troubles them. Your contribution is a separate set of eyes and filters and experiences, but you may forget those and adopt the clients'. During coaching you will have more time to self-adjust. Observe yourself—notice if you fail to keep your boundaries clear or to hold clients to their vision.

For Nines, notice if you fail to keep your boundaries clear or to hold clients to their vision.

Best of All

In the coaching process we are about to introduce, a good challenge for you is to embody the best of all the nine styles:

1. Be idealistic, focused on possibilities;

2. show your clients unconditional positive regard;

3. co-create outcomes in partnership with your clients;

4. treat each client as unique and use your own unique gifts;

5. balance your wise observations with emotional contact;

6. trust your inner guidance and take risks;

7. set free your spontaneity, inventiveness, playfulness;

8. be responsible and hold your clients accountable; and

9. put one foot into the client's world while keeping one foot in your own.

Coaching: An Inside Job

Each coach and each client is slightly different, so coaching is an art, not merely a body of information, a quiver of techniques, or even a set of skills. It is a partnership in which you use whatever resources of mind and heart and spirit you have to help your clients help themselves. Coaching is most effective when it begins from within you and reaches within your client. Knowledge of the Enneagram will enable you to refine and augment your existing resources.

You already use various successful coaching strategies: checklists, assumptions, standard probing questions, and intervention tools. So do we, and we encourage you to keep doing what works. As you learn to coach with the Enneagram, you will find that you don't have to unlearn anything. You will become more familiar with the characteristics of each style, and develop x-ray vision to see why certain behaviors are so difficult to understand, alter, or erase.

Spontaneous change occurs when perceptions no longer fit a worldview or actually contradict it. Some of your clients will have already experienced significant change — perhaps the result of a peak experience, a crisis, or an experience of unconditional love. They have seen something in a radically new light or behaved in a totally different way. But there is no reason to wait for spontaneous change to happen. You can encourage similar shifts by integrating our methods into your current coaching practices.

We have emphasized the difference between first-order change (solving a problem within someone's worldview) and second-order change (altering the worldview). You understand why it won't significantly change Eights, for example, only to teach them communication techniques such as active listening or principled negotiation. They may benefit from those changes — they might intimidate less, perhaps. But without second order change, they could still see the world as a battlefield — an outlook that excludes admitting vulnerability and burdens them

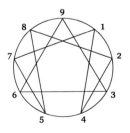

with responsibility. Instead of making a shift to spontaneous compassion, they might use these communication techniques as a new way to conquer and control.

Our approach is not always linear. We use examples, stories, symbolic behaviors, and metaphors. We know you will use them creatively in ways we cannot foresee nor prescribe. But even poetry has principles. We offer you three that might help:[1]

- **Acknowledge and Validate the Client's Worldview:** Transformational change is more likely to occur in a coaching relationship where there is deep rapport—where clients feel known. Knowing someone's inner world gives you both insight and compassion. Paradoxically, clients will be more open to change when they feel accepted exactly as they are. Once they have that assurance, you can help them realize how they create their worldview and how to change it.

- **Help Shift The Client's Worldview:** Many clients come to you having tried to avoid or overcome something they don't like about themselves. You will release energy for change if you suggest they pay attention to the patterns of thought and behavior you highlight for them. After that, look for inventive ways to help them alter the patterns they observe.

- **Focus on Solutions, Tapping Their Resources, Experience, and Ideas:** Our coaching and writing focuses on solutions. Sometimes a solution focus means merely encouraging more of what works. It can also mean framing the problem in the past and the solution in the present or future. Change occurs when a solution is specific enough that it can be solved and can be seen as a positive vision.

You will release energy for change in clients if you show insight and compassion toward their inner world, suggest they pay attention to their patterns of thought and behavior, and focus on solutions.

Hold these fundamentals in mind as you read the rest of this chapter. You'll see examples of all three principles interwoven throughout the following sections.

Participating in the Great Work

Alchemists believe that everything becomes something more advanced, given time, and that "the great work" is to speed up that process. This provides a rich metaphor for coaching as the crucible of change—envisioning yourself as a participant in *the great work*.

A certain synergy is on your side in the coaching process. You can realize and create more together than you could individually. You will both change from your interaction. You have expertise to share, but clients also learn in the act of relating with you as an equal.

[1] Mary and Clarence each teach a one-on-one, six-session, interactive phone clinic that applies the principles and practices outlined in this book to situations you bring for discussion. More information at www.breakoutofthebox.com/clinic.htm.

This book will only reach its full potential when you use it as a springboard to help you learn from your clients. They will act out each style's gifts and blind spots. Their struggles will enlighten you, and you will enlighten them. You will model openness and encourage clients when you acknowledge that they have inspired you, changed your thinking, or even caught you stuck in your own box. You will learn more about your own Enneagram style and how to work with all the other styles.

This kind of coaching relationship fosters mutual trust and respect. Clients invite you into their emotional home. They ask you to help them find the keys they may have misplaced. You bring a new set of eyes and some ability to help them see with their own. But they won't trust a stranger. You will need to listen and be authentic until they develop enough comfort to begin their search.

For example, one of Mary's clients wanted to work with his staff better. In conversation he described his son with affection, even though the son had some problems. Mary said, "I admire your ability to show love for your son in spite of his flaws. I hear that same quality in the way you treat the people who work for you." In this simple statement she conveyed, "I trust you enough to share my feelings with you." After that she underscored his strength: "You've been healthy enough to create a model of parenting and managing that goes beyond what you were taught." She did not pronounce like an expert; she affirmed more like a friend.

You will establish rapport when you help clients feel normal and acceptable. *Matching* means to play back behavior, language, and feelings in a way that meshes with the client's. You can also do more than reflect exactly what they offer. You introduce an element of change when you accept their current situation and at the same time point beyond it to their potential. For example, a client who is about Mary's height said she was overweight and wanted to lose 30 to 60 pounds. Mary reflected on her own experience: "I've weighed thirty pounds more than I weigh right now." "So you know what that's like," the client replied. A simple interaction without judgment or prescription. The client's response tells us she felt heard, and that her experience was normal. Also embedded in Mary's statement was the assurance that change was possible.

Establish rapport by matching clients' behavior, language, and feelings, and at the same time point beyond the current situation to their potential.

Inviting the Flow

How does someone learn to walk? You've seen small children taking their first steps. You can feel the desire, the fear, the need for support, and the equal opposite desire to do it all by themselves. No one can do it for them, but they need encouragement. Someone has to say, "C'mon, you can do this." Someone has to help them do what they know they can't do—they've never been able to—and at the same time is the only thing they want to do. Clients come to you because they want to do something they haven't been able to do. They need someone to hold out a hand. They have hope, or they wouldn't be with you. But they can't hear that inner voice that says, "You can do it!" Part of your job is to install or restore their confidence.

Clients will sometimes seem to resist the very changes they say they want. Some people speak of "overcoming resistance," which implies that convincing or persuading people will win them over. But if your suggestions don't persuade a client in the beginning, repetition won't help. Imagine trying to stop the flow of a river by standing in it. You can't. But you can divert the water by using its own energy, perhaps by digging a channel. A client's failure to agree to or follow your suggestions is not about you or your ideas. It is just behavior. Instead of labeling the behavior as negative, find a way to harness its energy. Take a calm, deep breath, look for where the water is flowing, and imagine how you might create a new channel.

A client's failure to agree to or follow your suggestions is not about you or your ideas. Instead of labeling a behavior as negative, find a way to harness its energy.

For example, Mary worked with a financially successful Three, Jeannene, who wanted to develop a deeper interior life. Jeannene had sold her business and taken some time to travel. She now wanted to earn some money but also to do more artwork and "get on an authentic beam so my real motivation comes from me, and I'm not acting out old messages of parents or society." She had used a few decision-making tools, yet found herself "frustrated that I can't seem to focus on a new career." Mary could hear her struggling for her soul. On a superficial level, Jeannene was frustrated that she wasn't getting out there right now and doing something. That was her Three script: "Make the decision and get moving." Her deeper, more real self was calling, "I'm going to keep you feeling frustrated, not letting you decide, so you don't fall into that ego trap."

Mary suggested that for the next week Jeannene focus on her ideas that seemed authentic—to stay with them and notice how her self-talk interfered. Jeannene came to the next session with many examples, which she reported with great emotion. She realized how effectively she had squelched her creativity. "A child in me wants to play," she said tearfully, "and doesn't know how." When Mary suggested that she spend the next week letting that child out to play and "see what happens," Jeannene asked, "Is that all? Will that keep me busy?" "Well," Mary replied, "the simple task of last week seemed to be full. You're learning a lot about yourself and also getting in touch with some deeply genuine feelings." Jeannene

204

then admitted that she "procrastinated" the whole week and did everything she'd described only that morning, in preparation for the call.

Was she resisting Mary's suggestions? If you interpret it that way, you would focus on the problem instead of the solution. We could explain this as Jeannene's seeking approval from Mary (common with a Three). But Mary said instead, "Ah, so procrastination is one way you've been holding your creative child in check. It's a real sign of progress that you're getting so many clues to how you can open the door to your own authenticity." Then Mary suggested that Jeannene observe any other procrastination more closely.

Here Mary carried out her intention to use everything that came up. You may have learned to hold clients accountable to do what they say they're going to do, but here's another way to think about that. What if clients do everything they've agreed to, yet remain stuck, getting better at what they've always done? They need to notice how their behavior is driven from a constricted or rigid worldview. The change needs to take place on the level of worldview, not behavior.

Reframing clients' behavior can interrupt their usual patterns of thought and behavior and free them to make deeper change.

When Mary re-interpreted and reframed procrastination, she momentarily disoriented Jeannene. This disorientation interrupted her usual pattern of thought and behavior and freed her to make deeper change. Consider our earlier metaphor of walking. To move forward means to shift from your securely planted back foot to the front foot that may not be entirely stable yet. If you had an injury that required you to learn to walk again, it would be like this disorientation of a client's worldview: new muscles, new patterns, new assumptions, and new possibilities.

Moreover, Mary went to the heart of what her client said she wanted. Jeannene wanted to be more authentic. Her reluctance to do the fieldwork was important information, not a barrier to progress. We don't remove blocks by ignoring or attacking them.

Clarence worked with a One client, Clint, who bemoaned his "perceptual problems." Clint said he was oblivious to the fact that he spouted moral tirades until people refused to work with him anymore because of them. "It's a blind spot," he lamented. "I feel hopeless." "Then we'll just have to get you a Seeing Eye dog," Clarence replied. Both of them laughed. At the very least, this broke the tension of Clint's hopelessness. More, it nudged his assumption that his "blindness" was a done deal, impossible to change. It also opened the door to possibilities. Blind people find ways to function in the world; so could he. The point: don't get into your head, analyze clients' words or moods, or think through what the best metaphor would be to shake them loose. Act spontaneously out of your positive intention; use everything that comes up as grist for the mill.

With positive intent, you will discover your clients' resources, whether buried deep or easily accessible. You know the value of listening, but certain ways of listening will help you identify clues you might otherwise miss. When you listen for the Enneagram pattern, you can respond in a whole new language: the language of change. You will learn to use your clients' experience and words to discover metaphors with meaning for them. A Four told Mary she felt she didn't fit in this world—she came "from a different planet." Mary could have taken the standard, logical approach and asked the client to list her frustrations, help her develop strategies to fit her present situation, to find a career or marriage or life where she does fit. But because Mary knew that more was possible, she first got on a spaceship with the client: "Take me to the planet where you live." There is a greater invitation to change in this statement than in, "What is it about the planet others live on that excludes you?" The latter question focuses on the problem. So it reinforces the worldview, "I am different, probably flawed."

Invite your intuitive powers. Learn to trust that losing your balance for a moment is an opportunity for something new to arise.

Realizing you have this freedom to explore can energize and encourage you. Not that you won't hear yourself thinking at times, "Oh, for Pete's sake, why did I suggest he do that?" or, "Good grief, I don't have a clue how to respond to her situation." Welcome to the underworld. Confusion is not limited to the client. Learn to trust that losing your balance for a moment is an opportunity for something new to arise. Suspend judgment; open yourself to a deep belief in the possibility of change. You can walk through your confusion, and tune into your intuition. You can also invite your intuitive powers by centering yourself before a coaching session. You've reviewed your notes, thought of questions to ask and possible next steps. Now, take a few deep breaths, let go of all thoughts about what you need to do or say, and anchor yourself in the present. Hold that state during your interaction with clients.

Illuminating the Path

Some experiences break through our usual worldview. If you hold a clear vision of what's possible, you can help your clients let go of a frame of reference based on how things have always been. One vision you can hold for them is an image of how they will be when not boxed in by their style.

Mary envisioned a Six client, for example, relying on his inner authority. This focus guided her to support every indication of self-trust. After he made a clear decision, she reflected back to him, "As you become more aware of the soundness of your own judgment, you will be less and less anxious about acting without concern for the status quo." She also helped him recognize his own competency when she reacted to a statement he made about his business mission: "Let me play back for you what you just said. It's brilliant that you created your own niche instead of marketing yourself under someone else's umbrella. I can hear the passion in your voice when you speak of it this way."

When you hold an image of how clients will be when not boxed in by their style, you can help them let go of a frame of reference based on how things have always been.

Clarence worked with a Nine, holding the vision with her of being focused and initiating. She was eager to create a strategy for a career change, but she said she didn't know how and wanted him to give her some ideas. Instead of taking the initiative away from her, Clarence recalled her telling him that she had established a theater group in college. So he pursued that, asking, "How did you decide to do that? And then…? And then…?" He walked her through the steps she took, drew out the empowering feelings that accompanied her efforts, got her to remember how she gauged her success, then played back her own strategy to her: "You already know how to create something you really want, and each time you remember yourself, you release more energy and sharpen your focus."

An Eight who worked with Mary had just revealed his feelings to such an extent that he was near tears. He complained (only half-jokingly) that she had "tricked him" into getting emotional. She gently held him to his vision. "It's hard, isn't it?" she acknowledged. "Your whole life up until now, you've felt you had to be tough. Here you can let yourself feel vulnerable, even awkward. As you get more practice and as you experience the relief of letting down that huge burden you've carried, you will feel compassion—for yourself first, and then for others."

The examples above presuppose the desired outcome. With the Eight, for example, it was a shift to compassion from a style whose worldview had always been one where "I must be in charge."

Below is a summary of how each of the styles moves to break out of the box:

1. Ones move from seeing primarily what's wrong to developing nuance and options.

2. Instead of losing themselves by taking care of others, Twos become loving and learn to give without strings.

3. Threes shift from succeeding at any price to being inner-directed and communal.

4. Fours, who are moody and blocked by melancholy when in their box, become effective in the external world.

5. Fives move from a reserved and reserving style to integrating action with thinking, and becoming generous.

6. The suspiciousness and self-doubt of Sixes is transformed into trust of self and others, as well as self-assured action.

7. Sevens can be scattered and unreliable; they break through as visionaries who are realistically enthusiastic.

8. From being driven by a war mentality and power seeking, Eights become compassionate and just.

9. Immobile and indecisive Nines become focused and initiating. They remain inclusive while remembering their own agenda.

Seeing the "I" With the "Eye"

In the case study chapters, we suggested that you help your clients break their patterns instead of automatically acting from fixed worldviews. To break through, clients must understand their Enneagram style and learn to observe without judgment how that style's dynamics play out specifically for them. Then they can find ways to interrupt their patterns. In short, they need to stop doing what they've been doing habitually and do something different. Stella knew she was a perfectionist, but previously what she had tried to do was fix herself. For her, "fixing" was fruitless—all it did was reinforce her underlying pattern. To interrupt that pattern she did something different: she observed judgmental labels around her and translated them into descriptive language. When she did, she noticed her own language beginning to change spontaneously. Even her former self-criticism became more and more descriptive. After a week's observation she reported it was easiest to hear labeling in talk shows and news reports. She added that she had "totally spaced out" in conversations with friends. Instead of judging herself for "failing" in the task, she gave this very descriptive self-assessment: "I may be missing something valuable by not doing this with friends."

To break through, clients must understand their Enneagram style and learn to observe without judgment how that style's dynamics play out specifically for them. Then they can find ways to interrupt the pattern.

Increasing self-awareness without judgment is the key to freedom. Enneagram worldviews, when unobserved, support and are supported by compulsive behaviors. These behaviors keep giving us filtered data to reinforce our habitual perspective. The value of impartial self-observation rests on the paradox that when we embrace ourselves as we are, our behavior becomes less driven and new choices open up.

As we become able to notice non-judgmentally how our habits show up, we quite naturally begin to interrupt those patterns. Jane, the Five you read about in chapter seven, first noticed that she was withholding questions because she didn't want to appear stupid. Jane broke the pattern of having to know everything by "trying really hard to appear stupid." When she observed herself feeling stupid, she said, "I just noticed it and said, 'Oh, I'm feeling stupid' and decided to make it happen more. It was empowering to actually cause it." Pattern recognition leads easily to pattern interruption.

Generalizations sustain a worldview. Specific observations reveal that illusory worldview and make change easier.

Beaming In

After clients describe problem behavior, note the same behavior in their interactions with you. It's important to break the behavior down into specific, descriptive observations. Generalizations sustain a worldview. Specific observations reveal that illusory worldview and make change easier.

Mike, a Four, told Mary, "I'm too driven by my feelings." Mary asked for more details. "I want to be able to pay more attention to what's really out there instead of responding to my inner reality," he explained. "One day I come in to work and it's the greatest place in the world; the next day it's the worst. And nothing has changed in my external environment. By my 'inner reality' I mean that nobody else knows this is going on. It's all happening inside. But it affects my creativity and energy." Mary began to watch for this pattern as she worked with him.

She noticed in the first two calls that Mike started out by saying, "Everything is fine," then half-way into the session he would say something dramatic such as, "I wake up at 2 a.m. in a cold sweat, feeling existential terror." He started the third call by saying, "I guess I'm doing all right. I can't complain too much." He was behaving with Mary as he did at work. ("Nobody else knows what is going on.") So Mary responded, "I've noticed in our conversations that you start off with some version of, 'I'm fine,' and then 20 minutes into the call you tell me your deeper feelings, such as waking up in the night feeling terror. If you could know right now what's below the surface, what might that be?" After a moment's pause he said, "I'm almost at the point where retirement is on the horizon. As I see what I've been doing coming to an end, there's a vacuum there." Bingo.

Make process observations, noting clients' problem behaviors in their interactions with you.

209

An Eight client, Butch, told Clarence that others said he was intimidating. Clarence asked him to be specific. Butch said he hurt people's feelings and described how he told a subordinate she gave an inferior review of someone. "Ah," Clarence reflected, "so one way you have intimidated was to use words that could hurt people's feelings because you made global judgments like *inferior.* What exactly was inferior about her review? How can you be more descriptive?"[2]

Later in the conversation, Butch described his sister to Clarence as weak and whining. Clarence pushed him again by saying, "You described your sister as whining. What are some more descriptive terms for whining that are not likely to hurt her when you talk to her?"

Catching clients in their habitual patterns is effective, but so is reinforcing change. Clarence had helped Butch be less judgmental by breaking down generalizations like "inferior," or "weak." Butch was a physician, but when Clarence used the metaphor of "spontaneous remission" to describe how Butch would notice himself changing, he didn't like it. He told Clarence, "The idea of spontaneous remission bugs me because it implies there's nothing we can do but wait for something good to come of this. I need to believe there's something I can do." Clarence noticed that Butch was being quite specific, so he reinforced Butch's progress: "That was a constructive way to tell me why that metaphor doesn't work for you. You gave me very specific, useful feedback. You've helped me know how to work with you better."

Protecting the Flame

The psychologist Carl Jung had a dream in which he was walking in a strong wind, holding a small flame in his hand. He knew that his task was to protect the flame as he continued into the wind. Your job as a coach is to help clients protect the flame of their potential as they face the winds of change. You can't just help them avoid pain or confrontation. Jane, in the example above, had to face her fear of appearing stupid, not avoid it.

Clients make real progress when you help them change self-defeating habitual responses to experience.

Clients make real progress when you help them change self-defeating habitual responses to experience. It doesn't work to fight against undesirable behavior. It does work to interrupt the underlying pattern of processing information that supports that behavior. This is why Mary asked Jeannene, the Three who procrastinated, to stay with any procrastination that showed up and observe it more closely. By doing this, Jeannene got in touch with the remembered voices that told her it was selfish

---

[2] Notice in this response the implicit reframing of the client's report that he "hurt people's feelings" by restating what he said in more conditional terms ("words that *could* hurt people's feelings"). Clarence also put the problem in the past ("one way you *have intimidated*") and the solution in the present ("How *can you be* more descriptive?").

[3] See Eugene Gendlin's book, *Focusing.*

to spend time creating art when she could be out making money. With Mary's help, she broke the habit of doing, and focused on being with herself.

There are many techniques to face into the wind. Jerry, a Five, was feeling overwhelmed with the burdens of work and felt "entrapped." When asked to locate that experience in his body and exaggerate it,[3] he said it was like "being in a chokehold."[4] Knowing that Jerry had studied martial arts, Clarence asked him how he might release a chokehold in *aikido* fashion. Later they worked with these images of freeing oneself from a chokehold.

Coach clients to face their fears instead of avoiding them.

Sue, a Nine, said she "froze" when giving formal presentations. She reported a dream in which her mother wanted to die and asked Sue to kill her. Mary asked Sue to talk to the mother in her dream.[5] "Why are you here?" Sue questioned her mother. When Mary asked how the mother might respond, Sue answered as the mother: "I am the mother in you who tells you that what you have to say is unimportant. I'm here to be killed because it's time to 'kill' your fear of speaking out."

Further into the process, Sue expressed her vague discomfort as "cloudy," which she interpreted as protecting herself from "blinding sunlight." She asked herself as the cloud what she could do to change this. The answer: "Picture yourself in the space where you are anxious. Imagine that the light is set low on a dimmer. Gradually turn the dimmer up until your eyes get used to bright light." This internal dialogue, and her own metaphor of turning up the dimmer, helped Sue break free of her performance anxiety. She was delighted (and a little surprised) that her anxiety dimmed as she allowed herself to be in the spotlight.

Karen, a Four, disliked doing the mundane tasks on her to-do list. But omitting follow-up calls after an introductory letter was costing her business. She would retreat and play the piano instead of calling, and then feel shame about falling behind in her work. Clarence asked Karen what kind of music she disliked playing. "I don't like contemporary classical music," she admitted. He invited her to consider, "How could you improvise in such a way that you'd enjoy playing contemporary classical music?" She answered right away, "By jazzing it up!" "Great," Clarence encouraged her. "Now, how could you jazz up your introductory letter so that making follow-up calls attracts you?"[6] He further requested that Karen not try to answer that question right away, but to "put it on the back burner and notice the innovative ideas that begin to occur to you."

[4] This was interesting to Clarence, because a Seven had recently described feeling "entrapped," but said it was like "being in prison." Two very different meanings attributed to the same word.

[5] Based on the Jungian technique of Active Imagination.

[6] Drawn from a creativity technique where you isolate the central aspect of a problem, take an excursion to a completely different arena, solve the problem there, then bring the solution back to the original problem and try it on for fit.

This suggestion presupposed that innovative ideas would occur to Karen. It was also based on an understanding of creative thinking—that after a certain amount of logical clarity, the most innovative solutions come at unexpected, unplanned moments, often in images.

Captivating with Stories[7]

When clients seem unable to initiate action or can't respond to direct suggestions, stories that parallel their situation can help them. For example, Clarence told a Three, "You will come to understand that your longing for efficiency has been based on a belief that you would be loved for what you accomplished. This has hurt you, because you've had this lurking fear that they loved your achievement but not the real you. You've been left still wanting to be loved for yourself." His client said, "I'm in a high-powered corporate setting. I don't relate to 'love' in that context." Clarence then added, "Well, the Enneagram deals with our deepest longings, and corporate striving is only one step removed from our inner world." The client still didn't buy it. A breakthrough occurred when Clarence told him this story:

> Once there was a wealthy developer who bought up all the houses in a section he wanted to develop, except for one old house owned by an elderly couple. He offered them three or four times the house's valuation, but they would not sell. They said they had lived there all their lives and they just didn't want to move. The developer fumed to his accountant, "That's purely emotional!" The accountant serenely answered, "So is the desire to be fabulously wealthy."

You can create stories for your clients, but often you can elicit theirs. For example, Linette, a Two that Mary coached, felt her boss had betrayed her by passing over her for promotion. She now worked for one of her former teammates. The only explanation offered to Linette was that the other person had "better organizational skills." "Of all the people in the group, I am the best manager," she fumed. "I know I could have walked out and taken something else." But Linette had not walked out, in spite of the blow to her pride. "When I was younger," she continued, "I felt confident I could win people over. More than that, I always felt there was some other power there, watching over my shoulder. Now I've lost that. I have no watchful spirit."

A useful story has a structure similar to the client's situation, including the underlying problem and an embedded solution.

Linette talked about her Chinese heritage and the devastating effects of losing face in that culture. In fact, one of her uncles had committed suicide when his

---

[7] Webster's defines *captivate* as "attract and hold irresistibly by some special charm or art." Our worldview is a kind of trance, where we operate on automatic according to the dictates of our Enneagram style. It is a coaching *art* to lure clients out of their worldview.

business failed. Mary asked if she could remember a situation where someone regained face. Linette then recalled a story of a young, unwed mother in her grandmother's village. "She was urged by her family to leave the village in shame, but she refused to go." Mary inquired, "What happened to her?" The answer: "She raised her child well and eventually earned an honorable reputation through her good works in the community."

A useful story has a structure similar to the client's situation, including the underlying problem and an embedded resolution. These elements were present in the above story. The young woman losing face when she became pregnant was analogous to losing face by not being promoted. The woman in the story regained face by choosing to be self-defined. Mary pointed out these parallels. The lessons in Linette's story helped her set her sights on expressing her own needs and talents.

Creating Room to Play

The word "metaphor" is from the Greek *pherein*, "to carry," and *meta*, "beyond" or "over." We are carried beyond our worldview by breakthrough experiences; metaphors illuminate the path. When clients shrink from a new perspective, that's a clue that intellectual understanding has not freed them to move. This is your chance to be spontaneous, playful, inventive—anything that will reach them at a symbolic level. We've just written about the power of stories. You can also create openings through the symbolic use of humor, behavior, gifts, or even poetry.

When intellectual understanding has not freed clients to move, this is your chance to be spontaneous, playful, inventive — anything that will reach them at a symbolic level.

Use your own imagination and creativity to develop metaphors for each style. Sometimes you can ask clients for a metaphor of how they see themselves and work with it. Don't worry about getting it just right. The meaning of a metaphor is often individual. Listen to your clients. They'll give you the metaphors that have meaning for them. An Eight told Clarence, "I'm a junkyard dog." Clarence stayed within that metaphor: "Who is the dog loyal to? Who cares for him? Whom does he let pet him? What is he protecting and from whom? In what way is he trapped by what he is protecting?"

Sometimes you'll hear clients using metaphors that illustrate a change in their worldview. For example, Mary had Stella, a One, study labeling. Mary asked her to observe the world around her (ads, articles, billboards, conversations) for global, judgmental words, then to translate each label into neutral behavioral descriptors. When Stella described her observations the next week, it was evident that she was learning how pervasive judgmental (negative and positive) language is in our culture. She was also learning how to make such labels more descriptive. For example, she had translated the term "credit card abuse" into "using a credit card to buy items you do not have money to cover, so you cannot pay your credit card bill when it comes." Then Stella asked, "What are we doing here?"

Mary explained that Stella's efforts in the past to fix herself had not worked, and had actually reinforced her underlying perfectionism. This work was to help Stella begin to use more descriptive language as a result of her ability to observe without judgment. After this summary, Mary asked, "Do you understand what I'm saying?"

Stella responded, "Here's how I understand it. When you paddle a canoe and you see a rock, you don't look at the rock because you're more likely to run into it; you look in the direction you want to go." It doesn't get any better than this.

Humor is one good antidote to untested assumptions. It shakes us loose. An Eight small business owner had told his team that he wanted them to stand up to him. But they didn't trust his sincerity. He always prevailed in any disagreement. Mary thought playfully about his war mentality. She suggested that he hand out water pistols at their next meeting and ask them to "shoot" him when he came on too strong. She had reframed war as a humorous interaction that would bring laughter instead of escalating attack. He loved it, and so did they.

Humor and metaphor can shake clients loose: An Eight handed out water pistols to his team and asked them to "shoot" him when he came on too strong.

Clarence had a Two client who admitted that as the company's financial officer she dogged her peers for financial reports at budget time, even though that was her boss's job. Although she didn't agree with her boss's insistence that she do his dirty work, she liked being the "power behind the throne." She had engendered the dislike of her peers, though, and she wanted to win back their approval. Clarence went to a toy store, found a puppet on strings, and gave it to her as a gift. The message was clear. She put it in a prominent place on her office bookshelf as a reminder that she was letting the boss pull her strings.

In working with teams Mary offers symbolic prizes for manifesting their patterns. In one retreat she gave a Seven a t-shirt with the slogan, "Kiss me... I'm a prince!" She'd faced him into his narcissistic behaviors. He was amused. His laughter reduced his defensiveness and opened the door to direct feedback from his teammates.

Clarence coached a depressed Nine who used to be a dancer. He'd tried everything he or she could think of, yet she couldn't seem to break free. Finally, Clarence asked her to dance her depression. She was startled out of her reverie, agreed to do it, and came back the next week with a new awareness about how she had kept herself stuck.

A Six client of Mary's had mixed feelings about an intense relationship. When it was good, it was very, very good. But his Seven girlfriend was addicted to alcohol and ran from problems by partying all night with friends. The Six asked if Mary thought these were "red flags," then waxed romantic about all the good things he and his girlfriend shared, then suspected that nothing would change, then doubted his own suspicions. He hadn't been able to integrate his opposing voices. Mary read to him Theodore Roethke's poem, *In a Dark Time,* emphasizing the lines, "A fallen man, I climb out of my fear," and, "The mind enters itself." His eyes welled up with tears. Somehow, these poetic images had set him free. He chose to leave the relationship.

We even know of a talented coach who introduces astrology as a metaphor. Maybe that's a little far-out for you, but it works for him. Free yourself to discover what works for you and your clients. Create more room to play.

Going Where No One Has Gone Before

When you think of fieldwork, you probably have some ready at hand. You have templates for personal or corporate strategy and mission development, communication techniques, time management, and weight control. You have structured exercises that clients can do between coaching sessions. These work well to solve many problems. But for our purposes, we ask you to consider fieldwork that will help clients shift their worldview. Dreaming up this kind of practice is creative and energizing. It doesn't matter how quirky or unusual your suggestions are if they get clients' attention and encourage them to do something different. Clients will often lead you exactly where they need to go if you pay attention.

Create fieldwork that will help clients shift their worldview. It doesn't matter how quirky or unusual your suggestions are if they encourage clients to do something different.

For example, a One named Barb told Mary she was dismayed with some of her own recent behavior. She had told a new acquaintance about a mutual friend, but noticed halfway through the conversation that she was describing only bad things about her friend. "I was just awful," Barb said. "Why do I have to be so critical of others?" She admitted, "I'm probably trying to avoid self-criticism by projecting it onto others." "Does it work?" Mary probed. "Well, no, now I'm criticizing myself for being so critical!" They both laughed. "Really, then," Mary observed, "criticizing others is guaranteed to lead you into the very thing you're trying to avoid—criticizing yourself."

Mary showed her how to work with her projections[8] to break this self-defeating habit: First she had Barb list all the things she didn't like about her friend, Jean. Then she asked her to try them on, one at a time, by speaking as if Jean were a part of her. Barb began gingerly, "I abhor the Jean in me who escalates someone else's mistakes until I become verbally abusive." She tried it on and the fit was snug. Mary knew that once Barb understood how to do this, she could break the pattern of projection and self-criticism.

But there's more to the story. Still being self-critical, Barb said, "I'm ashamed that I need to use a defense mechanism as crude as projection!" Mary grinned, "Well, you're right, projection is pretty common. What would be a more sophisticated defense mechanism? "Reaction formation," Barb joked back. (She knew that answer is in all the Enneagram texts.) "Great," Mary agreed. "That's your fieldwork for this week; to observe yourself for signs of reaction formation.[9] But by the way, it's such a sophisticated defense mechanism that I don't have an easy technique for it the way I do for projection. So see if you can think of a way to interrupt that pattern. If not, we'll figure it out together."

Mary did a number of things here. She validated her client's worldview (though disturbing it gently with humor). Instead of trying to overcome the problem, Mary showed her how to dive into it and use its energy for change. She emphasized the *how*, not the why. Mary also encouraged Barb to take responsibility for her own behavior while offering her support and ideas.

Fieldwork is especially fertile ground for inventing new responses to familiar situations. Instead of letting her client bemoan her imperfection in using a "crude" defense mechanism, Mary went with it and reframed it as an opportunity for change. She encouraged Barb to look for the presence of yet another defense mechanism that they could reframe together as a source of positive energy. Everything can be used in service of change.

Mary reframed Barb's view of projection as "awful" by redefining it as a vehicle for increased self-awareness. There's an implicit reframing here, too: The more defense mechanisms the merrier. Also, Mary added an element of confusion to the meaning of "perfectionism." In Barb's old view a perfect person wouldn't use defense mechanisms. The new view Mary offered was a facilitative double bind: "You can only be perfect by being imperfect."[10]

---

[8] Attributing to others your own undesirable traits or impulses. A clue to projection is experiencing strong feelings (negative or positive) out of proportion to the stimulus.

[9] The act of publicly criticizing what you privately desire.

[10] A double-bind communication is one that contains two contradictory messages. In a *facilitative* double-bind, clients' habitual thinking patterns are of no use—they *must* break free.

You may have seen the TV Star Trek episode where a computer has taken over a planet:

Captain Kirk tells the computer, "Everything I say is true."

"Compute."

"What I just said is a lie."

"Does not compute, does not compute!" (as the computer's programs disintegrate).

That is what happens when you help clients create new experiences that are incompatible with their old worldviews. The links holding together their habitual programs become inoperative: "Does not compute, does not compute!"

When you help clients create new experiences that are incompatible with their old worldviews, the links holding together their habitual programs become inoperative: "Does not compute, does not compute!"

If something works, do more of it; if it doesn't work do something else. When clients do their fieldwork, take advantage of that. If they don't do the fieldwork, take advantage of that, too. Hark back to our earlier discussion of the Three who procrastinated. You can use whatever clients give you to interrupt their Enneagram patterns.

Push them to take a risk. If they do their fieldwork too easily, it probably won't break them free. Pay attention to what happens when they risk. Don't assume you have the franchise on the best way to free them.

A Six client wanted to get rid of her anxiety about work, which had always been strongest on Monday mornings. Clarence showed her how to focus on, exaggerate, and gauge her level of anxiety, first raising it, and then lowering it.[11] He then asked her to practice what she'd learned if she began to feel anxious the following Monday morning. When he checked during the next session she said, "I tried the exercise you suggested, but when I got to maybe a 4 or a 5 on a scale of 10, I stopped. I couldn't have stayed with it if you'd put a gun to my head!" When Clarence probed for how her week went, she announced that on Monday morning as she headed into work, she didn't feel anxious at all! "How did you make that happen? What did you do differently?" he asked. "Well, over the weekend I remembered from a course on intuition the naming of characters that represent states of mind. Monday morning when I woke up, I found myself talking to two characters. One was kind of a bullwhip-wielding, challenging Indiana Jones; the other was a Wizard of Oz type who seemed like part of my higher self. As I drove to work I had a moment of choice. I could hear the Jones character telling me I was running late, then the Oz character stepped in and said, 'Let it go.' It was a

---

[11] Ordinarily we act as if our fears control us. This becomes self-fulfilling because trying to hold them in check only gives them energy. In contrast, exaggerating the physical manifestations sends a message to the unconscious: "I am able to change this." And, of course, if you can increase the feelings, you can also decrease them.

real breakthrough for me." Clarence praised her: "You created your own way to break free from your anxiety!"

Make the purpose of the fieldwork specific enough that both you and your client can test its effectiveness. The client above had the goal of feeling free of anxiety. The technique Clarence suggested might have worked. The one the client chose certainly did, and that's what he reinforced. When the purpose is clear the assignment itself can even be ambiguous, in the sense that neither of you knows exactly how it will play out. The assumption behind an ambiguous assignment is that clients know how to solve their problems and will remember how while searching for an answer.

For example, Mary worked with a very successful artist—a Four who owned several galleries featuring his sculptures and paintings. He couldn't possibly oversee all the details of managing the business side, and was happy to find a senior bookkeeper he could trust. Yet he spoke somewhat condescendingly of the bookkeeper's lack of cultivated knowledge in fine art. He agreed that he should forgive the woman, but made jokes about her taste in her presence. Consequently she had become more and more withdrawn. Mary wanted to help break his pattern of rejecting others who didn't match his subjective, idealized self-image. She suggested the following fieldwork: "Go to the flea market, find the homeliest, most distasteful person you can find, and talk to that person until you find something beautiful in them." Mary wasn't quite sure what would happen, but she knew even a small shift would weaken his Enneagram pattern.

Use your common sense. Be flexible, listen carefully, and then invent fieldwork that matches both your values and style and the client's. Some tasks may not relate directly to Enneagram styles, but often the clients' efforts between sessions provide an opportunity to shift their worldview. We've described possibilities for a One, a Six, and a Four. Here are brief examples for the remaining styles. Don't take them as rules. Each style has personal variety, and each client will offer you unique behavior. So generate more ideas on your own:

- A Two agency director was angry with a team member because of his lack of interest in promotion. As a Two, her anger was for him as much as it was against him. Mary asked her to make a list of all the reasons why she should do his emotional work. At the next session they explored the client's list and determined together what secondary gains she got from doing her team member's feeling for him.

- A Three who fancied herself quite sexy was stressed from overwork. Clarence suggested that she listen to the top 20 songs and read 20 poems. At the next session he asked her how many of them were about money. She had found none. Then he talked about why not, and asked if one of her goals was to inspire a song in someone's heart. That redefined success and possibly her life's goal.

- A Five client told Mary she had more information than anyone she worked with. Mary asked her to define *information*. The client's definition was quite cerebral. The fieldwork was to write down in great detail as much non-verbal and emotional information as she could about every personal interaction. This broke her tight focus and increased her emotional sensitivity.

- A very messy Seven had piles of clutter all over his office. He was a macho guy, so Clarence played with that: "A pile of work is a visual nag. Why do you allow your office to nag you?" The client's task before the next call was to figure out how to stop the nagging. By reframing the piles as nagging, Clarence found a way to move the client into behavior he'd characteristically avoided.

- An Eight Clarence coached had little insight into the motivations of people who worked for him. Clarence asked him to take notes in conversations with them, particularly how they looked and how they seemed to feel. The client learned to use active listening with a specific goal: to understand their thoughts and feelings so thoroughly that he felt like he was in their shoes looking back at himself. Clarence introduced him to empathy by eroding his habit of getting others to do what he wanted without considering their needs or feelings.

- A Nine client who wanted to lose weight described her strategy for exercising and eating healthier food, but after losing a certain amount of weight she would reach a plateau where her very attractive figure began to get noticed, and she would stop the program. Mary suggested that before the client would eat anything when she felt hungry, she first write down the answer to the question, "What do I really want in my life?" Mary reframed what used to be the onerous task of dieting by making the client's hunger an opportunity to remember herself.

Opening Up New Worlds

One simple way to open the door to a new world is with verb tense. Instead of reflecting, "Anger is a real problem for you," put the problem in the past: "So anger has been a real problem for you." Use the present tense to make the solution

Put problems in the past and solutions in the present or future.

present. For example, say, "How do you occasionally control your anger in similar situations?" The solution can also be placed in the future as a suggestion: "When you are enthusiastic without being angry or critical you will be more credible, better able to make your case, and bring people along with your ideas."

Also pay attention to how clients maintain their worldviews partially by seeing situations as either/or:

- One: "Either do what I should or do what I want."
- Two: "Either meet others' needs or meet my own."
- Three: "Either succeed or have my own emotional life."
- Four: "Either be accepted or be my real (defective) self."
- Five: "Either have what I want or share."
- Six: "Either be safe or be creative."
- Seven: "Either have joy or fulfill commitments."
- Eight: "Either be strong or be vulnerable."
- Nine: "Either let others have their way or have my own way."

Help them see new possibilities by thinking in terms of both/and. Your overall goal is to help them become more aware of their patterns and to reorganize their thinking.

A simple method encourages both/and thinking:

Identify either/or thinking and help clients see new possibilities by asking, "How can you do both X and Y?"

1. First, identify the key components of the "either" and the "or" (think of one as X and the other as Y). One of Mary's clients, for example, debated how to spend her time the next weekend. She said, "An instructor from out of town is giving a workshop with some new methods that build on what I've already learned from him. I really want to go, but I don't relish sitting through the parts I already know." (This is X.) She continued, "My son is sick and my husband has a lot to do this weekend, so I'd like to help them, but I can't do both." (This is Y.)

2. Then push the client's both/and button ("How can you do both X and Y?") Mary asked the client, "How can you both get the fine-tuning you need from this instructor and still spend time with your son?" The client quickly got a new idea: "I can call the event organizer and ask to schedule a private session with the instructor while he's in town." Then another one: "If he's not willing

or doesn't have the time this weekend, we can schedule our vacation where he lives. I can arrange private time with him while we're there." She found a solution to her immediate problem, and developed her both/and thinking capability.

Notice the stem of the opening phrase: "How can you…?" This is a presupposition ("You *can*") and it's open-ended, increasing the likelihood that clients will access their own resources. Every time you offer them an alternative to an either/or perspective you free them from it, at least a little.

When we suggest that you focus on solutions, this doesn't mean that you completely ignore problems. But we do encourage you to explore problems only as necessary to find keys to doors that can be opened. Here's another approach:

1. Help clients formulate the problem briefly: "I avoid making follow-up calls after sending an introductory letter, and that costs me business."

2. Clarify specifically what the client will be doing when there is no longer a problem: "So, when you make follow-up calls consistently, what will be happening?"

3. Search for exceptions to the problem: "Tell me about the times when you have made follow-up calls."

4. Guide clients to realize they do know how to solve their problems. "What did you do to get yourself to make the calls?" "How can you do more of that?"

5. If they can't find any exceptions (usually they will), encourage small steps that are likely to succeed: "How can you jazz up your introductory letters so you'll want to make follow-up calls?"

6. Look for and reinforce spontaneous change. Your combined efforts will invoke deliberate change. You will also notice spontaneous changes. This happens quite naturally because the links that held an Enneagram style together no longer hold. We also apply the principles of appreciative feedback: Once the goal is clear, instead of noticing ways the client falls short of the goal, reinforce any incremental steps in the direction of the goal.

7. Expect relapses and reframe them positively. Every period of change has ebbs and flows. But once we become aware of our Enneagram patterns, we are changed. No matter how often these patterns show up again and in what guises, we move toward greater and greater self-awareness. So it is the truth to

When clients can envision a solution, ask for examples where at least part of the solution is already happening. Encourage them to do more of what works.

When the goal is clear, instead of noticing ways the client falls short, reinforce incremental steps in the direction of the goal.

tell a client, "You will never be the same. Even when you feel disappointed in yourself, you see the pattern and that's change—you are more self-aware."

Take this to heart as a coach: change always occurs. You can influence and accelerate that process. We've given you a lot of material, so give yourself time and appreciation as you try out some of our suggestions that may be new to you. And practice, practice, practice—but remember to have fun with it.

Of course we could say a lot more. It's exciting to know that coaches can influence and accelerate the process of change. It delights us as we watch our own clients transform. We are pleased to share as much with you as we can. And we leave you with this final presupposition: "We wonder if you realize how much your view of coaching has already changed because of reading this book?"

Appendix: Out of the Box Coaching Resources

Out of the Box Coaching Skills Teleclinic

Whether you are a coach, counselor, teacher, minister, manager, or simply someone with whom friends like to brainstorm about events and issues in their lives, there are many ideas in this book about how to inspire significant change. To further develop your expertise, Mary and Clarence each offer six one-on-one phone sessions that apply these principles and practices to situations you bring for discussion: www.breakoutofthebox.com/clinic.htm.

Personal Coaching and Mentoring

The authors are available to coach individuals who want to enrich their own lives by learning more about the Enneagram and to professionals who want a mentor to help them use the Enneagram in their work. Contact Mary or Clarence for a free 45-minute phone consult:

Mary Bast
Gainesville, FL, USA
352-271-0010
coach@breakoutofthebox.com
www.breakoutofthebox.com

Clarence Thomson
Louisburg, KS, USA
913-376-3337
coach@enneagramcentral.com
www.enneagramcentral.com

Determining Your Enneagram Style

You probably have a good idea of your Enneagram style from having read this book, especially Chapter One. You will find more in-depth Enneagram descriptions in many books at your local bookstore, including those listed in our Bibliography. There's also an on-line Enneagram test at Clarence's web site: www.enneagramcentral.com/testa.htm. If you'd like to use your free 45-minute consult as an opportunity to confirm your Enneagram style, answer some or all of these questions, then contact Clarence or Mary by e-mail or phone to set up an appointment.

1. If you were a car, what kind would you be? Why?

2. If you were a room in a house, which room would you be? Why?

3. Describe your perfect job.

4. Describe your job from hell.

5. What is your pet peeve?

6. What category of fault do you never commit?

7. Describe your perfect meal.

8. How do you usually handle conflict?

9. We're writing your biography. What shall we title it?

10. We're also making a movie. Who should play you? Why?

11. How would you spend a perfect day off?

12. What is your favorite book? Why?

Bibliography

For clear, accurate Enneagram style descriptions

Baron, Renee and Elizabeth Wagele. *The Enneagram Made Easy: Discover the Nine Types of People.* (New York, NY: HarperCollins, 1994)

Goldberg, Michael J. *The 9 Ways of Working.* (New York, NY: Marlowe & Co., 1999)

Palmer, Helen. *The Enneagram: Understanding Yourself and the Others in Your Life.* (New York, NY: HarperCollins, 1991)

Riso, Don Richard and Russ Hudson. *The Wisdom of the Enneagram.* (New York, NY: Bantam Books, 1999)

Wagner, Jerome, Ph.D. *The Enneagram Spectrum of Personality Styles: An Introductory Guide.* (Portland, OR: Metamorphous Press, 1996)

To experience each of the Enneagram styles

Condon, Thomas. *The Enneagram Movie and Video Guide: How to See Personality Styles in the Movies.* (Portland, OR: Metamorphous Press, 1999)

Searle, Judith. *The Literary Enneagram: Characters from the Inside Out.* (Portland, OR: Metamorphous Press, 2001)

For deeper understanding of the principles of change

Gordon, David. *Therapeutic Metaphors.* (Cupertino, CA: META Publications, 1978)

O'Hanlon Bill. *Do One Thing Different: Ten Simple Ways to Change Your Life.* (New York, NY: HarperCollins, 2000)

Walter, John L. and Jane E. Peller. *Becoming Solution-Focused in Brief Therapy.* (New York, NY: Brunner/Mazel, 1992)

Watzlawick, Paul. *The Language of Change: Elements of Therapeutic Communication.* (New York, NY: Basic Books, 1978)